The BEAMER class User Guide

A catalogue record for this book is available from the Hong Kong Public Libraries.

Published in Hong Kong by Samurai Media Limited.

Email: info@samuraimedia.org

ISBN 978-988-8406-29-6

The BEAMER *class*
http://bitbucket.org/rivanvx/beamer
User Guide for version 3.36.

Till Tantau, Joseph Wright, Vedran Miletić

March 8, 2015

Contents

1 Introduction

BEAMER is a LaTeX class for creating presentations that are held using a projector, but it can also be used to create transparency slides. Preparing presentations with BEAMER is different from preparing them with WYSIWYG programs like OpenOffice.org Impress, Apple Keynote, KOffice KPresenter or Microsoft PowerPoint. A BEAMER presentation is created like any other LaTeX document: It has a preamble and a body, the body contains \sections and \subsections, the different slides (called *frames* in BEAMER) are put in environments, they are structured using itemize and enumerate environments, and so on. The obvious disadvantage of this approach is that you have to know LaTeX in order to use BEAMER. The advantage is that if you know LaTeX, you can use your knowledge of LaTeX also when creating a presentation, not only when writing papers.

1.1 Main Features

The list of features supported by BEAMER is quite long (unfortunately, so is presumably the list of bugs supported by BEAMER). The most important features, in our opinion, are:

- You can use BEAMER with `pdflatex`, `latex+dvips`, `lualatex` and `xelatex`. `latex+dvipdfm` isn't supported (but we accept patches!).

- The standard commands of LaTeX still work. A \tableofcontents will still create a table of contents, \section is still used to create structure, and itemize still creates a list.

- You can easily create overlays and dynamic effects.

- Themes allow you to change the appearance of your presentation to suit your purposes.

- The themes are designed to be usable in practice, they are not just for show. You will not find such nonsense as a green body text on a picture of a green meadow.

- The layout, the colors, and the fonts used in a presentation can easily be changed globally, but you still also have control over the most minute detail.

- A special style file allows you to use the LaTeX-source of a presentation directly in other LaTeX classes like `article` or `book`. This makes it easy to create presentations out of lecture notes or lecture notes out of presentations.

- The final output is typically a PDF-file. Viewer applications for this format exist for virtually every platform. When bringing your presentation to a conference on a memory stick, you do not have to worry about which version of the presentation program might be installed there. Also, your presentation is going to look exactly the way it looked on your computer.

1.2 History

Till Tantau created BEAMER mainly in his spare time. Many other people have helped by sending him emails containing suggestions for improvement or corrections or patches or whole new themes (by now, this amounts to over a thousand emails concerning BEAMER). Indeed, most of the development was only initiated by feature requests and bug reports. Without this feedback, BEAMER would still be what it was originally intended to be: a small private collection of macros that make using the seminar class easier. Till created the first version of BEAMER for his PhD defense presentation in February 2003. A month later, he put the package on CTAN at the request of some colleagues. After that, things somehow got out of hand.

After being unmaintained since 2007, in April 2010 Till handed over the maintenance to Joseph Wright and Vedran Miletić, who are still maintaining it: improving code, fixing bugs, adding new features and helping users.

1.3 Acknowledgments

Till Tantau: *"Where to begin? BEAMER's development depends not only on me, but on the feedback I get from other people. Many features have been implemented because someone requested them and I thought that these features would be nice to have and reasonably easy to implement. Other people have given valuable feedback on themes, on the user's guide, on features of the class, on the internals of the implementation, on special LaTeX features, and on life in general. A small selection of these people includes (in no particular order and I have surely forgotten to name lots of people who really, really deserve being in this list): Carsten (for everything), Birgit (for being the first person to use BEAMER besides me), Tux (for his silent criticism), Rolf Niepraschk (for showing me how to program LaTeX correctly), Claudio Beccari (for writing part of the documentation on font encodings), Thomas Baumann (for the emacs stuff), Stefan Müller (for not loosing hope), Uwe Kern (for XCOLOR), Hendri Adriaens (for HA-PROSPER), Ohura Makoto (for spotting typos). People who have contributed to the themes include Paul Gomme, Manuel Carro, and Marlon Régis Schmitz."*

Joseph Wright: *"Thanks to Till Tantau for the huge development effort in creating BEAMER. Sincere thanks to Vedran Miletić for taking the lead in continuing development."*

Vedran Miletić: *"First, I would like to thank Karl Berry and Sanda Bujačić for encouragement, without which I wouldn't ever be anything but a LaTeX user. I would also like to thank Ana Meštrović, my colleague, who was excited by the prospect of using BEAMER for preparing class material; Ivona Franković and Marina Rajnović, my students at Department of Informatics, who were the first to hear about LaTeX, BEAMER and how it can help in preparing class material. I would like to thank Heiko Oberdiek (for HYPERREF), Johannes Braams (for BABEL) and Philipp Lehman (for BIBLATEX). Above all, I owe a lot to Till Tantau for developing BEAMER in the first place and to Joseph Wright for developing SIUNITX and for helping me develop BEAMER further."*

1.4 How to Read this User's Guide

You should start with the first part. If you have not yet installed the package, please read Section 2 first. If you are new to BEAMER, you should next read the tutorial in Section 3. When you sit down to create your first real presentation using BEAMER, read Section 4 where the technical details of a possible workflow are discussed. If you are still new to creating presentations in general, you might find Section 5 helpful, where many guidelines are given on what to do and what not to do. Finally, you should browse through Section 6, where you will find ready-to-use solution templates for creating talks, possibly even in the language you intend to use.

The second part of this user's guide goes into the details of all the commands defined in BEAMER, but it also addresses other technical issues having to do with creating presentations (like how to include graphics or animations).

The third part explains how you can change the appearance of your presentation easily either using themes or by specifying colors or fonts for specific elements of a presentation (like, say, the font used for the numbers in an enumeration).

The fourth part talks about handouts and lecture notes, so called "support material". You will frequently have create some kind of support material to give to your audience during the talk or after it, and this part will explain how to do it using the same source that you created your presentation from.

The last part contains "howtos," which are explanations of how to get certain things done using BEAMER.

This user's guide contains descriptions of all "public" commands, environments, and concepts defined by the BEAMER-class. The following examples show how things are documented. As a general rule, red text is *defined*, green text is *optional*, blue text indicates special mode considerations.

\somebeamercommand[⟨*optional arguments*⟩]{⟨*first argument*⟩}{⟨*second argument*⟩}

> Here you will find the explanation of what the command \somebeamercommand does. The green argument(s) is optional. The command of this example takes two parameters.
>
> *Example:* \somebeamercommand[opt]{my arg}{xxx}

\begin{somebeamerenvironment}[⟨*optional arguments*⟩]{⟨*first argument*⟩}
⟨*environment contents*⟩

`\end{somebeamerenvironment}`

Here you will find the explanation of the effect of the environment `somebeamerenvironment`. As with commands, the green arguments are optional.

Example:
```
\begin{somebeamerenvironment}{Argument}
  Some text.
\end{somebeamerenvironment}
```

Beamer-Template/-Color/-Font `some beamer element`

Here you will find an explanation of the template, color, and/or font `some beamer element`. A "BEAMER-element" is a concept that is explained in more detail in Section 16. Roughly speaking, an *element* is a part of a presentation that is potentially typeset in some special way. Examples of elements are frame titles, the author's name, or the footnote sign. For most elements there exists a *template*, see Section 16 once more, and also a BEAMER-color and a BEAMER-font.

For each element, it is indicated whether a template, a BEAMER-color, and/or a BEAMER-font of the name `some beamer element` exist. Typically, all three exist and are employed together when the element needs to be typeset, that is, when the template is inserted the BEAMER-color and -font are installed first. However, sometimes templates do not have a color or font associated with them (like parent templates). Also, there exist BEAMER-colors and -fonts that do not have an underlying template.

Using and changing templates is explained in Section 16.3. Here is the essence: To change a template, you can say

`\setbeamertemplate{some beamer element}{your definition for this template}`

Unfortunately, it is not quite trivial to come up with a good definition for some templates. Fortunately, there are often *predefined options* for a template. These are indicated like this:

- `[square]` causes a small square to be used to render the template.
- `[circle]{⟨radius⟩}` causes circles of the given radius to be used to render the template.

You can install such a predefined option like this:
```
\setbeamertemplate{some beamer element}[square]
% Now squares are used
```
```
\setbeamertemplate{some beamer element}[circle]{3pt}
% Now a circle is used
```

BEAMER-colors are explained in Section 17. Here is the essence: To change the foreground of the color to, say, red, use

`\setbeamercolor{some beamer element}{fg=red}`

To change the background to, say, black, use:

`\setbeamercolor{some beamer element}{bg=black}`

You can also change them together using `fg=red,bg=black`. The background will not always be "honoured," since it is difficult to show a colored background correctly and an extra effort must be made by the templates (while the foreground color is usually used automatically).

BEAMER-fonts are explained in Section 18. Here is the essence: To change the size of the font to, say, large, use:

`\setbeamerfont{some beamer element}{size=\large}`

In addition to the size, you can use things like `series=\bfseries` to set the series, `shape=\itshape` to change the shape, `family=\sffamily` to change the family, and you can use them in conjunction. Add a star to the command to first "reset" the font.

11

As next to this paragraph, you will sometimes find the word PRESENTATION in blue next to some paragraph. This means that the paragraph applies only when you "normally typeset your presentation using LaTeX or pdfLaTeX."

Opposed to this, a paragraph with ARTICLE next to it describes some behavior that is special for the `article` mode. This special mode is used to create lecture notes out of a presentation (the two can coexist in one file).

1.5 Getting Help

When you need help with BEAMER, please do the following:

1. Read the user guide, at least the part that has to do with your problem.

2. If that does not solve the problem, try searching TeX-sx (`tex.stackexchange.com`). Perhaps someone has already reported a similar problem and someone has found a solution.

3. If you find no answers there, or if you are sure you have found a bug in BEAMER, please report it *via* `bitbucket.org/rivanvx/beamer/issues`.

4. Before you file a bug report, especially a bug report concerning the installation, make sure that this is really a bug. In particular, have a look at the `.log` file that results when you TeX your files. This `.log` file should show that all the right files are loaded from the right directories. Nearly all installation problems can be resolved by looking at the `.log` file.

   If you can, before reporting the bug, retest using latest version of BEAMER with latest version of TeX Live. This can help isolate bugs from other packages that might affect BEAMER.

5. *As a last resort* you can try emailing authors. We do not mind getting emails, we simply get way too many of them. Because of this, we cannot guarantee that your emails will be answered timely or even at all. Reporting an issue is usually a better approach as they don't get lost.

Part I
Getting Started

This part helps you getting started. It starts with an explanation of how to install the class. Hopefully, this will be very simple, with a bit of luck the whole class is already correctly installed! You will also find an explanation of special things you should consider when using certain other packages.

Next, a short tutorial is given that explains most of the features that you'll need in a typical presentation. Following the tutorial you will find a "possible workflow" for creating a presentation. Following this workflow may help you avoid problems later on.

This part includes a guidelines sections. Following these guidelines can help you create good presentations (no guarantees, though). This guideline section is kept as general as possible; most of what is said in that section applies to presentations in general, independent of whether they have been created using BEAMER or not.

At the end of this part you will find a summary of the solutions templates that come with BEAMER. You can use solutions templates to kick-start the creation of your presentation.

2 Installation

There are different ways of installing the BEAMER class, depending on your installation and needs. When installing the class, you may have to install some other packages as well as described below. Before installing, you may wish to review the licenses under which the class is distributed, see Section 7.

Fortunately, most likely your system will already have BEAMER preinstalled, so you can skip this section.

2.1 Versions and Dependencies

This documentation is part of version 3.36 of the BEAMER class. BEAMER needs a reasonably recent version of several standard packages to run and also the following versions of two special packages (later versions should work, but not necessarily):

- `pgf.sty` version 1.00,
- `xcolor.sty` version 2.00.

If you use `pdflatex`, which is optional, you need

- `pdflatex` version 0.14 or higher. Earlier versions do not work.

2.2 Installation of Pre-bundled Packages

We do not create or manage pre-bundled packages of BEAMER, but, fortunately, other nice people do. We cannot give detailed instructions on how to install these packages, since we do not manage them, but we *can* tell you were to find them and we can tell you what these nice people told us on how to install them. If you have a problem with installing, you might wish to have a look at the following first.

2.2.1 TeX Live and MacTeX

In TeX Live, use the `tlmgr` tool to install the packages called `beamer`, `pgf`, and `xcolor`. If you have a fairly recent version of TeX Live, and you have done full installation, BEAMER is included.

2.2.2 MiKTeX and proTeXt

For MiKTeX and proTeXt, use the update wizard or package manager to install the (latest versions of the) packages called `beamer`, `pgf`, and `xcolor`.

2.2.3 Debian and Ubuntu

The command "`aptitude install latex-beamer`" should do the trick. If necessary, the packages `pgf` and `latex-xcolor` will be automatically installed. Sit back and relax. In detail, the following packages are installed:

http://packages.debian.org/latex-beamer
http://packages.debian.org/pgf
http://packages.debian.org/latex-xcolor

Debian 5.0 "lenny" includes TeX Live 2007, and version 6.0 "squeeze" will include TeX Live 2009. This also allows you to manually install newer versions of BEAMER (into your local directory, see below) without having to update any other LaTeX packages.

Ubuntu 8.04, 9.04 and 9.10 include TeX Live 2007, and version 10.04 includes TeX Live 2009.

2.2.4 Fedora

Fedora 9, 10, 11, 12 and 13 include TeX Live 2007, which includes BEAMER. It can be installed by running the command "`yum install texlive-texmf-latex`". As with Debian, this allows you to manually install newer versions of BEAMER into your local directory (explained below).

Jindrich Novy provides TeX Live 2010 `rpm` packages for Fedora 12 and 13, at

http://fedoraproject.org/wiki/Features/TeXLive

Fedora 14 will contain TeX Live 2010 once it's released.

14

2.3 Installation in a texmf Tree

If, for whatever reason, you do not wish to use a prebundled package, the "right" way to install BEAMER is to put it in a so-called `texmf` tree. In the following, we explain how to do this.

Obtain the latest source version (ending `.tar.gz` or `.zip`) of the BEAMER package from

`http://bitbucket.org/rivanvx/beamer`

(most likely, you have already done this). Next, you also need the PGF package and the XCOLOR packages, which you need to install separately (see their installation instructions).

The package contains a bunch of files; `beamer.cls` is one of these files and happens to be the most important one. You now need to put these files in an appropriate `texmf` tree.

When you ask TEX to use a certain class or package, it usually looks for the necessary files in so-called `texmf` trees. These trees are simply huge directories that contain these files. By default, TEX looks for files in three different `texmf` trees:

- The root `texmf` tree, which is usually located at `/usr/share/texmf/`, `/usr/local/texlive/texmf/`, `c:\texmf\`, or
  `c:\texlive\texmf\`.

- The local `texmf` tree, which is usually located at `/usr/local/share/texmf/`, `/usr/local/texlive/texmf-local`, `c:\localtexmf\`, or
  `c:\texlive\texmf-local\`.

- Your personal `texmf` tree, which is usually located in your home directory at `~/texmf/` or `~/Library/texmf/`.

You should install the packages either in the local tree or in your personal tree, depending on whether you have write access to the local tree. Installation in the root tree can cause problems, since an update of the whole TEX installation will replace this whole tree.

Inside whatever `texmf` directory you have chosen, create the sub-sub-sub-directory

`texmf/tex/latex/beamer`

and place all files of the package in this directory.

Finally, you need to rebuild TEX's filename database. This is done by running the command `texhash` or `mktexlsr` (they are the same). In MiKTEX package manager and TEX Live `tlmgr`, there is a menu option to do this.

For a more detailed explanation of the standard installation process of packages, you might wish to consult `http://www.ctan.org/installationadvice/`. However, note that the BEAMER package does not come with a `.ins` file (simply skip that part).

2.4 Updating the Installation

To update your installation from a previous version, simply replace everything in the directory

`texmf/tex/latex/beamer`

with the files of the new version. The easiest way to do this is to first delete the old version and then to proceed as described above.

Note that if you have two versions installed, one in `texmf` and other in `texmf-local` directory, TEX distribution will prefer one in `texmf-local` directory. This generally allows you to update packages manually without administrator privileges.

2.5 Testing the Installation

To test your installation, copy the file `generic-ornate-15min-45min.en.tex` from the directory

`beamer/solutions/generic-talks`

to some place where you usually create presentations. Then run the command `pdflatex` several times on the file and check whether the resulting PDF file looks correct. If so, you are all set.

2.6 Compatibility with Other Packages and Classes

When using certain packages or classes together with the beamer class, extra options or precautions may be necessary.

\usepackage{AlDraTex}

Graphics created using AlDraTex must be treated like verbatim text. The reason is that DraTex fiddles with catcodes and spaces much like verbatim does. So, in order to insert a picture, either add the fragile option to the frame or use the \defverbatim command to create a box containing the picture.

\usepackage{alltt}

Text in an alltt environment must be treated like verbatim text. So add the fragile option to frames containing this environment or use \defverbatim.

\usepackage{amsthm}

This package is automatically loaded since BEAMER uses it for typesetting theorems. If you do not wish it to be loaded, which can be necessary especially in article mode if the package is incompatible with the document class, you can use the class option noamsthm to suppress its loading. See Section 12.4 for more details.

\usepackage[french]{babel}

When using the french style, certain features that clash with the functionality of the BEAMER class will be turned off. For example, enumerations are still produced the way the theme dictates, not the way the french style does.

\usepackage[spanish]{babel}

PRESEN-TATION When using the spanish style, certain features that clash with the functionality of the BEAMER class will be turned off. In particular, the special behavior of the pointed brackets < and > is deactivated.

ARTICLE To make the characters < and > active in article mode, pass the option activeospeccharacters to the package beamerbasearticle. This will lead to problems with overlay specifications.

\usepackage{color}

PRESEN-TATION The color package is automatically loaded by beamer.cls. This makes it impossible to pass options to color in the preamble of your document in the normal manner. To pass a ⟨list of options⟩ to color, you can use the following class option:

\documentclass[color=⟨list of options⟩]{beamer}

Causes the ⟨list of options⟩ to be passed on to the color package. If the ⟨list of options⟩ contains more than one option you must enclose it in curly brackets.

ARTICLE The color package is not loaded automatically if beamerarticle is loaded with the noxcolor option.

\usepackage{colortbl}

PRESEN-TATION With newer versions of xcolor.sty, you need to pass the option table to xcolor.sty if you wish to use colortbl. See the notes on xcolor below, on how to do this.

\usepackage{CJK}

PRESEN-TATION When using the CJK package for using Asian fonts, you must use the class option CJK.

\usepackage{deluxetable}

PRESEN-TATION The caption generation facilities of deluxetable are deactivated. Instead, the caption template is used.

`\usepackage{DraTex}`

See `AlDraTex`.

`\usepackage{enumerate}`

ARTICLE This package is loaded automatically in the `presentation` modes, but not in the `article` mode. If you use its features, you have to load the package "by hand" in the `article` mode.

`\documentclass{foils}`

If you wish to emulate the `foils` class using BEAMER, please see Section 24.3.

`\usepackage[T1,EU1,EU2]{fontenc}`

Use the `T1` option *only* with fonts that have outline fonts available in the T1 encoding like `times` or the `lmodern` fonts. In a standard installation standard Computer Modern fonts (the fonts Donald Knuth originally designed and which are used by default) are *not* available in the T1 encoding. Using this option with them will result in very poor rendering of your presentation when viewed with PDF viewer applications like Acrobat, `xpdf`, `evince` or `okular`. To use the Computer Modern fonts with the T1 encoding, use the package `lmodern`. See also Section 18.2.3. This applies both to `latex+dvips` and `pdflatex`

Use the `EU1` option with `xelatex`, and `EU2` option with `lualatex`. Note that `xelatex` and `luatex` support OpenType fonts, and font encodings work very different compared to `pdflatex`. Again, see Section 18.2.3 for more information.

`\usepackage{fourier}`

The package switches to a T1 encoding, but it does not redefine all fonts such that outline fonts (non-bitmapped fonts) are used by default. For example, the sans-serif text and the typewriter text are not replaced. To use outline fonts for these, write `\usepackage{lmodern}` *before* including the `fourier` package.

`\usepackage{HA-prosper}`

You cannot use this package with BEAMER. However, you might try to use the package `beamerprosper` instead, see Section 24.1.

`\usepackage{hyperref}`

PRESEN-
TATION The `hyperref` package is automatically loaded by `beamer.cls` and certain options are set up. In order to pass additional options to `hyperref` or to override options, you can use the following class option:

`\documentclass[hyperref=`⟨*list of options*⟩`]{beamer}`

Causes the ⟨*list of options*⟩ to be passed on to the `hyperref` package.

Example: `\documentclass[hyperref={bookmarks=false}]{beamer}`

Alternatively, you can also use the `\hypersetup` command.

ARTICLE In the `article` version, you must include `hyperref` manually if you want to use it. You can do so by passing option `hyperref` to `beamerarticle`. It is not included automatically.

`\usepackage[utf8,utf8x]{inputenc}`

PRESEN-
TATION When using Unicode, you may wish to use *some* of the following class options:

`\documentclass[ucs]{beamer}`

Loads the package `ucs` and passes the correct Unicode options to `hyperref`. Also, it preloads the Unicode code pages zero and one.

`\documentclass[utf8x]{beamer}`

Same as the option `ucs`, but also sets the input encoding to `utf8x`. You could also use the option `ucs` and say `\usepackage[utf8x]{inputenc}` in the preamble. This also automatically loads `ucs` package in most TeX systems.

If you use a Unicode character outside the first two code pages (which includes the Latin alphabet and the extended Latin alphabet) in a section or subsection heading, you have to use the command `\PreloadUnicodePage{`⟨*code page*⟩`}` to give ucs a chance to preload these code pages. You will know that a character has not been preloaded, if you get a message like "Please insert into preamble." The code page of a character is given by the unicode number of the character divided by 256.

`\documentclass[utf8]{beamer}`

> This option sets the input encoding to utf8. It's designed to be used *without* ucs. It's the same as saying `\usepackage[utf8]{inputenc}` in the preamble.

Note that *none* of these options apply to lualatex and xelatex, since both support Unicode natively without any extra packages. Most of the time using these options actually harms output quality, so be careful about what you use. If you want to have a document that allows compiling with multiple drivers, take a look at iftex, ifxetex and ifluatex packages.

ARTICLE Passing option utf8 to `beamerarticle` has the same effect as saying `\usepackage[utf8]{inputenc}` in the preamble.

Again, take care if you use lualatex or xelatex.

`\usepackage{listings}`

PRESEN- Note that you must treat `lstlisting` environments exactly the same way as you would treat `verbatim`
TATION environments. When using `\defverbatim` that contains a colored `lstlisting`, use the `colored` option of `\defverbatim`.

Example:

```
\usepackage{listings}

\begin{document}
\defverbatim[colored]\mycode{%
  \begin{lstlisting}[frame=single, emph={cout}, emphstyle={\color{blue}}]
    cout << "Hello world!";
  \end{lstlisting}
  }

\begin{frame}
  \mycode
\end{frame}
\end{document}
```

`\usepackage{msc}`

PRESEN- Since this package uses `pstricks` internally, everything that applies to pstricks also applies to `msc`.
TATION

`\usepackage{musixtex}`

When using MusiXTEX to typeset musical scores, you have to have ε-TEXextensions enabled. Most modern distributions enable that by default both in `pdflatex` and `latex`. However, if you have an older distribution, the document must be compiled with `pdfelatex` or `elatex` instead of `pdflatex` or `latex`.

Inside a `music` environment, the `\pause` is redefined to match MusiXTEX's definition (a rest during one quarter of a whole). You can use the `\beamerpause` command to create overlays in this environment.

`\usepackage{pdfpages}`

Commands like `\includepdf` only work *outside* frames as they produce pages "by themselves." You may also wish to say

`\setbeamercolor{background canvas}{bg=}`

when you use such a command since the background (even a white background) will otherwise be printed over the image you try to include.

Example:

```
\begin{document}
\begin{frame}
  \titlepage
\end{frame}

{
  \setbeamercolor{background canvas}{bg=}
  \includepdf{somepdfimages.pdf}
}

\begin{frame}
  A normal frame.
\end{frame}
\end{document}
```

\usepackage{⟨*professional font package*⟩}

PRESEN-
TATION
If you use a professional font package, BEAMER's internal redefinition of how variables are typeset may interfere with the font package's superior way of typesetting them. In this case, you should use the class option `professionalfont` to suppress any font substitution. See Section 18.2.2 for details.

\documentclass{prosper}

If you wish to (partly) emulate the **prosper** class using BEAMER, please see Section 24.1.

\usepackage{pstricks}

You should add the option `xcolor=pst` to make `xcolor` aware of the fact that you are using `pstricks`.

\documentclass{seminar}

If you wish to emulate the **seminar** class using BEAMER, please see Section 24.2.

\usepackage{texpower}

You cannot use this package with BEAMER. However, you might try to use the package `beamertexpower` instead, see Section 24.4.

\usepackage{textpos}

PRESEN-
TATION
BEAMER automatically installs a white background behind everything, unless you install a different background template. Because of this, you must use the `overlay` option when using `textpos`, so that it will place boxes *in front of* everything. Alternatively, you can install an empty background template, but this may result in an incorrect display in certain situtations with older versions of the Acrobat Reader.

\usepackage{ucs}

See \usepackage[utf8,utf8x]{inputenc}.

\usepackage{xcolor}

PRESEN-
TATION
The `xcolor` package is automatically loaded by `beamer.cls`. The same applies as to `color`.

\documentclass[xcolor=⟨*list of options*⟩]{beamer}

Causes the ⟨*list of options*⟩ to be passed on to the `xcolor` package.

When using BEAMER together with the `pstricks` package, be sure to pass the `xcolor=pst` option to BEAMER (and hence to `xcolor`).

ARTICLE
The `color` package is not loaded automatically if `beamerarticle` is loaded with the `noxcolor` option.

19

3 Tutorial: Euclid's Presentation

This section presents a short tutorial that focuses on those features of BEAMER that you are likely to use when you start using BEAMER. It leaves out all the glorious details that are explained in great detail later on.

3.1 Problem Statement

We wish to help Prof. Euclid of the University of Alexandria to create a presentation on his latest discovery: There are infinitely many prime numbers! Euclid wrote a paper on this and it got accepted at the 27th International Symposium on Prime Numbers -280 (ISPN '80). Euclid wishes to use the BEAMER class to create a presentation for the conference. On the conference webpage he found out that he will have twenty minutes for his talk, including questions.

3.2 Solution Template

The first thing Euclid should do is to look for a solution template for his presentation. Having a look at Section 6, he finds that the file

```
beamer/solutions/conference-talks/conference-ornate-20min.en.tex
```

might be appropriate. He creates a subdirectory `presentation` in the directory that contains the actual paper and copies the solution template to this subdirectory, renaming to `main.tex`.

He opens the file in his favorite editor. It starts

```
\documentclass{beamer}
```

which Euclid finds hardly surprising. Next comes a line reading

```
\mode<presentation>
```

which Euclid does not understand. Since he finds more stuff in the file that he does not understand, he decides to ignore all of that for time being, hoping that it all serves some good purpose.

3.3 Title Material

The next thing that seems logical is the place where the `\title` command is used. Naturally, he replaces it with

```
\title{There Is No Largest Prime Number}
```

since this was the title of the paper. He sees that the command `\title` also takes an optional "short" argument in square brackets, which is shown in places where there is little space, but he decides that the title is short enough by itself.

Euclid next adjusts the `\author` and `\date` fields as follows:

```
\author{Euclid of Alexandria}
\date[ISPN '80]{27th International Symposium of Prime Numbers}
```

For the date, he felt that the name was a little long, so a short version is given (ISPN '80). On second thought, Euclid decides to add his email address and replaces the `\author` field as follows:

```
\author[Euclid]{Euclid of Alexandria \\ \texttt{euclid@alexandria.edu}}
```

Somehow Euclid does not like the fact that there is no "`\email`" command in BEAMER. He decides to write an email to BEAMER's author, asking him to fix this, but postpones this for later when the presentation is finished.

There are two fields that Euclid does not know, but whose meaning he can guess: `\subtitle` and `\institute`. He adjusts them. (Euclid does not need to use the `\and` command, which is used to separate several authors, nor the `\inst` command, which just makes its argument a superscript).

3.4   The Title Page Frame

The next thing in the file that seems interesting is where the first "frame" is created, right after the \begin{document}:

```
\begin{frame}
  \titlepage
\end{frame}
```

In BEAMER, a presentation consists of a series of frames. Each frame in turn may consist of several slides (if there is more than one, they are called overlays). Normally, everything between \begin{frame} and \end{frame} is put on a single slide. No page breaking is performed. So Euclid infers that the first frame is "filled" by the title page, which seems quite logical.

3.5   Creating the Presentation PDF File

Eager to find out how the first page will look, he invokes pdflatex on his file main.tex (twice). He could also use latex (twice), followed by dvips, and then possibly ps2pdf, or lualatex (twice), or xelatex (twice). Then he uses the Acrobat Reader, xpdf, evince or okular to view the resulting main.pdf. Indeed, the first page contains all the information Euclid has provided until now. It even looks quite impressive with the colorful title and the rounded corners and the shadows, but he is doubtful whether he should leave it like that. He decides to address this problem later.

Euclid is delighted to find out that clicking on a section or subsection in the navigation bar at the top hyperjumps there. Also, the small symbols at the bottom seem to be clickable. Toying around with them for a while, he finds that clicking on the arrows left or right of a symbol hyperjumps him backward or forward one slide / frame / subsection / section. He finds the symbols quite small, but decides not to write an email to BEAMER's authors since he also thinks that bigger symbols would be distracting.

3.6   The Table of Contents

The next frame contains a table of contents:

```
\begin{frame}
  \frametitle{Outline}
  \tableofcontents
\end{frame}
```

Furthermore, this frame has an individual title (Outline). A comment in the frame says that Euclid might wish to try to add the [pausesections] option. He tries this, changing the frame to:

```
\begin{frame}
  \frametitle{Outline}
  \tableofcontents[pausesections]
\end{frame}
```

After re-pdfLATEXing the presentation, he finds that instead of a single slide, there are now two "table of contents" slides in the presentation. On the first of these, only the first section is shown, on the second both sections are shown (scanning down in the file, Euclid finds that, indeed, there are \section commands introducing these sections). The effect of the pausesections seems to be that one can talk about the first section before the second one is shown. Then, Euclid can press the down- or right-key, to show the complete table of contents and can talk about the second section.

3.7   Sections and Subsections

The next commands Euclid finds are

```
\section{Motivation}
\subsection{The Basic Problem That We Studied}
```

These commands are given *outside* of frames. So Euclid assumes that at the point of invocation they have no direct effect, they only create entries in the table of contents. Having a "Motivation" section seems reasonable to Euclid, but he changes the \subsection title.

As he looks at the presentation, he notices that his assumption was not quite true: each \subsection command seems to insert a frame containing a table of contents into the presentation. Doubling back he finds the command that causes this: The \AtBeginSubsection inserts a frame with only the current subsection highlighted at the beginning of each section. If Euclid does not like this, he can just delete the whole \AtBeginSubsection stuff and the table of contents at the beginning of each subsection disappears.

The \section and \subsection commands take optional short arguments. These short arguments are used whenever a short form of the section of subsection name is needed. While this is in keeping with the way BEAMER treats the optional arguments of things like \title, it is *different* from the usual way LaTeX treats an optional argument for sections (where the optional argument dictates what is shown in the table of contents and the main argument dictates what is shown everywhere else; in BEAMER things are exactly the other way round).

3.8 Creating a Simple Frame

Euclid then modifies the next frame, which is the first "real" frame of the presentation, as follows:

```
\begin{frame}
  \frametitle{What Are Prime Numbers?}
  A prime number is a number that has exactly two divisors.
\end{frame}
```

This yields the desired result. It might be a good idea to put some emphasis on the object being defined (prime numbers). Euclid tries \emph but finds that too mild an emphasis. BEAMER offers the command \alert, which is used like \emph and, by default, typesets its argument in bright red.

Next, Euclid decides to make it even clearer that he is giving a definition by putting a definition environment around the definition.

```
\begin{frame}
  \frametitle{What Are Prime Numbers?}
  \begin{definition}
    A \alert{prime number} is a number that has exactly two divisors.
  \end{definition}
\end{frame}
```

Other useful environments like theorem, lemma, proof, corollary, or example are also predefined by BEAMER. As in amsmath, they take optional arguments that they show in brackets. Indeed, amsmath is automatically loaded by BEAMER.

Since it is always a good idea to add examples, Euclid decides to add one:

```
\begin{frame}
  \frametitle{What Are Prime Numbers?}
  \begin{definition}
    A \alert{prime number} is a number that has exactly two divisors.
  \end{definition}
  \begin{example}
    \begin{itemize}
    \item 2 is prime (two divisors: 1 and 2).
    \item 3 is prime (two divisors: 1 and 3).
    \item 4 is not prime (\alert{three} divisors: 1, 2, and 4).
    \end{itemize}
  \end{example}
\end{frame}
```

3.9 Creating Simple Overlays

The frame already looks quite nice, though, perhaps a bit colorful. However, Euclid would now like to show the three items one after another, not all three right away. To achieve this, he adds \pause commands after the first and second items:

```
\begin{itemize}
\item 2 is prime (two divisors: 1 and 2).
  \pause
\item 3 is prime (two divisors: 1 and 3).
  \pause
\item 4 is not prime (\alert{three} divisors: 1, 2, and 4).
\end{itemize}
```

By showing them incrementally, he hopes to focus the audience's attention on the item he is currently talking about. On second thought, he deletes the \pause stuff once more since in simple cases like the above the pausing is rather silly. Indeed, Euclids has noticed that good presentations make use of this uncovering mechanism only in special circumstances.

Euclid finds that he can also add a \pause between the definition and the example. So, \pauses seem to transcede environments, which Euclid finds quite useful. After some experimentation he finds that \pause only does not work in align environments. He immediately writes an email about this to BEAMER's author, but receives a polite answer stating that the implementation of align does wicked things and there is no fix for this. Also, Euclid is pointed to the last part of the user's guide, where a workaround is described.

3.10 Using Overlay Specifications

The next frame is to show his main argument and is put in a "Results" section. Euclid desires a more complicated overlay behavior for this frame: In an enumeration of four points he wishes to uncover the points one-by-one, but he wishes the fourth point to be shown at the same time as the first. The idea is to illustrate his new proof method, namely proof by contradiction, where a wrong assumption is brought to a contradiction at the end after a number of intermediate steps that are not important at the beginning. For this, Euclid uses *overlay specifications*:

```
\begin{frame}
  \frametitle{There Is No Largest Prime Number}
  \framesubtitle{The proof uses \textit{reductio ad absurdum}.}

  \begin{theorem}
    There is no largest prime number.
  \end{theorem}
  \begin{proof}
    \begin{enumerate}
    \item<1-> Suppose $p$ were the largest prime number.
    \item<2-> Let $q$ be the product of the first $p$ numbers.
    \item<3-> Then $q + 1$ is not divisible by any of them.
    \item<1-> But $q + 1$ is greater than $1$, thus divisible by some prime
      number not in the first $p$ numbers.\qedhere
    \end{enumerate}
  \end{proof}
  \uncover<4->{The proof used \textit{reductio ad absurdum}.}
\end{frame}
```

The overlay specifications are given in pointed brackets. The specification <1-> means "from slide 1 on." Thus, the first and fourth item are shown on the first slide of the frame, but the other two items are not shown. Rather, the second point is shown only from the second slide onward. BEAMER automatically computes the number of slides needed for each frame. More generally, overlay specification are lists of numbers or number ranges where the start or ending of a range can be left open. For example -3,5-6,8- means "on all slides, except for slides 4 and 7."

The \qedhere is used to put the QED symbol at the end of the line *inside* the enumeration. Normally, the QED symbol is automatically inserted at the end of a proof environment, but that would be on an ugly empty line here.

The \item command is not the only command that takes overlay specifications. Another useful command that takes one is the \uncover command. It only shows its argument on the slides specified in the overlay specification. On all other slides, the argument is hidden (though it still occupies space). The command \only is similar and Euclid could also have tried

```
\only<4->{The proof used \textit{reductio ad absurdum}.}
```

On non-specified slides the \only command simply "throws its argument away" and the argument does not occupy any space. This leads to different heights of the text on the first three slides and on the fourth slide. If the text is centered vertically, this will cause the text to "wobble" and thus \uncover should be used. However, you sometimes wish things to "really disappear" on some slides and then \only is useful. Euclid could also have used the class option t, which causes the text in frames to be vertically flushed to the top. Then a differing text height does not cause wobbling. Vertical flushing can also be achieved for only a single frame by giving the optional argument [t] like this to the frame environment as in

```
\begin{frame}[t]
  \frametitle{There Is No Largest Prime Number}
  ...
\end{frame}
```

Vice versa, if the t class option is given, a frame can be vertically centered using the [c] option for the frame.

It turns out that certain environments, including the theorem and proof environments above, also take overlay specifications. If such a specification is given, the whole theorem or proof is only shown on the specified slides.

3.11 Structuring a Frame

On the next frame, Euclid wishes to contrast solved and open problems on prime numbers. Since there is no "Solved problem" environment similar to the theorem environment, Euclid decides to use the block environment, which allows him to give an arbitrary title:

```
\begin{frame}
  \frametitle{What's Still To Do?}
  \begin{block}{Answered Questions}
    How many primes are there?
  \end{block}
  \begin{block}{Open Questions}
    Is every even number the sum of two primes?
  \end{block}
\end{frame}
```

He could also have defined his own theorem-like environment by putting the following in the preamble:

```
\newtheorem{answeredquestions}[theorem]{Answered Questions}
\newtheorem{openquestions}[theorem]{Open Questions}
```

The optional argument [theorem] ensures that these environments are numbered the same way as everything else. Since these numbers are not shown anyway, it does not really matter whether they are given, but it's a good practice and, perhaps, Euclid might need these numbers some other time.

An alternative would be nested itemize:

```
\begin{frame}
  \frametitle{What's Still To Do?}
  \begin{itemize}
  \item Answered Questions
    \begin{itemize}
    \item How many primes are there?
    \end{itemize}
  \item Open Questions
    \begin{itemize}
```

```
  \item Is every even number the sum of two primes?
    \end{itemize}
  \end{itemize}
\end{frame}
```

Pondering on the problem some more, Euclid decides that it would be even nicer to have the "Answered Questions" on the left and the "Open Questions" on the right, so as to create a stronger visual contrast. For this, he uses the `columns` environment. Inside this environment, `\column` commands create new columns.

```
\begin{frame}
  \frametitle{What's Still To Do?}
  \begin{columns}
    \column{.5\textwidth}
      \begin{block}{Answered Questions}
        How many primes are there?
      \end{block}

    \column{.5\textwidth}
      \begin{block}{Open Questions}
        Is every even number the sum of two primes?
      \end{block}
  \end{columns}
\end{frame}
```

Trying this, he is not quite satisfied with the result as the block on the left has a different height than the one on the right. He thinks it would be nicer if they were vertically top-aligned. So he adds the `[t]` option to the `columns` environment.

Euclid is somewhat pleased to find out that a `\pause` at the end of the first column allows him to "uncover" the second column only on the second slide of the frame.

3.12   Adding References

Euclid decides that he would like to add a citation to his open questions list, since he would like to attribute the question to his good old friend Christian. Euclid is not really sure whether using a bibliography in his talk is a good idea, but he goes ahead anyway.

To this end, he adds an entry to the bibliography, which he fortunately already finds in the solution file. Having the bibliography in the appendix does not quite suit Euclid, so he removes the `\appendix` command. He also notices `<presentation>` overlay specifications and finds them a bit strange, but they don't seem to hurt either. Hopefully they do something useful. His bibliography looks like this:

```
\begin{thebibliography}{10}
\bibitem{Goldbach1742}[Goldbach, 1742]
  Christian Goldbach.
  \newblock A problem we should try to solve before the ISPN '43 deadline,
  \newblock \emph{Letter to Leonhard Euler}, 1742.
\end{thebibliography}
```

and he can then add a citation:

```
\begin{block}{Open Questions}
  Is every even number the sum of two primes?
  \cite{Goldbach1742}
\end{block}
```

3.13   Verbatim Text

On another frame, Euclid would like to show a listing of an algorithm his friend Eratosthenes has sent him (saying he came up with it while reorganizing his sieve collection). Euclid normally uses the `verbatim` environment and sometimes also similar environments like `lstlisting` to typeset listings. He can also use them in BEAMER, but he must add the `fragile` option to the frame:

```
\begin{frame}[fragile]
  \frametitle{An Algorithm For Finding Prime Numbers.}

\begin{verbatim}
int main (void)
{
  std::vector<bool> is_prime (100, true);
  for (int i = 2; i < 100; i++)
    if (is_prime[i])
      {
        std::cout << i << " ";
        for (int j = i; j < 100; is_prime [j] = false, j+=i);
      }
  return 0;
}
\end{verbatim}

  \begin{uncoverenv}<2>
    Note the use of \verb|std::|.
  \end{uncoverenv}
\end{frame}
```

On second thought, Euclid would prefer to uncover part of the algorithm stepwise and to add an emphasis on certain lines or parts of lines. He can use package like `alltt` for this, but in simple cases the environment {semiverbatim} defined by BEAMER is more useful: It works like {verbatim}, except that \, {, and } retain their meaning (one can typeset them by using \\, \{, and \}). Euclid might now typeset his algorithm as follows:

```
\begin{frame}[fragile]
  \frametitle{An Algorithm For Finding Primes Numbers.}

\begin{semiverbatim}
\uncover<1->{\alert<0>{int main (void)}}
\uncover<1->{\alert<0>{\{}}
\uncover<1->{\alert<1>{  \alert<4>{std::}vector<bool> is_prime (100, true);}}
\uncover<1->{\alert<1>{  for (int i = 2; i < 100; i++)}}
\uncover<2->{\alert<2>{    if (is_prime[i])}}
\uncover<2->{\alert<0>{      \{}}
\uncover<3->{\alert<3>{        \alert<4>{std::}cout << i << " ";}}
\uncover<3->{\alert<3>{        for (int j = i; j < 100;}}
\uncover<3->{\alert<3>{          is_prime [j] = false, j+=i);}}
\uncover<2->{\alert<0>{      \}}}
\uncover<1->{\alert<0>{  return 0;}}
\uncover<1->{\alert<0>{\}}}
\end{semiverbatim}

  \visible<4->{Note the use of \alert{\texttt{std::}}.}
\end{frame}
```

The \visible command does nearly the same as \uncover. A difference occurs if the command \setbeamercovered{t has been used to make covered text "transparent" instead, \visible still makes the text completely "invisible" on non-specified slides. Euclid has the feeling that the naming convention is a bit strange, but cannot quite pinpoint the problem.

3.14 Changing the Way Things Look I: Theming

With the contents of this talk fixed, Euclid decides to have a second look at the way things look. He goes back to the beginning and finds the line

```
\usetheme{Warsaw}
```

By substituting other cities (he notices that these cities seem to have in common that there has been a workshop or conference on theoretical computer science there at which always the same person had a paper, attended, or gave a talk) Euclid can change the way his presentation is going to look. He decides to choose some theme that is reasonably simple but, since his talk is not too short, shows a bit of navigational information.

He settles on the `Frankfurt` theme but decides that the light-dark contrast is too strong. He adds

```
\usecolortheme{seahorse}
\usecolortheme{rose}
```

The result seems some more subdued to him.

Euclid decides that the font used for the titles is not quite classical enough (classical fonts are the latest chic in Alexandria). So, he adds

```
\usefonttheme[onlylarge]{structuresmallcapsserif}
```

Euclid notices that the small fonts in the navigation bars are a bit hard to read as they are so thin. Adding the following helps:

```
\usefonttheme[onlysmall]{structurebold}
```

3.15 Changing the Way Things Look II: Colors and Fonts

Since Euclid wants to give a *perfect* talk, he decides that the font used for the title simply has to be a serif italics. To change only the font used for the title, Euclid uses the following command:

```
\setbeamerfont{title}{shape=\itshape,family=\rmfamily}
```

He notices that the font is still quite large (which he likes), but wonders why this is the case since he did not specify this. The reason is that calls of `\setbeamerfont` accumulate and the size was already set to `\large` by some font theme. Using the starred version of `\setbeamerfont` "resets" the font.

Euclid decides that he would also like to change the color of the title to a dashing red, though, perhaps, with a bit of black added. He uses the following command:

```
\setbeamercolor{title}{fg=red!80!black}
```

Trying the following command, Euclid is delighted to find that specifying a background color also has an effect:

```
\setbeamercolor{title}{fg=red!80!black,bg=red!20!white}
```

Finally, Euclid is satisfied with the presentation and goes ahead and gives a great talk at the conference, making many new friends. He also writes that email to BEAMER's author containing that long list of things that he missed in BEAMER or that do not work. He is a bit disappointed to learn that it might take till ISPN '79 for all these things to be taken care of, but he also understands that BEAMER's authors also need some time to do research or otherwise he would have nothing to give presentations about.

4 Workflow For Creating a Beamer Presentation

This section presents a possible workflow for creating a BEAMER presentation and possibly a handout to go along with it. Technical questions are addressed, like which programs to call with which parameters.

4.1 Step One: Setup the Files

SEN-
TION It is advisable that you create a folder for each presentation. Even though your presentation will usually reside in a single file, TeX produces so many extra files that things can easily get very confusing otherwise. The folder's name should ideally start with the date of your talk in ISO format (like 2003-12-25 for a Christmas talk), followed by some reminder text of what the talk is all about. Putting the date at the front in this format causes your presentation folders to be listed nicely when you have several of them residing in one directory. If you use an extra directory for each presentation, you can call your main file `main.tex`.

To create an initial `main.tex` file for your talk, copy an existing file from the `beamer/solutions` directory and adapt it to your needs. A list of possible BEAMER solutions that contain templates for presentation TeX-files can be found below.

If you wish your talk to reside in the same file as some different, non-presentation article version of your text, it is advisable to setup a more elaborate file scheme. See Section 21.2.2 for details.

4.2 Step Two: Structure Your Presentation

The next step is to fill the presentation file with `\section` and `\subsection` to create a preliminary outline. You'll find some hints on how to create a good outline in Section 5.1.

Put `\section` and `\subsection` commands into the (more or less empty) main file. Do not create any frames until you have a first working version of a possible table of contents. The file might look like this:

```
\documentclass{beamer}
% This is the file main.tex

\usetheme{Berlin}

\title{Example Presentation Created with the Beamer Package}
\author{Till Tantau}
\date{\today}

\begin{document}

\begin{frame}
  \titlepage
\end{frame}


\section*{Outline}
\begin{frame}
  \tableofcontents
\end{frame}

\section{Introduction}
\subsection{Overview of the Beamer Class}
\subsection{Overview of Similar Classes}

\section{Usage}
\subsection{...}
\subsection{...}

\section{Examples}
\subsection{...}
```

```
\subsection{...}

\begin{frame}
\end{frame} % to enforce entries in the table of contents

\end{document}
```

The empty frame at the end (which should be deleted later) ensures that the sections and subsections are actually part of the table of contents. This frame is necessary since a \section or \subsection command following the last page of a document has no effect.

4.3   Step Three: Creating a PDF or PostScript File

Once a first version of the structure is finished, you should try to create a first PDF or PostScript file of your (still empty) talk to ensure that everything is working properly. This file will only contain the title page and the table of contents.

4.3.1   Creating PDF

To create a PDF version of this file, run the program pdflatex on main.tex at least twice. You need to run it twice, so that TeX can create the table of contents. (It may even be necessary to run it more often since all sorts of auxiliary files are created.) In the following example, the greater-than-sign is the prompt.

```
> pdflatex main.tex
    ... lots of output ...
> pdflatex main.tex
    ... lots of output ...
```

Alternatively, you can use lualatex or xelatex instead of pdflatex in above commands.

You can next use a program like the Acrobat Reader, xpdf, evince or okular to view the resulting presentation.

```
> acroread main.pdf
```

4.3.2   Creating PostScript

To create a PostScript version, you should first ascertain that the HYPERREF package (which is automatically loaded by the BEAMER class) uses the option dvips or some compatible option, see the documentation of the HYPERREF package for details. Whether this is the case depends on the contents of your local hyperref.cfg file. You can enforce the usage of this option by passing dvips or a compatible option to the BEAMER class (write \documentclass[dvips]{beamer}), which will pass this option on to the HYPERREF package.

You can then run latex twice, followed by dvips.

```
> latex main.tex
    ... lots of output ...
> latex main.tex
    ... lots of output ...
> dvips -P pdf main.dvi
```

The option (-P pdf) tells dvips to use Type 1 outline fonts instead of the usual Type 3 bitmap fonts. You may wish to omit this option if there is a problem with it.

You can convert a PostScript file to a pdf file using

```
> ps2pdf main.ps main.pdf
```

4.3.3 Ways of Improving Compilation Speed

While working on your presentation, it may sometimes be useful to TeX your .tex file quickly and have the presentation contain only the most important information. This is especially true if you have a slow machine. In this case, you can do several things to speed up the compilation. First, you can use the draft class option.

`\documentclass[draft]{beamer}`

> Causes the headlines, footlines, and sidebars to be replaced by gray rectangles (their sizes are still computed, though). Many other packages, including pgf and hyperref, also "speed up" when this option is given.

Second, you can use the following command:

`\includeonlyframes{⟨frame label list⟩}`

> This command behaves a little bit like the \includeonly command: Only the frames mentioned in the list are included. All other frames are suppressed. Nevertheless, the section and subsection commands are still executed, so that you still have the correct navigation bars. By labeling the current frame as, say, current and then saying \includeonlyframes{current}, you can work on a single frame quickly.
>
> The ⟨frame label list⟩ is a comma-separated list (without spaces) of the names of frames that have been labeled. To label a frame, you must pass the option label=⟨name⟩ to the \frame command or frame environment.
>
> *Example:*
>
> ```
> \includeonlyframes{example1,example3}
>
> \frame[label=example1]
> {This frame will be included. }
>
> \frame[label=example2]
> {This frame will not be included. }
>
> \frame{This frame will not be included.}
>
> \againframe{example1} % Will be included
> ```

4.4 Step Four: Create Frames

Once the table of contents looks satisfactory, start creating frames for your presentation by adding frame environments. You'll find guidelines on what to put on a frame in Section 5.1.3.

4.5 Step Five: Test Your Presentation

Always test your presentation. For this, you should vocalize or subvocalize your talk in a quiet environment. Typically, this will show that your talk is too long. You should then remove parts of the presentation, such that it fits into the allotted time slot. Do *not* attempt to talk faster in order to squeeze the talk into the given amount of time. You are almost sure to lose your audience this way.

Do not try to create the "perfect" presentation immediately. Rather, test and retest the talk and modify it as needed.

4.6 Step Six: Create a Handout

4.6.1 Creating the Handout

Once your talk is fixed, you can create a handout, if this seems appropriate. For this, you can use the class option handout as explained in Section 21.1. Typically, you might wish to put several handout slides on one page, see below on how to do this easily.

You may also wish to create an article version of your talk. An "article version" of your presentation is a normal TeX text typeset using, for example, the document class article or perhaps llncs or a similar document class. The BEAMER class offers facilities to have this version coexist with your presentation version in one file and to share code. Also, you can include slides of your presentation as figures in your article version. Details on how to setup the article version can be found in Section 21.2.

4.6.2 Printing the Handout

The easiest way to print a presentation is to user the Acrobat Reader with the option "expand small pages to paper size" form the printer dialog enabled. This is necessary, because slides are by default only 128mm by 96mm large.

For the PostScript version and for printing multiple slides on a single page this simple approach does not work. In such cases you can use the `pgfpages` package, which works directly with `pdflatex`, `lualatex`, `xelatex` and `latex` plus `dvips`. Note however *that this package destroys hyperlinks*. This is due to fundamental flaws in the PDF-specification and it is not likely to change.

The `pgfpages` can do all sorts of tricks with pages. The most important one for printing BEAMER slides is the following command:

```
\usepackage{pgfpages}
\pgfpagesuselayout{resize to}[a4paper,border shrink=5mm,landscape]
```

This says "Resize all pages to landscape A4 pages, no matter what their original size was, but shrink the pages by 5mm, so that there is a bit of a border around everything." Naturally, instead of `a4paper` you can also use `letterpaper` or any of the other standard paper sizes. For further options and details see the documentation of `pgfpages`.

The second thing you might wish to do is to put several slides on a single page. This can be done as follows:

```
\usepackage{pgfpages}
\pgfpagesuselayout{2 on 1}[a4paper,border shrink=5mm]
```

This says "Put two pages on one page and then resize everything so that it fits on A4 paper." Note that this time we do not need landscape as the resulting page is, after all, not in landscape mode.

Instead of `2 on 1` you can also use `4 on 1`, but then with `landscape` once more, and also `8 on 1` and even `16 on 1` to get a grand (though unreadable) overview.

If you put several slides on one page and if these slides normally have a white background, it may be useful to write the following in your preamble:

```
\mode<handout>{\setbeamercolor{background canvas}{bg=black!5}}
```

This will cause the slides of the handout version to have a very light gray background. This makes it easy to discern the slides' border if several slides are put on one page.

5 Guidelines for Creating Presentations

In this section we sketch the guidelines that we try to stick to when we create presentations. These guidelines either arise out of experience, out of common sense, or out of recommendations by other people or books. These rules are certainly not intended as commandments that, if not followed, will result in catastrophe. The central rule of typography also applies to creating presentations: *Every rule can be broken, but no rule may be ignored.*

5.1 Structuring a Presentation

5.1.1 Know the Time Constraints

When you start to create a presentation, the very first thing you should worry about is the amount of time you have for your presentation. Depending on the occasion, this can be anything between 2 minutes and two hours.

- A simple rule for the number of frames is that you should have at most one frame per minute.

- In most situations, you will have less time for your presentation that you would like.

- *Do not try to squeeze more into a presentation than time allows for.* No matter how important some detail seems to you, it is better to leave it out, but get the main message across, than getting neither the main message nor the detail across.

In many situations, a quick appraisal of how much time you have will show that you won't be able to mention certain details. Knowing this can save you hours of work on preparing slides that you would have to remove later anyway.

5.1.2 Global Structure

To create the "global structure" of a presentation, with the time constraints in mind, proceed as follows:

- Make a mental inventory of the things you can reasonably talk about within the time available.

- Categorize the inventory into sections and subsections.

- For very long talks (like a 90 minute lecture), you might also divide your talk into independent parts (like a "review of the previous lecture part" and a "main part") using the \part command. Note that each part has its own table of contents.

- Do not feel afraid to change the structure later on as you work on the talk.

Parts, Section, and Subsections.

- Do not use more than four sections and not less than two per part.

Even four sections are usually too much, unless they follow a very easy pattern. Five and more sections are simply too hard to remember for the audience. After all, when you present the table of contents, the audience will not yet really be able to grasp the importance and relevance of the different sections and will most likely have forgotten them by the time you reach them.

- Ideally, a table of contents should be understandable by itself. In particular, it should be comprehensible *before* someone has heard your talk.

- Keep section and subsection titles self-explaining.

- Both the sections and the subsections should follow a logical pattern.

- Begin with an explanation of what your talk is all about. (Do not assume that everyone knows this. The *Ignorant Audience Law* states: Someone important in the audience always knows less than you think everyone should know, even if you take the Ignorant Audience Law into account.)

- Then explain what you or someone else has found out concerning the subject matter.

- Always conclude your talk with a summary that repeats the main message of the talk in a short and simple way. People pay most attention at the beginning and at the end of talks. The summary is your "second chance" to get across a message.

- You can also add an appendix part using the `\appendix` command. Put everything into this part that you do not actually intend to talk about, but that might come in handy when questions are asked.

- Do not use subsubsections, they are evil.

Giving an Abstract   In papers, the abstract gives a short summary of the whole paper in about 100 words. This summary is intend to help readers appraise whether they should read the whole paper or not.

- Since your audience is unlikely to flee after the first slide, in a presentation you usually do not need to present an abstract.

- However, if you can give a nice, succinct statement of your talk, you might wish to include an abstract.

- If you include an abstract, be sure that it is *not* some long text but just a very short message.

- *Never, ever* reuse a paper abstract for a presentation, *except* if the abstract is "We show P = NP" or "We show P $\neq$ NP"

- If your abstract is one of the above two, double-check whether your proof is correct.

Numbered Theorems and Definitions.   A common way of globally structuring (math) articles and books is to use consecutively numbered definitions and theorems. Unfortunately, for presentations the situation is a bit more complicated and we would like to discourage using numbered theorems in presentations. The audience has no chance of remembering these numbers. *Never* say things like "now, by Theorem 2.5 that I showed you earlier, we have ..." It would be much better to refer to, say, Kummer's Theorem instead of Theorem 2.5. If Theorem 2.5 is some obscure theorem that does not have its own name (unlike Kummer's Theorem or Main Theorem or Second Main Theorem or Key Lemma), then the audience will have forgotten about it anyway by the time you refer to it again.

In our opinion, the only situation in which numbered theorems make sense in a presentation is in a lecture, in which the students can read lecture notes in parallel to the lecture where the theorems are numbered in exactly the same way.

If you do number theorems and definitions, number everything consecutively. Thus if there are one theorem, one lemma, and one definition, you would have Theorem 1, Lemma 2, and Definition 3. Some people prefer all three to be numbered 1. We would *strongly* like to discourage this. The problem is that this makes it virtually impossible to find anything since Theorem 2 might come after Definition 10 or the other way round. Papers and, worse, books that have a Theorem 1 and a Definition 1 are a pain.

- Do not inflict pain on other people.

Bibliographies.   You may also wish to present a bibliography at the end of your talk, so that people can see what kind of "further reading" is possible. When adding a bibliography to a presentation, keep the following in mind:

- It is a bad idea to present a long bibliography in a presentation. Present only very few references. (Naturally, this applies only to the talk itself, not to a possible handout.)

- If you present more references than fit on a single slide you can be almost sure that none of them will be remembered.

- Present references only if they are intended as "further reading." Do not present a list of all things you used like in a paper.

- You should not present a long list of all your other great papers *except* if you are giving an application talk.

- Using the `\cite` commands can be confusing since the audience has little chance of remembering the citations. If you cite the references, always cite them with full author name and year like "[Tantau, 2003]" instead of something like "[2,4]" or "[Tan01,NT02]".

- If you want to be modest, you can abbreviate your name when citing yourself as in "[Nickelsen and T., 2003]" or "[Nickelsen and T, 2003]". However, this can be confusing for the audience since it is often not immediately clear who exactly "T." might be. We recommend using the full name.

5.1.3 Frame Structure

Just like your whole presentation, each frame should also be structured. A frame that is solely filled with some long text is very hard to follow. It is your job to structure the contents of each frame such that, ideally, the audience immediately sees which information is important, which information is just a detail, how the presented information is related, and so on.

The Frame Title

- Put a title on each frame. The title explains the contents of the frame to people who did not follow all details on the slide.

- The title should really *explain* things, not just give a cryptic summary that cannot be understood unless one has understood the whole slide. For example, a title like "The Poset" will have everyone puzzled what this slide might be about. Titles like "Review of the Definition of Partially Ordered Sets (Posets)" or "A Partial Ordering on the Columns of the Genotype Matrix" are *much* more informative.

- Ideally, titles on consecutive frames should "tell a story" all by themselves.

- In English, you should *either always* capitalize all words in a frame title except for words like "a" or "the" (as in a title), *or* you *always* use the normal lowercase letters. Do *not* mix this; stick to one rule. The same is true for block titles. For example, do not use titles like "A short Review of Turing machines." Either use "A Short Review of Turing Machines." or "A short review of Turing machines." (Turing is still spelled with a capital letter since it is a name).

- In English, the title of the whole document should be capitalized, regardless of whether you capitalize anything else.

- In German and other languages that have lots of capitalized words, always use the correct upper-/lowercase letters. Never capitalize anything in addition to what is usually capitalized.

How Much Can I Put On a Frame?

- A frame with too little on it is better than a frame with too much on it. A usual frame should have between 20 and 40 words. The maximum should be at about 80 words.

- Do not assume that everyone in the audience is an expert on the subject matter. Even if the people listening to you should be experts, they may last have heard about things you consider obvious several years ago. You should always have the time for a quick reminder of what exactly a "semantical complexity class" or an "ω-complete partial ordering" is.

- Never put anything on a slide that you are not going to explain during the talk, not even to impress anyone with how complicated your subject matter really is. However, you may explain things that are not on a slide.

- Keep it simple. Typically, your audience will see a slide for less than 50 seconds. They will not have the time to puzzle through long sentences or complicated formulas.

- Lance Fortnow, a professor of computer science, claims: PowerPoint users give better talks. His reason: Since PowerPoint is so bad at typesetting math, they use less math, making their talks easier to understand.

  There is some truth in this in our opinion. The great math-typesetting capabilities of TeX can easily lure you into using many more formulas than is necessary and healthy. For example, instead of writing "Since $|\{x \in \{0,1\}^* \mid x \sqsubseteq y\}| < \infty$, we have..." use "Since y has only finitely many prefixes, we have..."

  You will be surprised how much mathematical text can be reformulated in plain English or can just be omitted. Naturally, if some mathematical argument is what you are actually talking about, as in a math lecture, make use of TeX's typesetting capabilities to your heart's content.

Structuring a Frame

- Use block environments like `block`, `theorem`, `proof`, `example`, and so on.

- Prefer enumerations and itemize environments over plain text.

- Use `description` when you define several things.

- Do not use more than two levels of "subitemizing." BEAMER supports three levels, but you should not use that third level. Mostly, you should not even use the second one. Use good graphics instead.

- Do not create endless `itemize` or `enumerate` lists.

- Do not uncover lists piecewise.

- Emphasis is an important part of creating structure. Use `\alert` to highlight important things. This can be a single word or a whole sentence. However, do not overuse highlighting since this will negate the effect.

- Use columns.

- *Never* use footnotes. They needlessly disrupt the flow of reading. Either what is said in the footnote is important and should be put in the normal text; or it is not important and should be omitted (*especially* in a presentation).

- Use `quote` or `quotation` to typeset quoted text.

- Do not use the option `allowframebreaks` except for long bibliographies.

- Do not use long bibliographies.

Writing the Text

- Use short sentences.

- Prefer phrases over complete sentences. For example, instead of "The figure on the left shows a Turing machine, the figure on the right shows a finite automaton." try "Left: A Turing machine. Right: A finite automaton." Even better, turn this into an itemize or a description.

- Punctuate correctly: no punctuation after phrases, complete punctuation in and after complete sentences.

- *Never* use a smaller font size to "fit more on a frame." *Never ever* use the *evil* option `shrink`.

- Do not hyphenate words. If absolutely necessary, hyphenate words "by hand," using the command `\-`.

- Break lines "by hand" using the command `\\`. Do not rely on automatic line breaking. Break where there is a logical pause. For example, good breaks in "the tape alphabet is larger than the input alphabet" are before "is" and before the second "the." Bad breaks are before either "alphabet" and before "larger."

- Text and numbers in figures should have the *same* size as normal text. Illegible numbers on axes usually ruin a chart and its message.

5.1.4 Interactive Elements

Ideally, during a presentation you would like to present your slides in a perfectly linear fashion, presumably by pressing the page-down-key once for each slide. However, there are different reasons why you might have to deviate from this linear order:

- Your presentation may contain "different levels of detail" that may or may not be skipped or expanded, depending on the audience's reaction.

- You are asked questions and wish to show supplementary slides.

- You present a complicated picture and you have to "zoom out" different parts to explain details.

- You are asked questions about an earlier slide, which forces you to find and then jump to that slide.

You cannot really prepare against the last kind of questions. In this case, you can use the navigation bars and symbols to find the slide you are interested in, see 8.2.3.

Concerning the first three kinds of deviations, there are several things you can do to prepare "planned detours" or "planned short cuts".

- You can add "skip buttons." When such a button is pressed, you jump over a well-defined part of your talk. Skip button have two advantages over just pressing the forward key is rapid succession: first, you immediately end up at the correct position and, second, the button's label can give the audience a visual feedback of what exactly will be skipped. For example, when you press a skip button labeled "Skip proof" nobody will start puzzling over what he or she has missed.

- You can add an appendix to your talk. The appendix is kept "perfectly separated" from the main talk. Only once you "enter" the appendix part (presumably by hyperjumping into it), does the appendix structure become visible. You can put all frames that you do not intend to show during the normal course of your talk, but which you would like to have handy in case someone asks, into this appendix.

- You can add "goto buttons" and "return buttons" to create detours. Pressing a goto button will jump to a certain part of the presentation where extra details can be shown. In this part, there is a return button present on each slide that will jump back to the place where the goto button was pressed.

- In BEAMER, you can use the `\againframe` command to "continue" frames that you previously started somewhere, but where certain details have been suppressed. You can use the `\againframe` command at a much later point, for example only in the appendix to show additional slides there.

- In BEAMER, you can use the `\framezoom` command to create links to zoomed out parts of a complicated slide.

5.2 Using Graphics

Graphics often convey concepts or ideas much more efficiently than text: A picture can say more than a thousand words. (Although, sometimes a word can say more than a thousand pictures.)

- Put (at least) one graphic on each slide, whenever possible. Visualizations help an audience enormously.

- Usually, place graphics to the left of the text. (Use the `columns` environment.) In a left-to-right reading culture, we look at the left first.

- Graphics should have the same typographic parameters as the text: Use the same fonts (at the same size) in graphics as in the main text. A small dot in a graphic should have exactly the same size as a small dot in a text. The line width should be the same as the stroke width used in creating the glyphs of the font. For example, an 11pt non-bold Computer Modern font has a stroke width of 0.4pt.

- While bitmap graphics, like photos, can be much more colorful than the rest of the text, vector graphics should follow the same "color logic" as the main text (like black = normal lines, red = highlighted parts, green = examples, blue = structure).

- Like text, you should explain everything that is shown on a graphic. Unexplained details make the audience puzzle whether this was something important that they have missed. Be careful when importing graphics from a paper or some other source. They usually have much more detail than you will be able to explain and should be radically simplified.

- Sometimes the complexity of a graphic is intentional and you are willing to spend much time explaining the graphic in great detail. In this case, you will often run into the problem that fine details of the graphic are hard to discern for the audience. In this case you should use a command like \framezoom to create anticipated zoomings of interesting parts of the graphic, see Section 11.3.

5.3 Using Animations and Transitions

- Use animations to explain the dynamics of systems, algorithms, etc.

- Do *not* use animations just to attract the attention of your audience. This often distracts attention away from the main topic of the slide. No matter how cute a rotating, flying theorem seems to look and no matter how badly you feel your audience needs some action to keep it happy, most people in the audience will typically feel you are making fun of them.

- Do *not* use distracting special effects like "dissolving" slides unless you have a very good reason for using them. If you use them, use them sparsely. They *can* be useful in some situations: For example, you might show a young boy on a slide and might wish to dissolve this slide into a slide showing a grown man instead. In this case, the dissolving gives the audience visual feedback that the young boy "slowly becomes" the man.

5.4 Choosing Appropriate Themes

BEAMER comes with a number of different themes. When choosing a theme, keep the following in mind:

- Different themes are appropriate for different occasions. Do not become too attached to a favorite theme; choose a theme according to occasion.

- A longer talk is more likely to require navigational hints than a short one. When you give a 90 minute lecture to students, you should choose a theme that always shows a sidebar with the current topic highlighted so that everyone always knows exactly what's the current "status" of your talk is; when you give a ten-minute introductory speech, a table of contents is likely to just seem silly.

- A theme showing the author's name and affiliation is appropriate in situations where the audience is likely not to know you (like during a conference). If everyone knows you, having your name on each slide is just vanity.

- First choose a presentation theme that has a layout that is appropriate for your talk.

- Next you might wish to change the colors by installing a different color theme. This can drastically change the appearance of your presentation. A "colorful" theme like Berkeley will look much less flashy if you use the color themes seahorse and lily.

- You might also wish to change the fonts by installing a different font theme.

5.5 Choosing Appropriate Colors

- Use colors sparsely. The prepared themes are already quite colorful (blue = structure, red = alert, green = example). If you add more colors for things like code, math text, etc., you should have a *very* good reason.

- Be careful when using bright colors on white background, *especially* when using green. What looks good on your monitor may look bad during a presentation due to the different ways monitors, beamers, and printers reproduce colors. Add lots of black to pure colors when you use them on bright backgrounds.

- Maximize contrast. Normal text should be black on white or at least something very dark on something very bright. *Never* do things like "light green text on not-so-light green background."

- Background shadings decrease the legibility without increasing the information content. Do not add a background shading just because it "somehow looks nicer."

- Inverse video (bright text on dark background) can be a problem during presentations in bright environments since only a small percentage of the presentation area is light up by the beamer. Inverse video is harder to reproduce on printouts and on transparencies.

5.6 Choosing Appropriate Fonts and Font Attributes

Text and fonts literally surround us constantly. Try to think of the last time when there was no text around you within ten meters. Likely, this has never happened in your life! (Whenever you wear clothing, even a swim suit, there is a lot of text right next to your body.) The history of fonts is nearly as long as the history of civilization itself. There are tens of thousands of fonts available these days, some of which are the product of hundreds of years of optimization.

Choosing the right fonts for a presentation is by no means trivial and wrong choices will either just "look bad" or, worse, make the audience have trouble reading your slides. This user's guide cannot replace a good book on typography, but in the present section you'll find several hints that should help you setup fonts for a BEAMER presentation that look good. A font has numerous attributes like weight, family, or size. All of these have an impact on the usability of the font in presentations. In the following, these attributes are described and advantages and disadvantages of the different choices are sketched.

5.6.1 Font Size

Perhaps the most obvious attribute of a font is its size. Fonts are traditionally measured in "points." How much a point is depends on whom you ask. TeX thinks a point is the 72.27th part of an inch, which is 2.54 cm. On the other hand, PostScript and Adobe think a point is the 72th part of an inch (TeX calls this a big point). There are differences between American and European points. Once it is settled how much a point is, claiming that a text is in "11pt" means that the "height" of the letters in the font are 11pt. However, this "height" stems from the time when letters where still cast in lead and refers to the vertical size of the lead letters. It thus does not need to have any correlation with the actual height of, say, the letter x or even the letter M. The letter x of an 11pt Times from Adobe will have a height that is different from the height of the letter x of an 11pt Times from UTC and the letter x of an 11pt Helvetica from Adobe will have yet another height.

Summing up, the font size has little to do with the actual size of letters. Rather, these days it is a convention that 10pt or 11pt is the size a font should be printed for "normal reading." Fonts are designed so that they can optimally be read at these sizes.

In a presentation the classical font sizes obviously lose their meaning. Nobody could read a projected text if it were actually 11pt. Instead, the projected letters need to be several centimetres high. Thus, it does not really make sense to specify "font sizes" for presentations in the usual way. Instead, you should try to think of the number of lines that will fit on a slide if you were to fill the whole slide with line-by-line text (you are never going to do that in practice, though). Depending on how far your audience is removed from the projection and on how large the projection is, between 10 and 20 lines should fit on each slide. The less lines, the more readable your text will be.

In BEAMER, the default sizes of the fonts are chosen in a way that makes it difficult to fit "too much" onto a slide. Also, it will ensure that your slides are readable even under bad conditions like a large room and only a small projection area. However, you may wish to enlarge or shrink the fonts a bit if you know this to be more appropriate in your presentation environment.

Once the size of the normal text is settled, all other sizes are usually defined relative to that size. For this reason, LaTeX has commands like \large or \small. The actual size these commands select depends on the size of normal text.

In a presentation, you will want to use a very small font for text in headlines, footlines, or sidebars since the text shown there is not vital and is read at the audience's leisure. Naturally, the text should still be large enough that it actually *can* be read without binoculars. However, in a normal presentation environment the audience will still be able to read even \tiny text when necessary.

However, using small fonts can be tricky. Many PostScript fonts are just scaled down when used at small sizes. When a font is used at less than its normal size, the characters should actually be stroked using a slightly thicker "pen" than the one resulting from just scaling things. For this reason, high quality multiple master fonts or the Computer Modern fonts use different fonts for small characters and for normal characters. However, when you use a normal Helvetica or Times font, the characters are just scaled down. A similar problem arises when you use a light font on a dark background. Even when printed on paper in high resolution, light-on-dark text tends to be "overflooded" by the dark background. When light-on-dark text is rendered in a presentation this effect can be much worse, making the text almost impossible to read.

You can counter both negative effects by using a bold version for small text.

In the other direction, you can use larger text for titles. However, using a larger font does not always have the desired effect. Just because a frame title is printed in large letters does not mean that it is read first. Indeed, have a look at the cover of your favorite magazine. Most likely, the magazine's name is the typeset in the largest font, but your attention will nevertheless first go to the topics advertised on the cover. Likewise, in the table of contents you are likely to first focus on the entries, not on the words "Table of Contents." Most likely, you would not spot a spelling mistake there (a friend of mine actually managed to misspell *his own name* on the cover of his master's thesis and nobody noticed until a year later). In essence, large text at the top of a page signals "unimportant since I know what to expect." So, instead of using a very large frame title, also consider using a normal size frame title that is typeset in bold or in italics.

5.6.2 Font Families

The other central property of any font is its family. Examples of font families are Times or Helvetica or Futura. As the name suggests, a lot of different fonts can belong to the same family. For example, Times comes in different sizes, there is a bold version of Times, an italics version, and so on. To confuse matters, font families like Times are often just called the "font Times."

There are two large classes of font families: serif fonts and sans-serif fonts. A sans-serif font is a font in which the letters do not have serifs (from French *sans*, which means "without"). Serifs are the little hooks at the ending of the strokes that make up a letter. The font you are currently reading is a serif font. By comparison, this text is in a sans-serif font. Sans-serif fonts are (generally considered to be) easier to read when used in a presentation. In low resolution rendering, serifs decrease the legibility of a font. However, on projectors with very high resolution serif text is just as readable as sans-serif text. A presentation typeset in a serif font creates a more conservative impression, which might be exactly what you wish to create.

Most likely, you'll have a lot of different font families preinstalled on your system. The default font used by TeX (and BEAMER) is the Computer Modern font. It is the original font family designed by Donald Knuth himself for the TeX program. It is a mature font that comes with just about everything you could wish for: extensive mathematical alphabets, outline PostScript versions, real small caps, real oldstyle numbers, specially designed small and large letters, and so on.

However, there are reasons for using font families other than Computer Modern:

- The Computer Modern fonts are a bit boring if you have seen them too often. Using another font (but not Times!) can give a fresh look.

- Other fonts, especially Times and Helvetica, are sometime rendered better since they seem to have better internal hinting.

- The sans-serif version of Computer Modern is not nearly as well-designed as the serif version. Indeed, the sans-serif version is, in essence, the serif version with different design parameters, not an independent design.

- Computer modern needs much more space than more economic fonts like Times (this explains why Times is so popular with people who need to squeeze their great paper into just twelve pages). To be fair, Times was specifically designed to be economic (the newspaper company publishing The Times needed robust, but space-economic font).

A small selection of alternatives to Computer Modern:

- Latin Modern is a Computer Modern derivate that provides more characters, so it's not considered a real alternative. It's recommended over Computer Modern, though.

- Helvetica is an often used alternative. However, Helvetica also tends to look boring (since we see it everywhere) and it has a very large x-height (the height of the letter x in comparison to a letter like M). A large x-height is usually considered good for languages (like English) that use uppercase letters seldom and not-so-good for languages (like German) that use uppercase letters a lot. (We have never been quite convinced by the argument for this, though.) Be warned: the x-height of Helvetica is so different from the x-height of Times that mixing the two in a single line looks strange. The packages for loading Times and Helvetica provide options for fixing this, though.

- Futura is, in our opinion, a beautiful font that is very well-suited for presentations. Its thick letters make it robust against scaling, inversion, and low contrast. Unfortunately, while it is most likely installed on your system somewhere in some form, getting TeX to work with it is a complicated process. However, it has been made a lot simpler with modern typesetting engines such as `luatex` and `xetex`.

- Times is a possible alternative to Computer Modern. Its main disadvantage is that it is a serif font, which requires a high-resolution projector. Naturally, it also used very often, so we all know it very well.

- DejaVu, a derivate of Bitstream Vera is also a very good and free alternative. TrueType version that comes with OpenOffice.org is complicated to get to work with TeX, but `arev` LaTeX package provides an easy way to use Type 1 version named Bera. It has both sans-serif and serif versions; `arev` provides both.

Families that you should *not* use for normal text include:

- All monospaced fonts (like Courier).

- Script fonts (which look like handwriting). Their stroke width is way too small for a presentation.

- More delicate serif fonts like Stempel and possibly even Garamond (though Garamond is really a beautiful font for books).

- Gothic fonts. Only a small fraction of your audience will be able to read them fluently.

There is one popular font that is a bit special: Microsoft's Comic Sans. On the one hand, there is a website lobbying for banning the use of this font. Indeed, the main trouble with the font is that it is not particularly well-readable and that math typeset partly using this font looks terrible. On the other hand, this font *does* create the impression of a slide "written by hand," which gives the presentation a natural look. Think twice before using this font, but do not let yourself be intimidated.

One of the most important rules of typography is that you should use as little fonts as possible in a text. In particular, typographic wisdom dictates that you should not use more than two different families on one page. However, when typesetting mathematical text, it is often necessary and useful to use different font families. For example, it used to be common practice to use Gothic letters to denote vectors. Also, program texts are often typeset in monospace fonts. If your audience is used to a certain font family for a certain type of text, use that family, regardless of what typographic wisdom says.

A common practice in typography is to use a sans-serif fonts for titles and serif fonts for normal text (check your favorite magazine). You can *also* use two different sans-serif fonts or two different serif fonts, but you then have to make sure that the fonts look "sufficiently different." If they look only slightly different, the page will look "somehow strange," but the audience will not be able to tell why. For example, do not mix Arial and Helvetica (they are almost identical) or Computer Modern and Baskerville (they are quite similar). A combination of Gills Sans and Helvetica is dangerous but perhaps possible. A combination like Futura and Optima is certainly OK, at least with respect to the fonts being very different.

5.6.3 Font Shapes: Italics and Small Capitals

LaTeX introduces the concept of the *shape* of a font. The only really important ones are italic and small caps. An *italic* font is a font in which the text is slightly slanted to the right *like this*. Things to know about italics:

- Italics are commonly used in novels to express emphasis. However, especially with sans-serif fonts, italics are typically not "strong enough" and the emphasis gets lost in a presentation. Using a different color or bold text seems better suited for presentations to create emphasis.

- If you look closely, you will notice that italic text is not only slanted but that different letters are actually used (compare a and *a*, for example). However, this is only true for serif text, not for sans-serif text. Text that is only slanted without using different characters is called "slanted" instead of "italic." Sometimes, the word "oblique" is also used for slanted, but it sometimes also used for italics, so it is perhaps best to avoid it. Using slanted serif text is very much frowned upon by typographers and is considered "cheap computer typography." However, people who use slanted text in their books include Donald Knuth.

  In a presentation, if you go to the trouble of using a serif font for some part of it, you should also use italics, not slanted text.

- The different characters used for serif italics have changed much less from the original handwritten letters they are based on than normal serif text. For this reason, serif italics creates the impression of handwritten text, which may be desirable to give a presentation a more "personal touch" (although you can't get very personal using Times italics, which everyone has seen a thousand times). However, it is harder to read than normal text, so do not use it for text more than a line long.

The second font shape supported by TeX are small capital letters. Using them can create a conservative, even formal impression, but some words of caution:

- Small capitals are different from all-uppercase text. A small caps text leaves normal uppercase letters unchanged and uses smaller versions of the uppercase letters for normal typesetting lowercase letters. Thus the word "German" is typeset as GERMAN using small caps, but as GERMAN using all uppercase letters.

- Small caps either come as "faked" small caps or as "real" small caps. Faked small caps are created by just scaling down normal uppercase letters. This leads to letters the look too thin. Real small caps are specially designed smaller versions of the uppercase letters that have the same stroke width as normal text.

- Computer Modern fonts and expert version of PostScript fonts come with real small caps (though the small caps of Computer Modern are one point size too large for some unfathomable reason—but your audience is going to pardon this since it will not be noticed anyway). "Simple" PostScript fonts like out-of-the-box Helvetica or Times only come with faked small caps.

- Text typeset in small caps is harder to read than normal text. The reason is that we read by seeing the "shape" of words. For example, the word "shape" is mainly recognized by seing one normal letter, one ascending letter, a normal letter, one descending letter, and a normal letter. One has much more trouble spotting a misspelling like "shepe" than "spape". Small caps destroy the shape of words since SHAPE, SHEPE and SPAPE all have the same shape, thus making it much harder to tell them apart. Your audience will read small caps more slowly than normal text. This is, by the way, why legal disclaimers are often written in uppercase letters: not to make them appear more important to you, but to make them much harder to actually read.

5.6.4 Font Weight

The "weight" of a font refers to the thickness of the letters. Usually, fonts come as regular or as bold fonts. There often also exist semibold, ultrabold (or black), thin, or ultrathin (or hair) versions.

In typography, using a bold font to create emphasis, especially within normal text, is frowned upon (bold words in the middle of a normal text are referred to as "dirt"). For presentations this rule of not using bold text does not really apply. On a presentation slide there is usually very little text and there are numerous elements that try to attract the viewer's attention. Using the traditional italics to create emphasis will often be overlooked. So, using bold text, seems a good alternative in a presentation. However, an even better alternative is using a bright color like red to attract attention.

As pointed out earlier, you should use bold text for small text unless you use an especially robust font like Futura or DejaVu.

6 Solution Templates

In the subdirectories of the directory `beamer/solutions` you will find *solution templates* in different languages. A solution template is a TeX-text that "solves" a specific problem. Such a problem might be "I need to create a 20 minute talk for a conference" or "I want to create a slide that introduces the next speaker" or "I want to create a table that is uncovered piecewise." For such a problem, a solution template consists of a mixture of a template and an example that can be used to solve this particular problem. Just copy the solution template file (or parts of it) and freely adjust them to your needs.

The collecting of BEAMER solution templates has only begun and currently there are only very few of them. We hope that in the future more solutions will become available and we would like to encourage users of the BEAMER class to send us solutions they develop. We would also like to encourage users to help in translating solutions to languages other than English and German. If you have written a solution or a translation, please feel free to send it to us (make sure however, that it contains about the same amount of explanations and justifications as do the existing solutions).

The following list of solution templates is sorted by the length of the talks for which they provide a template. As always, the solutions can be found in the directory `beamer/solutions`.

Solution Template `short-talks/speaker_introduction-ornate-2min`

- Introducing another speaker.
- Talk length is about 2min.
- Ornate style.

PRESEN- TeX-version available in languages `de`, `en`, and `fr`.
TATION

Solution Template `generic-talks/generic-ornate-15min-45min`

- Generic solution template for talks on any subject.
- Talk length is between 15min and 45min.
- Ornate style.

PRESEN- TeX-version available in languages `de`, `en`, and `fr`.
TATION

Solution Template `conference-talks/conference-ornate-20min`

- Talk at a conference/colloquium.
- Talk length is about 20 minutes.
- Ornate style.

PRESEN- TeX-version available in languages `de`, `en`, and `fr`.
TATION

7 Licenses and Copyright

7.1 Which License Applies?

Different parts of the BEAMER package are distributed under different licenses:

1. The *code* of the package is dual-license. This means that you can decide which license you wish to use when using the BEAMER package. The two options are:

    (a) You can use the GNU General Public License, Version 2 or any later version published by the Free Software Foundation.

    (b) You can use the LaTeX Project Public License, version 1.3c or (at your option) any later version.

2. The *documentation* of the package is also dual-license. Again, you can choose between two options:

    (a) You can use the GNU Free Documentation License, Version 1.3 or any later version published by the Free Software Foundation.

    (b) You can use the LaTeX Project Public License, version 1.3c or (at your option) any later version.

The "documentation of the package" refers to all files in the subdirectory doc of the BEAMER package. A detailed listing can be found in the file doc/licenses/manifest-documentation.txt. All files in other directories are part of the "code of the package." A detailed listing can be found in the file doc/licenses/manifest-code.txt.

In the rest of this section, the licenses are presented. The following text is copyrighted, see the plain text versions of these licenses in the directory doc/licenses for details.

7.2 The GNU General Public License, Version 2

7.2.1 Preamble

The licenses for most software are designed to take away your freedom to share and change it. By contrast, the GNU General Public License is intended to guarantee your freedom to share and change free software—to make sure the software is free for all its users. This General Public License applies to most of the Free Software Foundation's software and to any other program whose authors commit to using it. (Some other Free Software Foundation software is covered by the GNU Library General Public License instead.) You can apply it to your programs, too.

When we speak of free software, we are referring to freedom, not price. Our General Public Licenses are designed to make sure that you have the freedom to distribute copies of free software (and charge for this service if you wish), that you receive source code or can get it if you want it, that you can change the software or use pieces of it in new free programs; and that you know you can do these things.

To protect your rights, we need to make restrictions that forbid anyone to deny you these rights or to ask you to surrender the rights. These restrictions translate to certain responsibilities for you if you distribute copies of the software, or if you modify it.

For example, if you distribute copies of such a program, whether gratis or for a fee, you must give the recipients all the rights that you have. You must make sure that they, too, receive or can get the source code. And you must show them these terms so they know their rights.

We protect your rights with two steps: (1) copyright the software, and (2) offer you this license which gives you legal permission to copy, distribute and/or modify the software.

Also, for each author's protection and ours, we want to make certain that everyone understands that there is no warranty for this free software. If the software is modified by someone else and passed on, we want its recipients to know that what they have is not the original, so that any problems introduced by others will not reflect on the original authors' reputations.

Finally, any free program is threatened constantly by software patents. We wish to avoid the danger that redistributors of a free program will individually obtain patent licenses, in effect making the program proprietary. To prevent this, we have made it clear that any patent must be licensed for everyone's free use or not licensed at all.

The precise terms and conditions for copying, distribution and modification follow.

7.2.2 Terms and Conditions For Copying, Distribution and Modification

0. This License applies to any program or other work which contains a notice placed by the copyright holder saying it may be distributed under the terms of this General Public License. The "Program", below, refers to any such program or work, and a "work based on the Program" means either the Program or any derivative work under copyright law: that is to say, a work containing the Program or a portion of it, either verbatim or with modifications and/or translated into another language. (Hereinafter, translation is included without limitation in the term "modification".) Each licensee is addressed as "you".

   Activities other than copying, distribution and modification are not covered by this License; they are outside its scope. The act of running the Program is not restricted, and the output from the Program is covered only if its contents constitute a work based on the Program (independent of having been made by running the Program). Whether that is true depends on what the Program does.

1. You may copy and distribute verbatim copies of the Program's source code as you receive it, in any medium, provided that you conspicuously and appropriately publish on each copy an appropriate copyright notice and disclaimer of warranty; keep intact all the notices that refer to this License and to the absence of any warranty; and give any other recipients of the Program a copy of this License along with the Program.

   You may charge a fee for the physical act of transferring a copy, and you may at your option offer warranty protection in exchange for a fee.

2. You may modify your copy or copies of the Program or any portion of it, thus forming a work based on the Program, and copy and distribute such modifications or work under the terms of Section 1 above, provided that you also meet all of these conditions:

   (a) You must cause the modified files to carry prominent notices stating that you changed the files and the date of any change.

   (b) You must cause any work that you distribute or publish, that in whole or in part contains or is derived from the Program or any part thereof, to be licensed as a whole at no charge to all third parties under the terms of this License.

   (c) If the modified program normally reads commands interactively when run, you must cause it, when started running for such interactive use in the most ordinary way, to print or display an announcement including an appropriate copyright notice and a notice that there is no warranty (or else, saying that you provide a warranty) and that users may redistribute the program under these conditions, and telling the user how to view a copy of this License. (Exception: if the Program itself is interactive but does not normally print such an announcement, your work based on the Program is not required to print an announcement.)

   These requirements apply to the modified work as a whole. If identifiable sections of that work are not derived from the Program, and can be reasonably considered independent and separate works in themselves, then this License, and its terms, do not apply to those sections when you distribute them as separate works. But when you distribute the same sections as part of a whole which is a work based on the Program, the distribution of the whole must be on the terms of this License, whose permissions for other licensees extend to the entire whole, and thus to each and every part regardless of who wrote it.

   Thus, it is not the intent of this section to claim rights or contest your rights to work written entirely by you; rather, the intent is to exercise the right to control the distribution of derivative or collective works based on the Program.

   In addition, mere aggregation of another work not based on the Program with the Program (or with a work based on the Program) on a volume of a storage or distribution medium does not bring the other work under the scope of this License.

3. You may copy and distribute the Program (or a work based on it, under Section 2) in object code or executable form under the terms of Sections 1 and 2 above provided that you also do one of the following:

   (a) Accompany it with the complete corresponding machine-readable source code, which must be distributed under the terms of Sections 1 and 2 above on a medium customarily used for software interchange; or,

(b) Accompany it with a written offer, valid for at least three years, to give any third party, for a charge no more than your cost of physically performing source distribution, a complete machine-readable copy of the corresponding source code, to be distributed under the terms of Sections 1 and 2 above on a medium customarily used for software interchange; or,

(c) Accompany it with the information you received as to the offer to distribute corresponding source code. (This alternative is allowed only for noncommercial distribution and only if you received the program in object code or executable form with such an offer, in accord with Subsubsection b above.)

The source code for a work means the preferred form of the work for making modifications to it. For an executable work, complete source code means all the source code for all modules it contains, plus any associated interface definition files, plus the scripts used to control compilation and installation of the executable. However, as a special exception, the source code distributed need not include anything that is normally distributed (in either source or binary form) with the major components (compiler, kernel, and so on) of the operating system on which the executable runs, unless that component itself accompanies the executable.

If distribution of executable or object code is made by offering access to copy from a designated place, then offering equivalent access to copy the source code from the same place counts as distribution of the source code, even though third parties are not compelled to copy the source along with the object code.

4. You may not copy, modify, sublicense, or distribute the Program except as expressly provided under this License. Any attempt otherwise to copy, modify, sublicense or distribute the Program is void, and will automatically terminate your rights under this License. However, parties who have received copies, or rights, from you under this License will not have their licenses terminated so long as such parties remain in full compliance.

5. You are not required to accept this License, since you have not signed it. However, nothing else grants you permission to modify or distribute the Program or its derivative works. These actions are prohibited by law if you do not accept this License. Therefore, by modifying or distributing the Program (or any work based on the Program), you indicate your acceptance of this License to do so, and all its terms and conditions for copying, distributing or modifying the Program or works based on it.

6. Each time you redistribute the Program (or any work based on the Program), the recipient automatically receives a license from the original licensor to copy, distribute or modify the Program subject to these terms and conditions. You may not impose any further restrictions on the recipients' exercise of the rights granted herein. You are not responsible for enforcing compliance by third parties to this License.

7. If, as a consequence of a court judgment or allegation of patent infringement or for any other reason (not limited to patent issues), conditions are imposed on you (whether by court order, agreement or otherwise) that contradict the conditions of this License, they do not excuse you from the conditions of this License. If you cannot distribute so as to satisfy simultaneously your obligations under this License and any other pertinent obligations, then as a consequence you may not distribute the Program at all. For example, if a patent license would not permit royalty-free redistribution of the Program by all those who receive copies directly or indirectly through you, then the only way you could satisfy both it and this License would be to refrain entirely from distribution of the Program.

If any portion of this section is held invalid or unenforceable under any particular circumstance, the balance of the section is intended to apply and the section as a whole is intended to apply in other circumstances.

It is not the purpose of this section to induce you to infringe any patents or other property right claims or to contest validity of any such claims; this section has the sole purpose of protecting the integrity of the free software distribution system, which is implemented by public license practices. Many people have made generous contributions to the wide range of software distributed through that system in reliance on consistent application of that system; it is up to the author/donor to decide if he or she is willing to distribute software through any other system and a licensee cannot impose that choice.

This section is intended to make thoroughly clear what is believed to be a consequence of the rest of this License.

8. If the distribution and/or use of the Program is restricted in certain countries either by patents or by copyrighted interfaces, the original copyright holder who places the Program under this License may add an explicit geographical distribution limitation excluding those countries, so that distribution is permitted only in or among countries not thus excluded. In such case, this License incorporates the limitation as if written in the body of this License.

9. The Free Software Foundation may publish revised and/or new versions of the General Public License from time to time. Such new versions will be similar in spirit to the present version, but may differ in detail to address new problems or concerns.

    Each version is given a distinguishing version number. If the Program specifies a version number of this License which applies to it and "any later version", you have the option of following the terms and conditions either of that version or of any later version published by the Free Software Foundation. If the Program does not specify a version number of this License, you may choose any version ever published by the Free Software Foundation.

10. If you wish to incorporate parts of the Program into other free programs whose distribution conditions are different, write to the author to ask for permission. For software which is copyrighted by the Free Software Foundation, write to the Free Software Foundation; we sometimes make exceptions for this. Our decision will be guided by the two goals of preserving the free status of all derivatives of our free software and of promoting the sharing and reuse of software generally.

7.2.3 No Warranty

10. Because the program is licensed free of charge, there is no warranty for the program, to the extent permitted by applicable law. Except when otherwise stated in writing the copyright holders and/or other parties provide the program "as is" without warranty of any kind, either expressed or implied, including, but not limited to, the implied warranties of merchantability and fitness for a particular purpose. The entire risk as to the quality and performance of the program is with you. Should the program prove defective, you assume the cost of all necessary servicing, repair or correction.

11. In no event unless required by applicable law or agreed to in writing will any copyright holder, or any other party who may modify and/or redistribute the program as permitted above, be liable to you for damages, including any general, special, incidental or consequential damages arising out of the use or inability to use the program (including but not limited to loss of data or data being rendered inaccurate or losses sustained by you or third parties or a failure of the program to operate with any other programs), even if such holder or other party has been advised of the possibility of such damages.

7.3 The GNU Free Documentation License, Version 1.3, 3 November 2008

Copyright ©2000, 2001, 2002, 2007, 2008 Free Software Foundation, Inc.

http://fsf.org/

Everyone is allowed to distribute verbatim copies of this license document, but modification of it is not allowed.

7.3.1 Preamble

The purpose of this License is to make a manual, textbook, or other functional and useful document "free" in the sense of freedom: to assure everyone the effective freedom to copy and redistribute it, with or without modifying it, either commercially or noncommercially. Secondarily, this License preserves for the author and publisher a way to get credit for their work, while not being considered responsible for modifications made by others.

This License is a kind of "copyleft", which means that derivative works of the document must themselves be free in the same sense. It complements the GNU General Public License, which is a copyleft license designed for free software.

We have designed this License in order to use it for manuals for free software, because free software needs free documentation: a free program should come with manuals providing the same freedoms that the software does. But this License is not limited to software manuals; it can be used for any textual work, regardless of subject matter or whether it is published as a printed book. We recommend this License principally for works whose purpose is instruction or reference.

7.3.2 Applicability and definitions

This License applies to any manual or other work, in any medium, that contains a notice placed by the copyright holder saying it can be distributed under the terms of this License. Such a notice grants a world-wide, royalty-free license, unlimited in duration, to use that work under the conditions stated herein. The **"Document"**, below, refers to any such manual or work. Any member of the public is a licensee, and is addressed as **"you"**. You accept the license if you copy, modify or distribute the work in a way requiring permission under copyright law.

A **"Modified Version"** of the Document means any work containing the Document or a portion of it, either copied verbatim, or with modifications and/or translated into another language.

A **"Secondary Section"** is a named appendix or a front-matter section of the Document that deals exclusively with the relationship of the publishers or authors of the Document to the Document's overall subject (or to related matters) and contains nothing that could fall directly within that overall subject. (Thus, if the Document is in part a textbook of mathematics, a Secondary Section may not explain any mathematics.) The relationship could be a matter of historical connection with the subject or with related matters, or of legal, commercial, philosophical, ethical or political position regarding them.

The **"Invariant Sections"** are certain Secondary Sections whose titles are designated, as being those of Invariant Sections, in the notice that says that the Document is released under this License. If a section does not fit the above definition of Secondary then it is not allowed to be designated as Invariant. The Document may contain zero Invariant Sections. If the Document does not identify any Invariant Sections then there are none.

The **"Cover Texts"** are certain short passages of text that are listed, as Front-Cover Texts or Back-Cover Texts, in the notice that says that the Document is released under this License. A Front-Cover Text may be at most 5 words, and a Back-Cover Text may be at most 25 words.

A **"Transparent"** copy of the Document means a machine-readable copy, represented in a format whose specification is available to the general public, that is suitable for revising the document straightforwardly with generic text editors or (for images composed of pixels) generic paint programs or (for drawings) some widely available drawing editor, and that is suitable for input to text formatters or for automatic translation to a variety of formats suitable for input to text formatters. A copy made in an otherwise Transparent file format whose markup, or absence of markup, has been arranged to thwart or discourage subsequent modification by readers is not Transparent. An image format is not Transparent if used for any substantial amount of text. A copy that is not "Transparent" is called **"Opaque"**.

Examples of suitable formats for Transparent copies include plain ASCII without markup, Texinfo input format, LaTeX input format, SGML or XML using a publicly available DTD, and standard-conforming simple HTML, PostScript or PDF designed for human modification. Examples of transparent image formats include PNG, XCF and JPG. Opaque formats include proprietary formats that can be read and edited only by proprietary word processors, SGML or XML for which the DTD and/or processing tools are not generally available, and the machine-generated HTML, PostScript or PDF produced by some word processors for output purposes only.

The **"Title Page"** means, for a printed book, the title page itself, plus such following pages as are needed to hold, legibly, the material this License requires to appear in the title page. For works in formats which do not have any title page as such, "Title Page" means the text near the most prominent appearance of the work's title, preceding the beginning of the body of the text.

The **"publisher"** means any person or entity that distributes copies of the Document to the public.

A section **"Entitled XYZ"** means a named subunit of the Document whose title either is precisely XYZ or contains XYZ in parentheses following text that translates XYZ in another language. (Here XYZ stands for a specific section name mentioned below, such as **"Acknowledgements"**, **"Dedications"**, **"Endorsements"**, or **"History"**.) To **"Preserve the Title"** of such a section when you modify the Document means that it remains a section "Entitled XYZ" according to this definition.

The Document may include Warranty Disclaimers next to the notice which states that this License applies to the Document. These Warranty Disclaimers are considered to be included by reference in this License, but only as regards disclaiming warranties: any other implication that these Warranty Disclaimers may have is void and has no effect on the meaning of this License.

7.3.3 Verbatim Copying

You may copy and distribute the Document in any medium, either commercially or noncommercially, provided that this License, the copyright notices, and the license notice saying this License applies to the Document are reproduced in all copies, and that you add no other conditions whatsoever to those of this License. You may not use technical measures to obstruct or control the reading or further copying of the copies you make or distribute. However, you may accept compensation in exchange for copies. If you distribute a large enough number of copies you must also follow the conditions in section 3.

You may also lend copies, under the same conditions stated above, and you may publicly display copies.

7.3.4 Copying in Quantity

If you publish printed copies (or copies in media that commonly have printed covers) of the Document, numbering more than 100, and the Document's license notice requires Cover Texts, you must enclose the copies in covers that carry, clearly and legibly, all these Cover Texts: Front-Cover Texts on the front cover, and Back-Cover Texts on the back cover. Both covers must also clearly and legibly identify you as the publisher of these copies. The front cover must present the full title with all words of the title equally prominent and visible. You may add other material on the covers in addition. Copying with changes limited to the covers, as long as they preserve the title of the Document and satisfy these conditions, can be treated as verbatim copying in other respects.

If the required texts for either cover are too voluminous to fit legibly, you should put the first ones listed (as many as fit reasonably) on the actual cover, and continue the rest onto adjacent pages.

If you publish or distribute Opaque copies of the Document numbering more than 100, you must either include a machine-readable Transparent copy along with each Opaque copy, or state in or with each Opaque copy a computer-network location from which the general network-using public has access to download using public-standard network protocols a complete Transparent copy of the Document, free of added material. If you use the latter option, you must take reasonably prudent steps, when you begin distribution of Opaque copies in quantity, to ensure that this Transparent copy will remain thus accessible at the stated location until at least one year after the last time you distribute an Opaque copy (directly or through your agents or retailers) of that edition to the public.

It is requested, but not required, that you contact the authors of the Document well before redistributing any large number of copies, to give them a chance to provide you with an updated version of the Document.

7.3.5 Modifications

You may copy and distribute a Modified Version of the Document under the conditions of sections 2 and 3 above, provided that you release the Modified Version under precisely this License, with the Modified Version filling the role of the Document, thus licensing distribution and modification of the Modified Version to whoever possesses a copy of it. In addition, you must do these things in the Modified Version:

A. Use in the Title Page (and on the covers, if any) a title distinct from that of the Document, and from those of previous versions (which should, if there were any, be listed in the History section of the Document). You may use the same title as a previous version if the original publisher of that version gives permission.

B. List on the Title Page, as authors, one or more persons or entities responsible for authorship of the modifications in the Modified Version, together with at least five of the principal authors of the Document (all of its principal authors, if it has fewer than five), unless they release you from this requirement.

C. State on the Title page the name of the publisher of the Modified Version, as the publisher.

D. Preserve all the copyright notices of the Document.

E. Add an appropriate copyright notice for your modifications adjacent to the other copyright notices.

F. Include, immediately after the copyright notices, a license notice giving the public permission to use the Modified Version under the terms of this License, in the form shown in the Addendum below.

G. Preserve in that license notice the full lists of Invariant Sections and required Cover Texts given in the Document's license notice.

H. Include an unaltered copy of this License.

I. Preserve the section Entitled "History", Preserve its Title, and add to it an item stating at least the title, year, new authors, and publisher of the Modified Version as given on the Title Page. If there is no section Entitled "History" in the Document, create one stating the title, year, authors, and publisher of the Document as given on its Title Page, then add an item describing the Modified Version as stated in the previous sentence.

J. Preserve the network location, if any, given in the Document for public access to a Transparent copy of the Document, and likewise the network locations given in the Document for previous versions it was based on. These may be placed in the "History" section. You may omit a network location for a work that was published at least four years before the Document itself, or if the original publisher of the version it refers to gives permission.

K. For any section Entitled "Acknowledgements" or "Dedications", Preserve the Title of the section, and preserve in the section all the substance and tone of each of the contributor acknowledgements and/or dedications given therein.

L. Preserve all the Invariant Sections of the Document, unaltered in their text and in their titles. Section numbers or the equivalent are not considered part of the section titles.

M. Delete any section Entitled "Endorsements". Such a section may not be included in the Modified Version.

N. Do not retitle any existing section to be Entitled "Endorsements" or to conflict in title with any Invariant Section.

O. Preserve any Warranty Disclaimers.

If the Modified Version includes new front-matter sections or appendices that qualify as Secondary Sections and contain no material copied from the Document, you may at your option designate some or all of these sections as invariant. To do this, add their titles to the list of Invariant Sections in the Modified Version's license notice. These titles must be distinct from any other section titles.

You may add a section Entitled "Endorsements", provided it contains nothing but endorsements of your Modified Version by various parties–for example, statements of peer review or that the text has been approved by an organization as the authoritative definition of a standard.

You may add a passage of up to five words as a Front-Cover Text, and a passage of up to 25 words as a Back-Cover Text, to the end of the list of Cover Texts in the Modified Version. Only one passage of Front-Cover Text and one of Back-Cover Text may be added by (or through arrangements made by) any one entity. If the Document already includes a cover text for the same cover, previously added by you or by arrangement made by the same entity you are acting on behalf of, you may not add another; but you may replace the old one, on explicit permission from the previous publisher that added the old one.

The author(s) and publisher(s) of the Document do not by this License give permission to use their names for publicity for or to assert or imply endorsement of any Modified Version.

7.3.6 Combining Documents

You may combine the Document with other documents released under this License, under the terms defined in section 4 above for modified versions, provided that you include in the combination all of the Invariant Sections of all of the original documents, unmodified, and list them all as Invariant Sections of your combined work in its license notice, and that you preserve all their Warranty Disclaimers.

The combined work need only contain one copy of this License, and multiple identical Invariant Sections may be replaced with a single copy. If there are multiple Invariant Sections with the same name but different contents, make the title of each such section unique by adding at the end of it, in parentheses, the name of the original author or publisher of that section if known, or else a unique number. Make the same adjustment to the section titles in the list of Invariant Sections in the license notice of the combined work.

In the combination, you must combine any sections Entitled "History" in the various original documents, forming one section Entitled "History"; likewise combine any sections Entitled "Acknowledgements", and any sections Entitled "Dedications". You must delete all sections Entitled "Endorsements".

7.3.7 Collection of Documents

You may make a collection consisting of the Document and other documents released under this License, and replace the individual copies of this License in the various documents with a single copy that is included in the collection, provided that you follow the rules of this License for verbatim copying of each of the documents in all other respects.

You may extract a single document from such a collection, and distribute it individually under this License, provided you insert a copy of this License into the extracted document, and follow this License in all other respects regarding verbatim copying of that document.

7.3.8 Aggregating with Independent Works

A compilation of the Document or its derivatives with other separate and independent documents or works, in or on a volume of a storage or distribution medium, is called an "aggregate" if the copyright resulting from the compilation is not used to limit the legal rights of the compilation's users beyond what the individual works permit. When the Document is included in an aggregate, this License does not apply to the other works in the aggregate which are not themselves derivative works of the Document.

If the Cover Text requirement of section 3 is applicable to these copies of the Document, then if the Document is less than one half of the entire aggregate, the Document's Cover Texts may be placed on covers that bracket the Document within the aggregate, or the electronic equivalent of covers if the Document is in electronic form. Otherwise they must appear on printed covers that bracket the whole aggregate.

7.3.9 Translation

Translation is considered a kind of modification, so you may distribute translations of the Document under the terms of section 4. Replacing Invariant Sections with translations requires special permission from their copyright holders, but you may include translations of some or all Invariant Sections in addition to the original versions of these Invariant Sections. You may include a translation of this License, and all the license notices in the Document, and any Warranty Disclaimers, provided that you also include the original English version of this License and the original versions of those notices and disclaimers. In case of a disagreement between the translation and the original version of this License or a notice or disclaimer, the original version will prevail.

If a section in the Document is Entitled "Acknowledgements", "Dedications", or "History", the requirement (section 4) to Preserve its Title (section 1) will typically require changing the actual title.

7.3.10 Termination

You may not copy, modify, sublicense, or distribute the Document except as expressly provided under this License. Any attempt otherwise to copy, modify, sublicense, or distribute it is void, and will automatically terminate your rights under this License.

However, if you cease all violation of this License, then your license from a particular copyright holder is reinstated (a) provisionally, unless and until the copyright holder explicitly and finally terminates your license, and (b) permanently, if the copyright holder fails to notify you of the violation by some reasonable means prior to 60 days after the cessation.

Moreover, your license from a particular copyright holder is reinstated permanently if the copyright holder notifies you of the violation by some reasonable means, this is the first time you have received notice of violation of this License (for any work) from that copyright holder, and you cure the violation prior to 30 days after your receipt of the notice.

Termination of your rights under this section does not terminate the licenses of parties who have received copise or rights from you under this License. If your rights have been terminated and not permanently reinstated, receipt of a copy of some or all of the same material does not give you any rights to use it.

7.3.11   Future Revisions of this License

The Free Software Foundation may publish new, revised versions of the GNU Free Documentation License from time to time. Such new versions will be similar in spirit to the present version, but may differ in detail to address new problems or concerns. See http://www.gnu.org/copyleft/.

Each version of the License is given a distinguishing version number. If the Document specifies that a particular numbered version of this License "or any later version" applies to it, you have the option of following the terms and conditions either of that specified version or of any later version that has been published (not as a draft) by the Free Software Foundation. If the Document does not specify a version number of this License, you may choose any version ever published (not as a draft) by the Free Software Foundation. If the Document specifies that a proxy can decide which future versions of this License can be used, that proxy's public statement of acceptance of a version permanently authorizes you to choose that version for the Document.

7.3.12   Relicensing

"Massive Multiauthor Collaboration Site" (or "MMC Site") means any World Wide Web server that publishes copyrightable works and also provides prominent facilities for anybody to edit those works. A public wiki that anybody can edit is an example of such a server. A "Massive Multiauthor Collaboration" (or "MMC") contained in the site means any set of copyrightable works thus published on the MMC site.

"CC-BY-SA" means the Creative Commons Attribution-Share Alike 3.0 license published by Creative Commons Corporation, a not-for-profit corporation with a principal place of business in San Francisco, California, as well as future copyleft versions of that license published by that same organization.

"Incorporate" means to publish or republish a Document, in whole or in part, as part of another Document.

An MMC is "eligible for relicensing" if it is licensed under this License, and if all works that were first published under this License somewhere other than this MMC, and subsequently incorporated in whole or in part into the MMC, (1) had no cover texts or invariant sections, and (2) were thus incorporated prior to November 1, 2008.

The operator of an MMC Site may republish an MMC contained in the site under CC-BY-SA on the same site at any time before August 1, 2009, provided the MMC is eligible for relicensing.

7.3.13   Addendum: How to use this License for your documents

To use this License in a document you have written, include a copy of the License in the document and put the following copyright and license notices just after the title page:

> Copyright ©YEAR YOUR NAME.
>
> Permission is granted to copy, distribute and/or modify this document under the terms of the GNU Free Documentation License, Version 1.3 or any later version published by the Free Software Foundation; with no Invariant Sections, no Front-Cover Texts, and no Back-Cover Texts. A copy of the license is included in the section entitled "GNU Free Documentation License".

If you have Invariant Sections, Front-Cover Texts and Back-Cover Texts, replace the "with ... Texts." line with this:

> with the Invariant Sections being LIST THEIR TITLES, with the Front-Cover Texts being LIST, and with the Back-Cover Texts being LIST.

If you have Invariant Sections without Cover Texts, or some other combination of the three, merge those two alternatives to suit the situation.

If your document contains nontrivial examples of program code, we recommend releasing these examples in parallel under your choice of free software license, such as the GNU General Public License, to permit their use in free software.

7.4 The LaTeX Project Public License

LPPL Version 1.3c 2008-05-04
Copyright 1999, 2002–2008 LaTeX3 Project

> Everyone is allowed to distribute verbatim copies of this license document, but modification of it is not allowed.

7.4.1 Preamble

The LaTeX Project Public License (LPPL) is the primary license under which the LaTeX kernel and the base LaTeX packages are distributed.

You may use this license for any work of which you hold the copyright and which you wish to distribute. This license may be particularly suitable if your work is TeX-related (such as a LaTeX package), but it is written in such a way that you can use it even if your work is unrelated to TeX.

The section 'WHETHER AND HOW TO DISTRIBUTE WORKS UNDER THIS LICENSE', below, gives instructions, examples, and recommendations for authors who are considering distributing their works under this license.

This license gives conditions under which a work may be distributed and modified, as well as conditions under which modified versions of that work may be distributed.

We, the LaTeX3 Project, believe that the conditions below give you the freedom to make and distribute modified versions of your work that conform with whatever technical specifications you wish while maintaining the availability, integrity, and reliability of that work. If you do not see how to achieve your goal while meeting these conditions, then read the document 'cfgguide.tex' and 'modguide.tex' in the base LaTeX distribution for suggestions.

7.4.2 Definitions

In this license document the following terms are used:

Work Any work being distributed under this License.

Derived Work Any work that under any applicable law is derived from the Work.

Modification Any procedure that produces a Derived Work under any applicable law – for example, the production of a file containing an original file associated with the Work or a significant portion of such a file, either verbatim or with modifications and/or translated into another language.

Modify To apply any procedure that produces a Derived Work under any applicable law.

Distribution Making copies of the Work available from one person to another, in whole or in part. Distribution includes (but is not limited to) making any electronic components of the Work accessible by file transfer protocols such as FTP or HTTP or by shared file systems such as Sun's Network File System (NFS).

Compiled Work A version of the Work that has been processed into a form where it is directly usable on a computer system. This processing may include using installation facilities provided by the Work, transformations of the Work, copying of components of the Work, or other activities. Note that modification of any installation facilities provided by the Work constitutes modification of the Work.

Current Maintainer A person or persons nominated as such within the Work. If there is no such explicit nomination then it is the 'Copyright Holder' under any applicable law.

Base Interpreter A program or process that is normally needed for running or interpreting a part or the whole of the Work.

A Base Interpreter may depend on external components but these are not considered part of the Base Interpreter provided that each external component clearly identifies itself whenever it is used interactively. Unless explicitly specified when applying the license to the Work, the only applicable Base Interpreter is a 'LaTeX-Format' or in the case of files belonging to the 'LaTeX-format' a program implementing the 'TeX language'.

7.4.3 Conditions on Distribution and Modification

1. Activities other than distribution and/or modification of the Work are not covered by this license; they are outside its scope. In particular, the act of running the Work is not restricted and no requirements are made concerning any offers of support for the Work.

2. You may distribute a complete, unmodified copy of the Work as you received it. Distribution of only part of the Work is considered modification of the Work, and no right to distribute such a Derived Work may be assumed under the terms of this clause.

3. You may distribute a Compiled Work that has been generated from a complete, unmodified copy of the Work as distributed under Clause 2 above, as long as that Compiled Work is distributed in such a way that the recipients may install the Compiled Work on their system exactly as it would have been installed if they generated a Compiled Work directly from the Work.

4. If you are the Current Maintainer of the Work, you may, without restriction, modify the Work, thus creating a Derived Work. You may also distribute the Derived Work without restriction, including Compiled Works generated from the Derived Work. Derived Works distributed in this manner by the Current Maintainer are considered to be updated versions of the Work.

5. If you are not the Current Maintainer of the Work, you may modify your copy of the Work, thus creating a Derived Work based on the Work, and compile this Derived Work, thus creating a Compiled Work based on the Derived Work.

6. If you are not the Current Maintainer of the Work, you may distribute a Derived Work provided the following conditions are met for every component of the Work unless that component clearly states in the copyright notice that it is exempt from that condition. Only the Current Maintainer is allowed to add such statements of exemption to a component of the Work.

   (a) If a component of this Derived Work can be a direct replacement for a component of the Work when that component is used with the Base Interpreter, then, wherever this component of the Work identifies itself to the user when used interactively with that Base Interpreter, the replacement component of this Derived Work clearly and unambiguously identifies itself as a modified version of this component to the user when used interactively with that Base Interpreter.

   (b) Every component of the Derived Work contains prominent notices detailing the nature of the changes to that component, or a prominent reference to another file that is distributed as part of the Derived Work and that contains a complete and accurate log of the changes.

   (c) No information in the Derived Work implies that any persons, including (but not limited to) the authors of the original version of the Work, provide any support, including (but not limited to) the reporting and handling of errors, to recipients of the Derived Work unless those persons have stated explicitly that they do provide such support for the Derived Work.

   (d) You distribute at least one of the following with the Derived Work:

      i. A complete, unmodified copy of the Work; if your distribution of a modified component is made by offering access to copy the modified component from a designated place, then offering equivalent access to copy the Work from the same or some similar place meets this condition, even though third parties are not compelled to copy the Work along with the modified component;

      ii. Information that is sufficient to obtain a complete, unmodified copy of the Work.

7. If you are not the Current Maintainer of the Work, you may distribute a Compiled Work generated from a Derived Work, as long as the Derived Work is distributed to all recipients of the Compiled Work, and as long as the conditions of Clause 6, above, are met with regard to the Derived Work.

8. The conditions above are not intended to prohibit, and hence do not apply to, the modification, by any method, of any component so that it becomes identical to an updated version of that component of the Work as it is distributed by the Current Maintainer under Clause 4, above.

9. Distribution of the Work or any Derived Work in an alternative format, where the Work or that Derived Work (in whole or in part) is then produced by applying some process to that format, does not relax or nullify any sections of this license as they pertain to the results of applying that process.

10. (a) A Derived Work may be distributed under a different license provided that license itself honors the conditions listed in Clause 6 above, in regard to the Work, though it does not have to honor the rest of the conditions in this license.

    (b) If a Derived Work is distributed under a different license, that Derived Work must provide sufficient documentation as part of itself to allow each recipient of that Derived Work to honor the restrictions in Clause 6 above, concerning changes from the Work.

11. This license places no restrictions on works that are unrelated to the Work, nor does this license place any restrictions on aggregating such works with the Work by any means.

12. Nothing in this license is intended to, or may be used to, prevent complete compliance by all parties with all applicable laws.

7.4.4 No Warranty

There is no warranty for the Work. Except when otherwise stated in writing, the Copyright Holder provides the Work 'as is', without warranty of any kind, either expressed or implied, including, but not limited to, the implied warranties of merchantability and fitness for a particular purpose. The entire risk as to the quality and performance of the Work is with you. Should the Work prove defective, you assume the cost of all necessary servicing, repair, or correction.

In no event unless required by applicable law or agreed to in writing will The Copyright Holder, or any author named in the components of the Work, or any other party who may distribute and/or modify the Work as permitted above, be liable to you for damages, including any general, special, incidental or consequential damages arising out of any use of the Work or out of inability to use the Work (including, but not limited to, loss of data, data being rendered inaccurate, or losses sustained by anyone as a result of any failure of the Work to operate with any other programs), even if the Copyright Holder or said author or said other party has been advised of the possibility of such damages.

7.4.5 Maintenance of The Work

The Work has the status 'author-maintained' if the Copyright Holder explicitly and prominently states near the primary copyright notice in the Work that the Work can only be maintained by the Copyright Holder or simply that it is 'author-maintained'.

The Work has the status 'maintained' if there is a Current Maintainer who has indicated in the Work that they are willing to receive error reports for the Work (for example, by supplying a valid e-mail address). It is not required for the Current Maintainer to acknowledge or act upon these error reports.

The Work changes from status 'maintained' to 'unmaintained' if there is no Current Maintainer, or the person stated to be Current Maintainer of the work cannot be reached through the indicated means of communication for a period of six months, and there are no other significant signs of active maintenance.

You can become the Current Maintainer of the Work by agreement with any existing Current Maintainer to take over this role.

If the Work is unmaintained, you can become the Current Maintainer of the Work through the following steps:

1. Make a reasonable attempt to trace the Current Maintainer (and the Copyright Holder, if the two differ) through the means of an Internet or similar search.

2. If this search is successful, then enquire whether the Work is still maintained.

    (a) If it is being maintained, then ask the Current Maintainer to update their communication data within one month.

    (b) If the search is unsuccessful or no action to resume active maintenance is taken by the Current Maintainer, then announce within the pertinent community your intention to take over maintenance. (If the Work is a LaTeX work, this could be done, for example, by posting to `comp.text.tex`.)

3. (a) If the Current Maintainer is reachable and agrees to pass maintenance of the Work to you, then this takes effect immediately upon announcement.

    (b) If the Current Maintainer is not reachable and the Copyright Holder agrees that maintenance of the Work be passed to you, then this takes effect immediately upon announcement.

4. If you make an 'intention announcement' as described in 2b above and after three months your intention is challenged neither by the Current Maintainer nor by the Copyright Holder nor by other people, then you may arrange for the Work to be changed so as to name you as the (new) Current Maintainer.

5. If the previously unreachable Current Maintainer becomes reachable once more within three months of a change completed under the terms of 3b or 4, then that Current Maintainer must become or remain the Current Maintainer upon request provided they then update their communication data within one month.

A change in the Current Maintainer does not, of itself, alter the fact that the Work is distributed under the LPPL license.

If you become the Current Maintainer of the Work, you should immediately provide, within the Work, a prominent and unambiguous statement of your status as Current Maintainer. You should also announce your new status to the same pertinent community as in 2b above.

7.4.6 Whether and How to Distribute Works under This License

This section contains important instructions, examples, and recommendations for authors who are considering distributing their works under this license. These authors are addressed as 'you' in this section.

7.4.7 Choosing This License or Another License

If for any part of your work you want or need to use *distribution* conditions that differ significantly from those in this license, then do not refer to this license anywhere in your work but, instead, distribute your work under a different license. You may use the text of this license as a model for your own license, but your license should not refer to the LPPL or otherwise give the impression that your work is distributed under the LPPL.

The document 'modguide.tex' in the base LaTeX distribution explains the motivation behind the conditions of this license. It explains, for example, why distributing LaTeX under the GNU General Public License (GPL) was considered inappropriate. Even if your work is unrelated to LaTeX, the discussion in 'modguide.tex' may still be relevant, and authors intending to distribute their works under any license are encouraged to read it.

7.4.8 A Recommendation on Modification Without Distribution

It is wise never to modify a component of the Work, even for your own personal use, without also meeting the above conditions for distributing the modified component. While you might intend that such modifications will never be distributed, often this will happen by accident – you may forget that you have modified that component; or it may not occur to you when allowing others to access the modified version that you are thus distributing it and violating the conditions of this license in ways that could have legal implications and, worse, cause problems for the community. It is therefore usually in your best interest to keep your copy of the Work identical with the public one. Many works provide ways to control the behavior of that work without altering any of its licensed components.

7.4.9 How to Use This License

To use this license, place in each of the components of your work both an explicit copyright notice including your name and the year the work was authored and/or last substantially modified. Include also a statement that the distribution and/or modification of that component is constrained by the conditions in this license.

Here is an example of such a notice and statement:

```
%% pig.dtx
%% Copyright 2005 M. Y. Name
%
% This work may be distributed and/or modified under the
% conditions of the LaTeX Project Public License, either version 1.3
% of this license or (at your option) any later version.
% The latest version of this license is in
%    http://www.latex-project.org/lppl.txt
% and version 1.3 or later is part of all distributions of LaTeX
% version 2005/12/01 or later.
%
% This work has the LPPL maintenance status 'maintained'.
%
% The Current Maintainer of this work is M. Y. Name.
%
% This work consists of the files pig.dtx and pig.ins
% and the derived file pig.sty.
```

Given such a notice and statement in a file, the conditions given in this license document would apply, with the 'Work' referring to the three files 'pig.dtx', 'pig.ins', and 'pig.sty' (the last being generated from 'pig.dtx' using 'pig.ins'), the 'Base Interpreter' referring to any 'LaTeX-Format', and both 'Copyright Holder' and 'Current Maintainer' referring to the person 'M. Y. Name'.

If you do not want the Maintenance section of LPPL to apply to your Work, change 'maintained' above into 'author-maintained'. However, we recommend that you use 'maintained' as the Maintenance section was added in order to ensure that your Work remains useful to the community even when you can no longer maintain and support it yourself.

7.4.10 Derived Works That Are Not Replacements

Several clauses of the LPPL specify means to provide reliability and stability for the user community. They therefore concern themselves with the case that a Derived Work is intended to be used as a (compatible or incompatible) replacement of the original Work. If this is not the case (e.g., if a few lines of code are reused for a completely different task), then clauses 6b and 6d shall not apply.

7.4.11 Important Recommendations

Defining What Constitutes the Work The LPPL requires that distributions of the Work contain all the files of the Work. It is therefore important that you provide a way for the licensee to determine which files constitute the Work. This could, for example, be achieved by explicitly listing all the files of the Work near the copyright notice of each file or by using a line such as:

```
% This work consists of all files listed in manifest.txt.
```

in that place. In the absence of an unequivocal list it might be impossible for the licensee to determine what is considered by you to comprise the Work and, in such a case, the licensee would be entitled to make reasonable conjectures as to which files comprise the Work.

Part II
Building a Presentation

This part contains an explanation of all the commands that are used to create presentations. It starts with a section treating the commands and environments used to create *frames*, the basic building blocks of presentations. Next, the creation of overlays is explained.

The following three sections concern commands and methods of *structuring* a presentation. In order, the *static global* structure, the *interactive global* structure, and the *local* structure are treated.

Two further sections treat graphics and animations. Much of the material in these sections applies to other packages as well, not just to BEAMER.

8 Creating Frames

8.1 The Frame Environment

A presentation consists of a series of frames. Each frame consists of a series of slides. You create a frame using the command `\frame` or the environment `frame`, which do the same. The command takes one parameter, namely the contents of the frame. All of the text that is not tagged by overlay specifications is shown on all slides of the frame. (Overlay specifications are explained in more detail in later sections. For the moment, let's just say that an overlay specification is a list of numbers or number ranges in pointed brackets that is put after certain commands as in `\uncover<1,2>{Text}`.) If a frame contains commands that have an overlay specification, the frame will contain multiple slides; otherwise it contains only one slide.

`\begin{frame}`<*⟨overlay specification⟩*>`[`<*⟨default overlay specification⟩*>`]` `[`*⟨options⟩*`]` `{`*⟨title⟩*`}` `{`*⟨subtitle⟩*`}`
   ⟨environment contents⟩
`\end{frame}`

The *⟨overlay specification⟩* dictates which slides of a frame are to be shown. If left out, the number is calculated automatically. The *⟨environment contents⟩* can be normal LaTeX text, but may not contain `\verb` commands or `verbatim` environments or any environment that changes the character codes, unless the `fragile` option is given.

The optional *⟨title⟩* is detected by an opening brace, that is, if the first thing in the frame is an opening brace then it is assumed that a frame title follows. Likewise, the optional *⟨subtitle⟩* is detected the same way, that is, by an opening brace following the *⟨title⟩*. The title and subtitle can also be given using the `\frametitle` and `\framesubtitle` commands.

The normal LaTeX command `\frame` is available *inside* frames with its usual meaning. Both outside and inside frames it is always available as `\framelatex`.

Example:

```
\begin{frame}{A title}
  Some content.
\end{frame}
% Same effect:
\begin{frame}
  \frametitle{A title}
  Some content.
\end{frame}
```

Example:

```
\begin{frame}<beamer>{Outline}  % frame is only shown in beamer mode
  \tabelofcontent[current]
\end{frame}
```

Normally, the complete *⟨environment contents⟩* is put on a slide. If the text does not fit on a slide, being too high, it will be squeezed as much as possible, a warning will be issued, and the text just extends unpleasantly over the bottom. You can use the option `allowframebreaks` to cause the *⟨frame text⟩* to be split among several slides, though you cannot use overlays then. See the explanation of the `allowframebreaks` option for details.

The *⟨default overlay specification⟩* is an optional argument that is "detected" according to the following rule: If the first optional argument in square brackets starts with a <, then this argument is a *⟨default overlay specification⟩*, otherwise it is a normal *⟨options⟩* argument. Thus `\begin{frame}[<+->][plain]` would be legal, but also `\begin{frame}[plain]`.

The effect of the *⟨default overlay specification⟩* is the following: Every command or environment *inside the frame* that accepts an action specification, see Section 9.6.3, (this includes the `\item` command, the `actionenv` environment, `\action`, and all block environments) and that is not followed by an overlay specification gets the *⟨default overlay specification⟩* as its specification. By providing an incremental specification like <+->, see Section 9.6.4, this will essentially cause all blocks and all enumerations to be uncovered piece-wise (blocks internally employ action specifications).

58

Example: In this frame, the theorem is shown from the first slide on, the proof from the second slide on, with the first two itemize points shown one after the other; the last itemize point is shown together with the first one. In total, this frame will contain four slides.

```
\begin{frame}[<+->]
  \begin{theorem}
    $A = B$.
  \end{theorem}
  \begin{proof}
    \begin{itemize}
    \item Clearly, $A = C$.
    \item As shown earlier,  $C = B$.
    \item<3-> Thus $A = B$.
    \end{itemize}
  \end{proof}
\end{frame}
```

The following ⟨*options*⟩ may be given:

- `allowdisplaybreaks`=⟨*break desirability*⟩ causes the AMST_EX command `\allowdisplaybreaks[`⟨*break desirability*⟩`]` to be issued for the current frame. The ⟨*break desirability*⟩ can be a value between 0 (meaning formulas may never be broken) and 4 (the default, meaning that formulas can be broken anywhere without any penalty). The option is just a convenience and makes sense only together with the `allowsframebreaks` option.

- `allowframebreaks`=⟨*fraction*⟩. When this option is given, the frame will be automatically broken up into several frames if the text does not fit on a single slide. In detail, when this option is given, the following things happen:

  1. Overlays are not supported.
  2. Any notes for the frame created using the `\note` command will be inserted after the first page of the frame.
  3. Any footnotes for the frame will be inserted on the last page of the frame.
  4. If there is a frame title, each of the pages will have this frame title, with a special note added indicating which page of the frame that page is. By default, this special note is a Roman number. However, this can be changed using the following template.
     Beamer-Template/-Color/-Font `frametitle continuation`
     The text of this template is inserted at the end of every title of a frame with the `allowframebreaks` option set.
     The following template options are predefined:
     - [`default`] Installs a Roman number as the template. The number indicates the current page of the frame.
     - [`roman`] Alias for the default.
     - [`from second`] [⟨*text*⟩] Installs a template that inserts ⟨*text*⟩ from the second page of a frame on. By default, the text inserted is `\insertcontinuationtext`, which in turn is (`cont.`) by default.
     The following inserts are available:
     - `\insertcontinuationcount` inserts the current page of the frame as an arabic number.
     - `\insertcontinuationcountroman` inserts the current page of the frame as an (uppercase) Roman number.
     - `\insertcontinuationtext` just inserts the text (`cont.`) or, possibly, a translation thereof (like (`Forts.`) in German).

If a frame needs to be broken into several pages, the material on all but the last page fills only 95% of each page by default. Thus, there will be some space left at the top and/or bottom, depending on the vertical placement option for the frame. This yields a better visual result than a 100% filling, which typically looks crowded. However, you can change this percentage using the optional argument

59

⟨*fraction*⟩, where 1 means 100% and 0.5 means 50%. This percentage includes the frame title. Thus, in order to split a frame "roughly in half," you should give 0.6 as ⟨*fraction*⟩.

Most of the fine details of normal TeX page breaking also apply to this option. For example, when you wish equations to be broken automatically, be sure to use the `\allowdisplaybreaks` command. You can insert `\break`, `\nobreak`, and `\penalty` commands to control where breaks should occur. The commands `\pagebreak` and `\nopagebreak` also work, including their options. Since you typically do not want page breaks for the frame to apply also to the `article` mode, you can add a mode specification like `<presentation>` to make these commands apply only to the presentation modes. The command `\framebreak` is a shorthand for `\pagebreak<presentation>` and `\noframebreak` is a shorthand for `\nopagebreak<presentation>`.

The use of this option is *evil*. In a (good) presentation you prepare each slide carefully and think twice before putting something on a certain slide rather than on some different slide. Using the `allowframebreaks` option invites the creation of horrible, endless presentations that resemble more a "paper projected on the wall" than a presentation. Nevertheless, the option does have its uses. Most noticeably, it can be convenient for automatically splitting bibliographies or long equations.

Example:

```
\begin{frame}[allowframebreaks]{References}
  \begin{thebibliography}{XX}

  \bibitem...
  \bibitem...
     ...
  \bibitem...
  \end{thebibliography}
\end{frame}
```

Example:

```
\begin{frame}[allowframebreaks,allowdisplaybreaks]{A Long Equation}
  \begin{align}
    \zeta(2) &= 1 + 1/4 + 1/9 + \cdots \\
    &= ... \\
    ...
    &= \pi^2/6.
  \end{align}
\end{frame}
```

- b, c, t will cause the frame to be vertically aligned at the bottom/center/top. This overrides the global placement policy, which is governed by the class options t and c.

- `fragile=singleslide` tells BEAMER that the frame contents is "fragile." This means that the frame contains text that is not "interpreted as usual." For example, this applies to verbatim text, which is, obviously, interpreted somewhat differently from normal text.

  If a frame contains fragile text, different internal mechanisms are used to typeset the frame to ensure that inside the frame the character codes can be reset. The price of switching to another internal mechanism is that either you cannot use overlays or an external file needs to be written and read back (which is not always desirable).

  In detail, the following happens when this option is given for normal (pdf)LaTeX: The contents of the frame is scanned and then written to a special file named ⟨*jobname*⟩.vrb or, if a label has been assigned to the frame, ⟨*jobname*⟩.⟨*current frame number*⟩.vrb. Then, the frame is started anew and the content of this file is read back. Since, upon reading of a file, the character codes can be modified, this allows you to use both verbatim text and overlays.

  To determine the end of the frame, the following rule is used: The first occurence of a single line containing exactly `\end{`⟨*frame environment name*⟩`}` ends the frame. The ⟨*environment name*⟩ is normally `frame`, but it can be changed using the `environment` option. This special rule is needed since the frame contents is, after all, not interpreted when it is gathered.

You can also add the optional information =singleslide. This tells BEAMER that the frame contains only a single slide. In this case, the frame contents is *not* written to a special file, but interpreted directly, which is "faster and cleaner."

- environment=⟨*frame environment name*⟩. This option is useful only in conjunction with the fragile option (but it is not used for fragile=singleslide, only for the plain fragile). The ⟨*frame environment name*⟩ is used to determine the end of the scanning when gathering the frame contents. Normally, the frame ends when a line reading \end{frame} is reached. However, if you use \begin{frame} inside another environment, you need to use this option:

Example:

```
\newenvironment{slide}[1]
  {\begin{frame}[fragile,environment=slide]
     \frametitle{#1}}
  {\end{frame}}

\begin{slide}{My title}
  Text.
\end{slide}
```

If you did not specify the option environment=slide in the above example, TEX would "miss" the end of the slide since it does not interpret text while gathering the frame contents.

- label=⟨*name*⟩ causes the frame's contents to be stored under the name ⟨*name*⟩ for later resumption using the command \againframe. Furthermore, on each slide of the frame a label with the name ⟨*name*⟩<⟨*slide number*⟩> is created. On the *first* slide, furthermore, a label with the name ⟨*name*⟩ is created (so the labels ⟨*name*⟩ and ⟨*name*⟩<1> point to the same slide). Note that labels in general, and these labels in particular, can be used as targets for hyperlinks.

  You can use this option together with fragile.

- plain causes the headlines, footlines, and sidebars to be suppressed. This is useful for creating single frames with different head- and footlines or for creating frames showing big pictures that completely fill the frame.

Example: A frame with a picture completely filling the frame:

```
\begin{frame}[plain]
  \begin{centering}%
    \pgfimage[height=\paperheight]{somebigimagefile}%
    \par%
  \end{centering}%
\end{frame}
```

Example: A title page, in which the head- and footlines are replaced by two graphics.

```
\setbeamertemplate{title page}
{
  \pgfuseimage{toptitle}
  \vskip0pt plus 1filll

  \begin{centering}
    {\usebeamerfont{title}\usebeamercolor[fg]{title}\inserttitle}

    \insertdate
  \end{centering}

  \vskip0pt plus 1filll
  \pgfuseimage{bottomtitle}
}
\begin{frame}[plain]
  \titlepage
\end{frame}
```

- shrink=⟨*minimum shrink percentage*⟩. This option will cause the text of the frame to be shrunk if it is too large to fit on the frame. BEAMER will first normally typeset the whole frame. Then it has a look at vertical size of the frame text (excluding the frame title). If this vertical size is larger than the text height minus the frame title height, BEAMER computes a shrink factor and scales down the frame text by this factor such that the frame text then fills the frame completely. Using this option will automatically cause the squeeze option to be used, also.

  Since the shrinking takes place only after everything has been typeset, shrunk frame text will not fill the frame completely horizontally. For this reason, you can specify a ⟨*minimum shrink percentage*⟩ like 20. If this percentage is specified, the frame will be shrunk *at least* by this percentage. Since BEAMER knows this, it can increase the horizontal width proportionally such that the shrunk text once more fills the entire frame. If, however, the percentage is not enough, the text will be shrunk as needed and you will be punished with a warning message.

  The best way to use this option is to identify frames that are overly full, but in which all text absolutely has to be fit on a single frame. Then start specifying first shrink=5, then shrink=10, and so on, until no warning is issued any more (or just ignore the warning when things look satisfactory).

  Using this option is *very evil*. It will result in changes of the font size from slide to slide, which is a typographic nightmare. Its usage can *always* be avoided by restructuring and simplifying frames, which will result in a better presentation.

  Example:

  ```
  \begin{frame}[shrink=5]
    Some evil endless slide that is 5\% too large.
  \end{frame}
  ```

- squeeze causes all vertical spaces in the text to be squeezed together as much as possible. Currently, this just causes the vertical space in enumerations or itemizations to be reduced to zero.

  Using this option is not good, but also not evil.

ARTICLE In article mode, the frame environment does not create any visual reference to the original frame (no frame is drawn). Rather, the frame text is inserted into the normal text. To change this, you can modify the templates frame begin and frame end, see below. To suppress a frame in article mode, you can, for example, specify <presentation> as overlay specification.

Beamer-Template frame begin

The text of this template is inserted at the beginning of each frame in article mode (and only there). You can use it, say, to start a minipage environment at the beginning of a frame or to insert a horizontal bar or whatever.

Beamer-Template frame end

The text of this template is inserted at the end of each frame in article mode.

You *can* use the frame environment inside other environments like this

```
\newenvironment{slide}{\begin{frame}}{\end{frame}}
```

or like this

```
\newenvironment{myframe}[1]
  {\begin{frame}[fragile,environment=myframe]\frametitle{#1}}
  {\end{frame}}
```

However, the actual mechanics are somewhat sensitive since the "collecting" of the frame contents is not easy, so do not attempt anything too fancy. As a rule, the beginning of the environment can be pretty arbitrary, but the ending must end with \end{frame} and should not contain any \end{xxx}. Anything really complex is likely to fail. If you need some \end{xxx} there, define a new command that contains this stuff as in the following example:

```
\newenvironment{itemizeframe}
  {\begin{frame}\startitemizeframe}
  {\stopitemizeframe\end{frame}}

\newcommand\startitemizeframe{\begin{bfseries}\begin{itemize}}
\newcommand\stopitemizeframe{\end{itemize}\end{bfseries}}

\begin{itemizeframe}
\item First item
\end{itemizeframe}
```

8.2 Components of a Frame

Each frame consists of several components:

1. a headline and a footline,
2. a left and a right sidebar,
3. navigation bars,
4. navigation symbols,
5. a logo,
6. a frame title,
7. a background, and
8. some frame contents.

A frame need not have all of these components. Usually, the first three components are automatically setup by the theme you are using.

8.2.1 The Headline and Footline

The headline of a frame is the area at the top of the frame. If it is not empty, it should show some information that helps the audience orientate itself during your talk. Likewise, the footline is the area at the bottom of the frame.

BEAMER does not use the standard LATEX mechanisms for typesetting the headline and the footline. Instead, the special `headline` and `footline` templates are used to typeset them.

The size of the headline and the footline is determined as follows: Their width is always the paper width. Their height is determined by tentatively typesetting the headline and the footline right after the `\begin{document}` command. The head of the headline and the footline at that point is "frozen" and will be used throughout the whole document, even if the headline and footline vary in height later on (which they should not).

The appearance of the headline and footline is determined by the following templates:

Beamer-Template/-Color/-Font `headline`

> This template is used to typeset the headline. The BEAMER-color and -font `headline` are installed at the beginning. The background of the BEAMER-color is not used by default, that is, no background rectangle is drawn behind the headline and footline (this may change in the future with the introduction of a headline and a footline canvas).
>
> The width of the headline is the whole paper width. The height is determined automatically as described above. The headline is typeset in vertical mode with interline skip turned off and the paragraph skip set to zero.
>
> Inside this template, the \\ command is changed such that it inserts a comma instead.
>
> *Example:*
> ```
> \setbeamertemplate{headline}
> {%
>   \begin{beamercolorbox}{section in head/foot}
>     \vskip2pt\insertnavigation{\paperwidth}\vskip2pt
>   \end{beamercolorbox}%
> }
> ```

The following template options are predefined:

- [default] The default is just an empty headline. To get the default headline of earlier versions of the BEAMER class, use the compatibility theme.

- [infolines theme] This option becomes available (and is used) if the infolines outer theme is loaded. The headline shows current section and subsection.

- [miniframes theme] This option becomes available (and is used) if the miniframes outer theme is loaded. The headline shows the sections with small clickable mini frames below them.

- [sidebar theme] This option becomes available (and is used) if the sidebar outer theme is loaded and if the head height (and option of the sidebar theme) is not zero. In this case, the headline is an empty bar of the background color frametitle with the logo to the left or right of this bar.

- [smoothtree theme] This option becomes available (and is used) if the smoothtree outer theme is loaded. A "smoothed" navigation tree is shown in the headline.

- [smoothbars theme] This option becomes available (and is used) if the smoothbars outer theme is loaded. A "smoothed" version of the miniframes headline is shown.

- [tree] This option becomes available (and is used) if the tree outer theme is loaded. A navigational tree is shown in the headline.

- [split theme] This option becomes available (and is used) if the split outer theme is loaded. The headline is split into a left part showing the sections and a right part showing the subsections.

- [text line]{⟨*text*⟩} The headline is typeset more or less as if it were a normal text line with the ⟨*text*⟩ as contents. The left and right margin are setup such that they are the same as the margins of normal text. The ⟨*text*⟩ is typeset inside an \hbox, while the headline is normally typeset in vertical mode.

Inside the template numerous inserts can be used:

- \insertnavigation{⟨*width*⟩} Inserts a horizontal navigation bar of the given ⟨*width*⟩ into a template. The bar lists the sections and below them mini frames for each frame in that section.

- \insertpagenumber Inserts the current page number into a template.

- \insertsection Inserts the current section into a template.

- \insertsectionnavigation{⟨*width*⟩} Inserts a vertical navigation bar containing all sections, with the current section highlighted.

- \insertsectionnavigationhorizontal{⟨*width*⟩}{⟨*left insert*⟩}{⟨*right insert*⟩} Inserts a horizontal navigation bar containing all sections, with the current section highlighted. The ⟨*left insert*⟩ will be inserted to the left of the sections, the {⟨*right insert*⟩} to the right. By inserting a triple fill (a filll) you can flush the bar to the left or right.

  Example:

  \insertsectionnavigationhorizontal{.5\textwidth}{\hskip0pt plus1filll}{}

- \insertshortauthor[⟨*options*⟩] Inserts the short version of the author into a template. The text will be printed in one long line, line breaks introduced using the \\ command are suppressed. The following ⟨*options*⟩ may be given:

  - width=⟨*width*⟩ causes the text to be put into a multi-line minipage of the given size. Line breaks are still suppressed by default.

  - center centers the text inside the minipage created using the width option, rather than having it left aligned.

  - respectlinebreaks causes line breaks introduced by the \\ command to be honored.

  Example: \insertauthor[width={3cm},center,respectlinebreaks]

- \insertshortdate[⟨*options*⟩] Inserts the short version of the date into a template. The same options as for \insertshortauthor may be given.

- `\insertshortinstitute[`⟨*options*⟩`]` Inserts the short version of the institute into a template. The same options as for `\insertshortauthor` may be given.

- `\insertshortpart[`⟨*options*⟩`]` Inserts the short version of the part name into a template. The same options as for `\insertshortauthor` may be given.

- `\insertshorttitle[`⟨*options*⟩`]` Inserts the short version of the document title into a template. Same options as for `\insertshortauthor` may be given.

- `\insertshortsubtitle[`⟨*options*⟩`]` Inserts the short version of the document subtitle. Same options as for `\insertshortauthor` may be given.

- `\insertsubsection` Inserts the current subsection into a template.

- `\insertsubsubsection` Inserts the current subsection into a template.

- `\insertsubsectionnavigation{`⟨*width*⟩`}` Inserts a vertical navigation bar containing all subsections of the current section, with the current subsection highlighted.

- `\insertsubsectionnavigationhorizontal{`⟨*width*⟩`}{`⟨*left insert*⟩`}{`⟨*right insert*⟩`}` See `\insertsectionnav`

- `\insertverticalnavigation{`⟨*width*⟩`}` Inserts a vertical navigation bar of the given ⟨*width*⟩ into a template. The bar shows a little table of contents. The individual lines are typeset using the templates `section in head/foot` and `subsection in head/foot`.

- `\insertframenumber` Inserts the number of the current frame (not slide) into a template.

- `\inserttotalframenumber` Inserts the total number of the frames (not slides) into a template. The number is only correct on the second run of TEX on your document.

- `\insertframestartpage` Inserts the page number of the first page of the current frame.

- `\insertframeendpage` Inserts the page number of the last page of the current frame.

- `\insertsubsectionstartpage` Inserts the page number of the first page of the current subsection.

- `\insertsubsectionendpage` Inserts the page number of the last page of the current subsection.

- `\insertsectionstartpage` Inserts the page number of the first page of the current section.

- `\insertsectionendpage` Inserts the page number of the last page of the current section.

- `\insertpartstartpage` Inserts the page number of the first page of the current part.

- `\insertpartendpage` Inserts the page number of the last page of the current part.

- `\insertpresentationstartpage` Inserts the page number of the first page of the presentation.

- `\insertpresentationendpage` Inserts the page number of the last page of the presentation (excluding the appendix).

- `\insertappendixstartpage` Inserts the page number of the first page of the appendix. If there is no appendix, this number is the last page of the document.

- `\insertappendixendpage` Inserts the page number of the last page of the appendix. If there is no appendix, this number is the last page of the document.

- `\insertdocumentstartpage` Inserts 1.

- `\insertdocumentendpage` Inserts the page number of the last page of the document (including the appendix).

Beamer-Template/-Color/-Font `footline`

This template behaves exactly the same way as the headline. Note that, sometimes quite annoyingly, BEAMER currently adds a space of 4pt between the bottom of the frame's text and the top of the footline.

The following template options are predefined:

- `[default]` The default is an empty footline. Note that the navigational symbols are *not* part of the footline by default. Rather, they are part of an (invisible) right sidebar.

- `[infolines theme]` This option becomes available (and is used) if the `infolines` outer theme is loaded. The footline shows things like the author's name and the title of the talk.

- [miniframes theme] This option becomes available (and is used) if the miniframes outer theme is loaded. Depending on the exact options that are used when the miniframes theme is loaded, different things can be shown in the footline.

- [page number] Shows the current page number in the footline.

- [frame number] Shows the current frame number in the footline.

- [split] This option becomes available (and is used) if the split outer theme is loaded. The footline (just like the headline) is split into a left part showing the author's name and a right part showing the talk's title.

- [text line]{⟨text⟩} The footline is typeset more or less as if it were a normal text line with the ⟨text⟩ as contents. The left and right margin are setup such that they are the same as the margins of normal text. The ⟨text⟩ is typeset inside an \hbox, while the headline is normally typeset in vertical mode. Using the \strut command somewhere in such a line might be a good idea.

The same inserts as for headlines can be used.

Beamer-Color/-Font page number in head/foot

These BEAMER-color and -font are used to typeset the page number or frame number in the footline.

8.2.2 The Sidebars

Sidebars are vertical areas that stretch from the lower end of the headline to the top of the footline. There can be a sidebar at the left and another one at the right (or even both). Sidebars can show a table of contents, but they could also be added for purely aesthetic reasons.

When you install a sidebar template, you must explicitly specify the horizontal size of the sidebar using the command \setbeamersize with the option sidebar left width or sidebar right width. The vertical size is determined automatically. Each sidebar has its own background canvas, which can be setup using the sidebar canvas templates.

Adding a sidebar of a certain size, say 1 cm, will make the main text 1 cm narrower. The distance between the inner side of a side bar and the outer side of the text, as specified by the command \setbeamersize with the option text margin left and its counterpart for the right margin, is not changed when a sidebar is installed.

Internally, the sidebars are typeset by showing them as part of the headline. The BEAMER class keeps track of six dimensions, three for each side: the variables \beamer@leftsidebar and \beamer@rightsidebar store the (horizontal) sizes of the side bars, the variables \beamer@leftmargin and \beamer@rightmargin store the distance between sidebar and text, and the macros \Gm@lmargin and \Gm@rmargin store the distance from the edge of the paper to the edge of the text. Thus the sum \beamer@leftsidebar and \beamer@leftmargin is exactly \Gm@lmargin. Thus, if you wish to put some text right next to the left sidebar, you might write \hskip-\beamer@leftmargin to get there.

Beamer-Template/-Color/-Font sidebar left

Color/font parents: sidebar

The template is used to typeset the left sidebar. As mentioned above, the size of the left sidebar is set using the command

\setbeamersize{sidebar width left=2cm}

BEAMER will not clip sidebars automatically if they are too large.

When the sidebar is typeset, it is put inside a \vbox. You should currently setup things like the \hsize or the \parskip yourself.

The following template options are predefined:

- [default] installs an empty template.

- [sidebar theme] This option is available if the outer theme sidebar is loaded with the left option. In this case, this options is selected automatically. It shows a mini table of contents in the sidebar.

Beamer-Template/-Color/-Font `sidebar right`

Color/font parents: `sidebar`

This template works the same way as the template for the left.

The following template options are predefined:

- [`default`] The default right sidebar has zero width. Nevertheless, it shows navigational symbols and, if installed, a logo at the bottom of the sidebar, protruding to the left into the text.

- [`sidebar theme`] This option is available, if the outer theme `sidebar` is loaded with the `right` option. In this case, this option is selected automatically. It shows a mini table of contents in the sidebar.

Beamer-Template `sidebar canvas left`

Like the overall background canvas, this canvas is drawn behind the actual text of the sidebar. This template should normally insert a rectangle of the size of the sidebar, though a too large height will not lead to an error or warning. When this template is called, the BEAMER-color `sidebar left` will have been installed.

The following template options are predefined:

- [`default`] uses a large rectangle colored with `sidebar.bg` as the sidebar canvas. However, if the background of `sidebar` is empty, nothing is drawn and the canvas is "transparent."

- [`vertical shading`] [⟨*color options*⟩] installs a vertically shaded background. The following ⟨*color options*⟩ may be given:

    - `top`=⟨*color*⟩ specifies the color at the top of the sidebar. By default, 25% of the foreground of the BEAMER-color `palette primary` is used.

    - `bottom`=⟨*color*⟩ specifies the color at the bottom of the sidebar (more precisely, at a distance of the page height below the top of the sidebar). By default, the background of `normal text` at the moment of invocation of this command is used.

    - `middle`=⟨*color*⟩ specifies the color for the middle of the sidebar. Thus, if this option is given, the shading changes from the bottom color to this color and then to the top color.

    - `midpoint`=⟨*factor*⟩ specifies at which point of the page the middle color is used. A factor of `0` is the bottom of the page, a factor of `1` is the top. The default, which is `0.5`, is in the middle.

The following template options are predefined:

Note that you must give "real" LaTeX colors here. This often makes it necessary to invoke the command `\usebeamercolor` before this command can be used.

Also note, that the width of the sidebar should be setup before this option is used.

Example: A stylish, but not very useful shading:

```
{\usebeamercolor{palette primary}}
\setbeamertemplate{sidebar canvas}[vertical shading]
[top=palette primary.bg,middle=white,bottom=palette primary.bg]
```

- [`horizontal shading`] [⟨*color options*⟩] installs a horizontally shaded background. The following ⟨*color options*⟩ may be given:

    - `left`=⟨*color*⟩ specifies the color at the left of the sidebar.

    - `right`=⟨*color*⟩ specifies the color at the right of the sidebar.

    - `middle`=⟨*color*⟩ specifies the color in the middle of the sidebar.

    - `midpoint`=⟨*factor*⟩ specifies at which point of the sidebar the middle color is used. A factor of `0` is the left of the sidebar, a factor of `1` is the right. The default, which is `0.5`, is in the middle.

Example: Adds two "pillars"

```
\setbeamersize{sidebar width left=0.5cm,sidebar width right=0.5cm}
```

```
{\usebeamercolor{sidebar}}
```

```
\setbeamertemplate{sidebar canvas left}[horizontal shading]
```

```
[left=white,middle=sidebar.bg,right=white]
\setbeamertemplate{sidebar canvas right}[horizontal shading]
[left=white,middle=sidebar.bg,right=white]
```

Beamer-Template `sidebar canvas right`

Works exactly as for the left side.

8.2.3 Navigation Bars

Many themes install a headline or a sidebar that shows a *navigation bar*. Although these navigation bars take up quite a bit of space, they are often useful for two reasons:

- They provide the audience with a visual feedback of how much of your talk you have covered and what is yet to come. Without such feedback, an audience will often puzzle whether something you are currently introducing will be explained in more detail later on or not.

- You can click on all parts of the navigation bar. This will directly "jump" you to the part you have clicked on. This is particularly useful to skip certain parts of your talk and during a "question session," when you wish to jump back to a particular frame someone has asked about.

Some navigation bars can be "compressed" using the following option:

`\documentclass[compress]{beamer}`

Tries to make all navigation bars as small as possible. For example, all small frame representations in the navigation bars for a single section are shown alongside each other. Normally, the representations for different subsections are shown in different lines. Furthermore, section and subsection navigations are compressed into one line.

Some themes use the `\insertnavigation` to insert a navigation bar into the headline. Inside this bar, small icons are shown (called "mini frames") that represent the frames of a presentation. When you click on such an icon, the following happens:

- If you click on (the icon of) any frame other than the current frame, the presentation will jump to the first slide of the frame you clicked on.

- If you click on the current frame and you are not on the last slide of this frame, you will jump to the last slide of the frame.

- If you click on the current frame and you are on the last slide, you will jump to the first slide of the frame.

By the above rules you can:

- Jump to the beginning of a frame from somewhere else by clicking on it once.

- Jump to the end of a frame from somewhere else by clicking on it twice.

- Skip the rest of the current frame by clicking on it once.

We also tried making a jump to an already-visited frame jump automatically to the last slide of this frame. However, this turned out to be more confusing than helpful. With the current implementation a double-click always brings you to the end of a slide, regardless from where you "come" from.

Parent Beamer-Template `mini frames`

This parent template has the children `mini frame` and `mini frame in current subsection`.

Example: `\setbeamertemplate{mini frames}[box]`

The following template options are predefined:

- `[default]` shows small circles as mini frames.

- `[box]` shows small rectangles as mini frames.
- `[tick]` shows small vertical bars as mini frames.

Beamer-Template/-Color/-Font `mini frame`

The template is used to render the mini frame of the current frame in a navigation bar.

The width of the template is ignored. Instead, when multiple mini frames are shown, their position is calculated based on the BEAMER-sizes `mini frame size` and `mini frame offset`. See the command `\setbeamersize` for a description of how to change them.

Beamer-Template `mini frame in current subsection`

This template is used to render the mini frame of frames in the current subsection that are not the current frame. The BEAMER-color/-font `mini frame` installed prior to the usage of this template is invoked.

Beamer-Template `mini frame in other subsection`

This template is used to render mini frames of frames from subsections other than the current one.

The following template options are predefined:

- `[default]` `[⟨percentage⟩]` By default, this template shows `mini frame in current subsection`, except that the color is first changed to `fg!⟨percentage⟩!bg`. The default ⟨percentage⟩ is 50%.

  Example: To get an extremely "shaded" rendering of the frames outside the current subsection you can use the following:

  `\setbeamertemplate{mini frame in other subsection}[default][20]`

  Example: To render all mini frames other than the current one in the same way, use

  `\setbeamertemplate{mini frame in other subsection}[default][100]`

Some themes show sections and/or subsections in the navigation bars. By clicking on a section or subsection in the navigation bar, you will jump to that section. Clicking on a section is particularly useful if the section starts with a `\tableofcontents[currentsection]`, since you can use it to jump to the different subsections.

Beamer-Template/-Color/-Font `section in head/foot`

This template is used to render a section entry if it occurs in the headline or the footline. The background of the BEAMER-color is typically used as the background of the whole "area" where section entries are shown in the headline. You cannot usually use this template yourself since the insert `\insertsectionhead` is setup correctly only when a list of sections is being typeset in the headline.

The default template just inserts the section name. The following inserts are useful for this template:

- `\insertsectionhead` inserts the name of the section that is to be typeset in a navigation bar.
- `\insertsectionheadnumber` inserts the number of the section that is to be typeset in a navigation bar.
- `\insertpartheadnumber` inserts the number of the part of the current section or subsection that is to be typeset in a navigation bar.

Beamer-Template `section in head/foot shaded`

This template is used instead of `section in head/foot` for typesetting sections that are currently shaded. Such shading is usually applied to all sections but the current one.

Note that this template does *not* have its own color and font. When this template is called, the BEAMER-font and color `section in head/foot` will have been setup. Then, at the start of the template, you will typically change the current color or start a `colormixin` environment.

The following template options are predefined:

- [default] [⟨*percentage*⟩] The default template changes the current color to `fg!`⟨*percentage*⟩`!bg`. This causes the current color to become "washed out" or "shaded." The default percentage is 50.

  Example: You can use the following command to make the shaded entries very "light":

  `\setbeamertemplate{section in head/foot shaded}[default][20]`

Beamer-Template/-Color/-Font `section in sidebar`

This template is used to render a section entry if it occurs in the sidebar, typically as part of a mini table of contents shown there. The background of the BEAMER-color is used as background for the entry. Just like `section in head/foot`, you cannot usually use this template yourself and you should also use `\insertsectionhead` to insert the name of the section that is to be typeset.

For once, no default is installed for this template.

The following template options are predefined:

- [`sidebar theme`] This template, which is only available if the `sidebar` outer theme is loaded, inserts a bar with the BEAMER-color's foreground and background that shows the section name. The width of the bar is the same as the width of the whole sidebar.

The same inserts as for `section in head/foot` can be used.

Beamer-Template/-Color `section in sidebar shaded`

This template is used instead of `section in sidebar` for typesetting sections that are currently shaded. Such shading is usually applied to all sections but the current one.

Differently from `section in head/foot shaded`, this template *has* its own BEAMER-color.

The following template options are predefined:

- [`sidebar theme`] Does the same as for the nonshaded version, except that a different BEAMER-color is used.

Beamer-Template/-Color/-Font `subsection in head/foot`

This template behaves exactly like `section in head/foot`, only for subsections.

- `\insertsubsectionhead` works like `\insertsectionhead`.
- `\insertsubsectionheadnumber` works like `\insertsectionheadnumber`.

Beamer-Template `subsection in head/foot shaded`

This template behaves exactly like `section in head/foot shaded`, only for subsections.

The following template options are predefined:

- [default] [⟨*percentage*⟩] works like the corresponding option for sections.

  Example:

  `\setbeamertemplate{section in head/foot shaded}[default][20]`
  `\setbeamertemplate{subsection in head/foot shaded}[default][20]`

Beamer-Template/-Color/-Font `subsection in sidebar`

This template behaves exactly like `section in sidebar`, only for subsections.

Beamer-Template `subsection in sidebar shaded`

This template behaves exactly like `section in sidebar shaded`, only for subsections.

Beamer-Template/-Color/-Font `subsubsection in head/foot`

This template behaves exactly like `section in head/foot`, only for subsubsections. Currently, it is not used by the default themes.

- \insertsubsubsectionhead works like \insertsectionhead.
- \insertsubsubsectionheadnumber works like \insertsectionheadnumber.

Beamer-Template `subsubsection in head/foot shaded`

This template behaves exactly like `section in head/foot shaded`, only for subsubsections.

The following template options are predefined:

- [`default`] [⟨*percentage*⟩] works like the corresponding option for sections.

Beamer-Template/-Color/-Font `subsubsection in sidebar`

This template behaves exactly like `section in sidebar`, only for subsubsections.

Beamer-Template `subsubsection in sidebar shaded`

This template behaves exactly like `section in sidebar shaded`, only for subsubsections.

By clicking on the document title in a navigation bar (not all themes show it), you will jump to the first slide of your presentation (usually the title page) *except* if you are already at the first slide. On the first slide, clicking on the document title will jump to the end of the presentation, if there is one. Thus by *double* clicking the document title in a navigation bar, you can jump to the end.

8.2.4   The Navigation Symbols

Navigation symbols are small icons that are shown on every slide by default. The following symbols are shown:

1. A slide icon, which is depicted as a single rectangle. To the left and right of this symbol, a left and right arrow are shown.

2. A frame icon, which is depicted as three slide icons "stacked on top of each other". This symbol is framed by arrows.

3. A subsection icon, which is depicted as a highlighted subsection entry in a table of contents. This symbol is framed by arrows.

4. A section icon, which is depicted as a highlighted section entry (together with all subsections) in a table of contents. This symbol is framed by arrows.

5. A presentation icon, which is depicted as a completely highlighted table of contents.

6. An appendix icon, which is depicted as a completely highlighted table of contents consisting of only one section. (This icon is only shown if there is an appendix.)

7. Back and forward icons, depicted as circular arrows.

8. A "search" or "find" icon, depicted as a detective's magnifying glass.

Clicking on the left arrow next to an icon always jumps to (the last slide of) the previous slide, frame, subsection, or section. Clicking on the right arrow next to an icon always jumps to (the first slide of) the next slide, frame, subsection, or section.

Clicking *on* any of these icons has different effects:

1. If supported by the viewer application, clicking on a slide icon pops up a window that allows you to enter a slide number to which you wish to jump.

2. Clicking on the left side of a frame icon will jump to the first slide of the frame, clicking on the right side will jump to the last slide of the frame (this can be useful for skipping overlays).

3. Clicking on the left side of a subsection icon will jump to the first slide of the subsection, clicking on the right side will jump to the last slide of the subsection.

4. Clicking on the left side of a section icon will jump to the first slide of the section, clicking on the right side will jump to the last slide of the section.

5. Clicking on the left side of the presentation icon will jump to the first slide, clicking on the right side will jump to the last slide of the presentation. However, this does *not* include the appendix.

6. Clicking on the left side of the appendix icon will jump to the first slide of the appendix, clicking on the right side will jump to the last slide of the appendix.

7. If supported by the viewer application, clicking on the back and forward symbols jumps to the previously visited slides.

8. If supported by the viewer application, clicking on the search icon pops up a window that allows you to enter a search string. If found, the viewer application will jump to this string.

You can reduce the number of icons that are shown or their layout by adjusting the `navigation symbols` template.

Beamer-Template/-Color/-Font `navigation symbols`

This template is invoked in "three-star-mode" by themes at the place where the navigation symbols should be shown. "Three-star-mode" means that the command `\usebeamertemplate***` is used.

Note that, although it may *look* like the symbols are part of the footline, they are more often part of an invisible right sidebar.

The following template options are predefined:

- [default] Organizes the navigation symbols horizontally.
- [horizontal] This is an alias for the default.
- [vertical] Organizes the navigation symbols vertically.
- [only frame symbol] Shows only the navigational symbol for navigating frames.

Example: The following command suppresses all navigation symbols:

`\setbeamertemplate{navigation symbols}{}`

Inside this template, the following inserts are useful:

- `\insertslidenavigationsymbol` Inserts the slide navigation symbols, that is, the slide symbols (a rectangle) together with arrows to the left and right that are hyperlinked.
- `\insertframenavigationsymbol` Inserts the frame navigation symbol.
- `\insertsubsectionnavigationsymbol` Inserts the subsection navigation symbol.
- `\insertsectionnavigationsymbol` Inserts the section navigation symbol.
- `\insertdocnavigationsymbol` Inserts the presentation navigation symbol and (if necessary) the appendix navigation symbol.
- `\insertbackfindforwardnavigationsymbol` Inserts a back, a find, and a forward navigation symbol.

8.2.5 The Logo

To install a logo, use the following command:

`\logo{⟨logo text⟩}`

The ⟨*logo text*⟩ is usually a command for including a graphic, but it can be any text. The position where the logo is inserted is determined by the current theme; you cannot (currently) specify this position directly.

Example:

```
\pgfdeclareimage[height=0.5cm]{logo}{tu-logo}
\logo{\pgfuseimage{logo}}
```

Example:

`\logo{\includegraphics[height=0.5cm]{logo.pdf}}`

Currently, the effect of this command is just to setup the `logo` template. However, a more sophisticated effect might be implemented in the future.

ARTICLE This command has no effect.

Beamer-Template/-Color/-Font `logo`

This template is used to render the logo.

The following insert can be used to insert a logo somewhere:

- `\insertlogo` inserts the logo at the current position. This command has the same effect as `\usebeamertemplate*{logo}`.

8.2.6 The Frame Title

The frame title is shown prominently at the top of the frame and can be specified with the following command:

`\frametitle<`⟨*overlay specification*⟩`>[`⟨*short frame title*⟩`]{`⟨*frame title text*⟩`}`

You should end the ⟨*frame title text*⟩ with a period, if the title is a proper sentence. Otherwise, there should not be a period. The ⟨*short frame title*⟩ is normally not shown, but it's available via the `\insertshortframetitle` command. The ⟨*overlay specification*⟩ is mostly useful for suppressing the frame title in `article` mode.

Example:

```
\begin{frame}
  \frametitle{A Frame Title is Important.}
  \framesubtitle{Subtitles are not so important.}

  Frame contents.
\end{frame}
```

If you are using the `allowframebreaks` option with the current frame, a continuation text (like "(cont.)" or something similar, depending on the template `frametitle continuation`) is automatically added to the ⟨*frame title text*⟩ at the end, separated with a space.

PRESEN-   The frame title is not typeset immediately when the command `\frametitle` is encountered. Rather, the
TATION   argument of the command is stored internally and the frame title is only typeset when the complete frame has been read. This gives you access to both the ⟨*frame title text*⟩ and to the ⟨*subframe title text*⟩ that is possibly introduced using the `\framesubtitle` command.

ARTICLE By default, this command creates a new paragraph in `article` mode, entitled ⟨*frame title text*⟩. Using the ⟨*overlay specification*⟩ makes it easy to suppress a frame title once in a while. If you generally wish to suppress *all* frame titles in `article` mode, say `\setbeamertemplate<article>{frametitle}{}`.

Beamer-Template/-Color/-Font `frametitle`

Color/font parents: `titlelike`

When the frame title and subtitle are to be typeset, this template is invoked with the BEAMER-color and -font `frametitle` set. This template is *not* invoked when the commands `\frametitle` or `\framesubtitle` are called. Rather, it is invoked when the whole frame has been completely read. Till then, the frame title and frame subtitle text are stored in a special place. This way, when the template is invoked, both inserts are setup correctly. The resulting TeX-box is then magically put back to the top of the frame.

The following template options are predefined:

- [default] [⟨*alignment*⟩] The frame is typeset using the BEAMER-color `frametitle` and the BEAMER-font `frametitle`. The subtitle is put below using the color and font `framesubtitle`. If the color `frametitle` has a background, a background bar stretching the whole frame width is put behind the title. A background color of the subtitle is ignored. The ⟨*alignment*⟩ is passed on to the `beamercolorbox` environment. In particular, useful options are `left`, `center`, and `right`. As a special case, the `right` option causes the left border of the frame title to be somewhat larger than normal so that the frame title is more in the middle of the frame.

- [shadow theme] This option is available if the outer theme `shadow` is loaded. It draws the frame title on top of a horizontal shading between the background colors of `frametitle` and `frametitle right`. A subtitle is, if present, also put on this bar. Below the bar, a "shadow" is drawn.

- [sidebar theme] This option is available if the outer theme `sidebar` is loaded and if the headline height is not set to 0pt (which can be done using an option of the `sidebar` theme). With this option, the frame title is put inside a rectangular area that is part of the headline (some "negative space" is used to raise the frame title into this area). The background of the color `frametitle` is not used, this is the job of the headline template in this case.

- [smoothbars theme] This option is available if the outer theme `smoothbars` is loaded. It typesets the frame title on a colored bar with the background color of `frametitle`. The top and bottom of the bar smoothly blend over to backgrounds above and below.

- [smoothtree theme] Like `smoothbars theme`, only for the `smoothtree` theme.

The following commands are useful for this template:

- `\insertframetitle` yields the frame title.
- `\insertframesubtitle` yields the frame subtitle.

`\framesubtitle<`⟨*overlay specification*⟩`>{`⟨*frame subtitle text*⟩`}`

If present, a subtitle will be shown in a smaller font below the main title. Like the `\frametitle` command, this command can be given anywhere in the frame, since the frame title is actually typeset only when everything else has already been typeset.

Example:

```
\begin{frame}
  \frametitle<presentation>{Frame Title Should Be in Uppercase.}
  \framesubtitle{Subtitles can be in lowercase if they are full sentences.}

  Frame contents.
\end{frame}
```

ARTICLE By default, the subtitle is not shown in any way in `article` mode.

Beamer-Color/-Font `framesubtitle`

Color/font parents: `frametitle`

This element provides a color and a font for the subtitle, but no template. It is the job of the `frametitle` template to also typeset the subtitle.

Be default, all material for a slide is vertically centered. You can change this using the following class options:

`\documentclass[t]{beamer}`

Place text of slides at the (vertical) top of the slides. This corresponds to a vertical "flush." You can override this for individual frames using the `c` or `b` option.

`\documentclass[c]{beamer}`

Place text of slides at the (vertical) center of the slides. This is the default. You can override this for individual frames using the `t` or `b` option.

8.2.7 The Background

Each frame has a *background*, which—as the name suggests—is "behind everything." The background is a surprisingly complex object: in BEAMER, it consists of a *background canvas* and the *main background*.

The background canvas can be imagined as a large area on which everything (the main background and everything else) is painted on. By default, this canvas is a big rectangle filling the whole frame whose color is the background of the BEAMER-color `background canvas`. Since this color inherits from `normal text`, by changing the background color of the normal text, you can change this color of the canvas.

Example: The following command changes the background color to a light red.

`\setbeamercolor{normal text}{bg=red!20}`

The canvas need not be monochrome. Instead, you can install a shading or even make it transparent. Making it transparent is a good idea if you wish to include your slides in some other document.

Example: The following command makes the background canvas transparent:

`\setbeamercolor{background canvas}{bg=}`

Beamer-Template/-Color/-Font `background canvas`

   Color parents: `normal text`

   The template is inserted "behind everything." The template should typically be some TEX commands that produce a rectangle of height `\paperheight` and width `\paperwidth`.

   The following template options are predefined:

- [default] installs a large rectangle with the background color. If the background is empty, the canvas is "transparent." Since `background canvas` inherits from `normal text`, you can change the background of the BEAMER-color `normal text` to change the color of the default canvas. However, to make the canvas transparent, only set the background of the canvas empty; leave the background of normal text white.

- [vertical shading][⟨*color options*⟩] installs a vertically shaded background. *Use with care: Background shadings are often distracting!* The following ⟨*color options*⟩ may be given:
   - top=⟨*color*⟩ specifies the color at the top of the page. By default, 25% of the foreground of the BEAMER-color `palette primary` is used.
   - bottom=⟨*color*⟩ specifies the color at the bottom of the page. By default, the background of `normal text` at the moment of invocation of this command is used.
   - middle=⟨*color*⟩ specifies the color for the middle of the page. Thus, if this option is given, the shading changes from the bottom color to this color and then to the top color.
   - midpoint=⟨*factor*⟩ specifies at which point of the page the middle color is used. A factor of 0 is the bottom of the page, a factor of 1 is the top. The default, which is 0.5 is in the middle.

The main background is drawn on top of the background canvas. It can be used to add, say, a grid to every frame or a big background picture or whatever. If you plan to use a PNG image as a background image, use one with an alpha channel to avoid potential problems with transparency in some PDF viewers.

Beamer-Template/-Color/-Font `background`

   Color parents: `background canvas`

   The template is inserted "behind everything, but on top of the background canvas." Use it for pictures or grids or anything that does not necessarily fill the whole background. When this template is typeset, the BEAMER-color and -font `background` will be setup.

   The following template options are predefined:

- [default] is empty.
- [grid][⟨*grid options*⟩] places a grid on the background. The following ⟨*grid options*⟩ may be given:
   - step=⟨*dimension*⟩ specifies the distance between grid lines. The default is 0.5cm.
   - color=⟨*color*⟩ specifies the color of the grid lines. The default is 10% foreground.

8.3 Frame and Margin Sizes

The size of a frame is actually the "paper size" of a BEAMER presentation, and it is variable. By default, it amounts to 128mm by 96mm. The aspect ratio of this size is 4:3, which is exactly what most beamers offer these days. It is the job of the presentation program (like `acroread`, `xpdf`, `okular` or `evince`) to display the slides at full screen size. The main advantage of using a small "paper size" is that you can use all your normal fonts at their natural sizes. In particular, inserting a graphic with 11pt labels will result in reasonably sized labels during the presentation.

To change "paper size" and aspect ratio, you can use the following class options:

`\documentclass[aspectratio=1610]{beamer}`

   Sets aspect ratio to 16:10, and frame size to 160mm by 100mm.

`\documentclass[aspectratio=169]{beamer}`

   Sets aspect ratio to 16:9, and frame size to 160mm by 90mm.

`\documentclass[aspectratio=149]{beamer}`

   Sets aspect ratio to 14:9, and frame size to 140mm by 90mm.

`\documentclass[aspectratio=141]{beamer}`

   Sets aspect ratio to 1.41:1, and frame size to 148.5mm by 105mm.

`\documentclass[aspectratio=54]{beamer}`

   Sets aspect ratio to 5:4, and frame size to 125mm by 100mm.

`\documentclass[aspectratio=43]{beamer}`

   The default aspect ratio and frame size. You need not specify this option.

`\documentclass[aspectratio=32]{beamer}`

   Sets aspect ratio to 3:2, and frame size to 135mm by 90mm.

Aside from using these options, you should refrain from changing the "paper size." However, you *can* change the size of the left and right margins, which default to 1cm. To change them, you should use the following command:

`\setbeamersize{`⟨*options*⟩`}`

   The following ⟨*options*⟩ can be given:

   - `text margin left=`⟨*T_EX dimension*⟩ sets a new left margin. This excludes the left sidebar. Thus, it is the distance between the right edge of the left sidebar and the left edge of the text.
   - `text margin right=`⟨*T_EX dimension*⟩ sets a new right margin.
   - `sidebar width left=`⟨*T_EX dimension*⟩ sets the size of the left sidebar. Currently, this command should be given *before* a shading is installed for the sidebar canvas.
   - `sidebar width right=`⟨*T_EX dimension*⟩ sets the size of the right sidebar.
   - `description width=`⟨*T_EX dimension*⟩ sets the default width of description labels, see Section 12.1.
   - `description width of=`⟨*text*⟩ sets the default width of description labels to the width of the ⟨*text*⟩, see Section 12.1.
   - `mini frame size=`⟨*T_EX dimension*⟩ sets the size of mini frames in a navigation bar. When two mini frame icons are shown alongside each other, their left end points are ⟨*T_EX dimension*⟩ far apart.
   - `mini frame offset=`⟨*T_EX dimension*⟩ set an additional vertical offset that is added to the mini frame size when arranging mini frames vertically.

ARTICLE This command has no effect in `article` mode.

8.4 Restricting the Slides of a Frame

The number of slides in a frame is automatically calculated. If the largest number mentioned in any overlay specification inside the frame is 4, four slides are introduced (despite the fact that a specification like <4-> might suggest that more than four slides would be possible).

You can also specify the number of slides in the frame "by hand." To do so, you pass an overlay specification to the \frame command. The frame will contain only the slides specified in this argument. Consider the following example.

```
\begin{frame}<1-2,4->
  This is slide number \only<1>{1}\only<2>{2}\only<3>{3}%
  \only<4>{4}\only<5>{5}.
\end{frame}
```

This command will create a frame containing four slides. The first will contain the text "This is slide number 1," the second "This is slide number 2," the third "This is slide number 4," and the fourth "This is slide number 5."

A useful specification is just <0>, which causes the frame to have no slides at all. For example, \begin{frame}<handout:0> causes the frame to be suppressed in the handout version, but to be shown normally in all other versions. Another useful specification is <beamer>, which causes the frame to be shown normally in beamer mode, but to be suppressed in all other versions.

9 Creating Overlays

9.1 The Pause Commands

The `pause` command offers an easy, but not very flexible way of creating frames that are uncovered piecewise. If you say \pause somewhere in a frame, only the text on the frame up to the \pause command is shown on the first slide. On the second slide, everything is shown up to the second \pause, and so forth. You can also use \pause inside environments; its effect will last after the environment. However, taking this to extremes and using \pause deeply within a nested environment may not have the desired result.

A much more fine-grained control over what is shown on each slide can be attained using overlay specifications, see the next sections. However, for many simple cases the \pause command is sufficient.

The effect of \pause lasts till the next \pause, \onslide, or the end of the frame.

```
\begin{frame}
  \begin{itemize}
  \item
    Shown from first slide on.
  \pause
  \item
    Shown from second slide on.
    \begin{itemize}
    \item
      Shown from second slide on.
    \pause
    \item
      Shown from third slide on.
    \end{itemize}
  \item
    Shown from third slide on.
  \pause
  \item
    Shown from fourth slide on.
  \end{itemize}

Shown from fourth slide on.

  \begin{itemize}
  \onslide
  \item
    Shown from first slide on.
  \pause
  \item
    Shown from fifth slide on.
  \end{itemize}
\end{frame}
```

\pause [⟨*number*⟩]

> This command causes the text following it to be shown only from the next slide on, or, if the optional ⟨*number*⟩ is given, from the slide with the number ⟨*number*⟩. If the optional ⟨*number*⟩ is given, the counter `beamerpauses` is set to this number. This command uses the \onslide command, internally. This command does *not* work inside `amsmath` environments like `align`, since these do really wicked things.

> *Example:*

```
\begin{frame}
  \begin{itemize}
  \item
    A
  \pause
```

```
    \item
      B
    \pause
    \item
      C
  \end{itemize}
\end{frame}
```

ARTICLE This command is ignored.

To "unpause" some text, that is, to temporarily suspend pausing, use the command \onslide, see below.

9.2   The General Concept of Overlay Specifications

The approach taken by most presentation classes to overlays is somewhat similar to the above \pause command. These commands get a certain slide number as input and affect the text on the slide following this command in a certain way. For example, PROSPER's \FromSlide{2} command causes all text following this command to be shown only from the second slide on.

The BEAMER class uses a different approach (though the abovementioned command is also available: \onslide<2-> will have the same effect as \FromSlide{2}, except that \onslide transcends environments; likewise, \pause is internally mapped to a command with an appropriate overlay specification). The idea is to add *overlay specifications* to certain commands. These specifications are always given in pointed brackets and follow the command "as soon as possible," though in certain cases BEAMER also allows overlay specification to be given a little later. In the simplest case, the specification contains just a number. A command with an overlay specification following it will only have "effect" on the slide(s) mentioned in the specification. What exactly "having an effect" means, depends on the command. Consider the following example.

```
\begin{frame}
  \textbf{This line is bold on all three slides.}
  \textbf<2>{This line is bold only on the second slide.}
  \textbf<3>{This line is bold only on the third slide.}
\end{frame}
```

For the command \textbf, the overlay specification causes the text to be set in boldface only on the specified slides. On all other slides, the text is set in a normal font.

For a second example, consider the following frame:

```
\begin{frame}
  \only<1>{This line is inserted only on slide 1.}
  \only<2>{This line is inserted only on slide 2.}
\end{frame}
```

The command \only, which is introduced by BEAMER, normally simply inserts its parameter into the current frame. However, if an overlay specification is present, it "throws away" its parameter on slides that are not mentioned.

Overlay specifications can only be written behind certain commands, not every command. Which commands you can use and which effects this will have is explained in the next section. However, it is quite easy to redefine an existing command such that it becomes "overlay specification aware," see also Section 9.3.

The syntax of (basic) overlay specifications is the following: They are comma-separated lists of slides and ranges. Ranges are specified like this: 2-5, which means slide two through to five. The start or the end of a range can be omitted. For example, 3- means "slides three, four, five, and so on" and -5 means the same as 1-5. A complicated example is -3,6-8,10,12-15, which selects the slides 1, 2, 3, 6, 7, 8, 10, 12, 13, 14, and 15.

9.3   Commands with Overlay Specifications

Important: Due to the way overlay specifications are implemented, the commands documented here are *all* fragile even if the LaTeX 2_ε kernel versions are not.

For the following commands, adding an overlay specification causes the command to be simply ignored on slides that are not included in the specification: \textbf, \textit, \textsl, \textrm, \textsf, \color, \alert, \structure. If a command takes several arguments, like \color, the specification should directly follow the command as in the following example (but there are exceptions to this rule):

```
\begin{frame}
  \color<2-3>[rgb]{1,0,0} This text is red on slides 2 and 3, otherwise black.
\end{frame}
```

For the following commands, the effect of an overlay specification is special:

\onslide⟨*modifier*⟩<⟨*overlay specification*⟩>{⟨*text*⟩}

The behavior of this command depends on whether the optional argument ⟨*text*⟩ is given or not (note that the optional argument is given in *normal* braces, not in square brackets). If present, the ⟨*modifier*⟩ can be either a + or a *.

If no ⟨*text*⟩ is given, the following happens: All text following this command will only be shown (uncovered) on the specified slides. On non-specified slides, the text still occupies space. If no slides are specified, the following text is always shown. You need not call this command in the same TeX group, its effect transcends block groups. However, this command has a *different* effect inside an overprint environment, see the description of overprint.

If the ⟨*modifier*⟩ is +, hidden text will not be treated as covered, but as invisible. The difference is the same as the difference between \uncover and \visible. The modifier * may not be given if no ⟨*text*⟩ argument is present.

Example:

```
\begin{frame}
  Shown on first slide.
  \onslide<2-3>
  Shown on second and third slide.
  \begin{itemize}
  \item
    Still shown on the second and third slide.
  \onslide+<4->
  \item
    Shown from slide 4 on.
  \end{itemize}
  Shown from slide 4 on.
  \onslide
  Shown on all slides.
\end{frame}
```

If a ⟨*text*⟩ argument is present, \onslide (without a ⟨*modifier*⟩) is mapped to \uncover, \onslide+ is mapped to \visible, and \onslide* is mapped to \only.

Example:

```
\begin{frame}
  \onslide<1>{Same effect as the following command.}
  \uncover<1>{Same effect as the previous command.}

  \onslide+<2>{Same effect as the following command.}
  \visible<2>{Same effect as the previous command.}

  \onslide*<3>{Same effect as the following command.}
  \only<3>{Same effect as the previous command.}
\end{frame}
```

\only<⟨*overlay specification*⟩>{⟨*text*⟩}<⟨*overlay specification*⟩>

80

If either ⟨*overlay specification*⟩ is present (though only one may be present), the ⟨*text*⟩ is inserted only into the specified slides. For other slides, the text is simply thrown away. In particular, it occupies no space.

Example: `\only<3->{Text inserted from slide 3 on.}`

Since the overlay specification may also be given after the text, you can often use `\only` to make other commands overlay specification-aware in a simple manner:

Example:

```
\newcommand{\myblue}{\only{\color{blue}}}
\begin{frame}
  \myblue<2> This text is blue only on slide 2.
\end{frame}
```

`\uncover<`⟨*overlay specification*⟩`>{`⟨*text*⟩`}`

If the ⟨*overlay specification*⟩ is present, the ⟨*text*⟩ is shown ("uncovered") only on the specified slides. On other slides, the text still occupies space and it is still typeset, but it is not shown or only shown as if transparent. For details on how to specify whether the text is invisible or just transparent see Section 17.6.

Example: `\uncover<3->{Text shown from slide 3 on.}`

ARTICLE This command has the same effect as `\only`.

`\visible<`⟨*overlay specification*⟩`>{`⟨*text*⟩`}`

This command does almost the same as `\uncover`. The only difference is that if the text is not shown, it is never shown in a transparent way, but rather it is not shown at all. Thus, for this command the transparency settings have no effect.

Example: `\visible<2->{Text shown from slide 2 on.}`

ARTICLE This command has the same effect as `\only`.

`\invisible<`⟨*overlay specification*⟩`>{`⟨*text*⟩`}`

This command is the opposite of `\visible`.

Example: `\invisible<-2>{Text shown from slide 3 on.}`

`\alt<`⟨*overlay specification*⟩`>{`⟨*default text*⟩`}{`⟨*alternative text*⟩`}<`⟨*overlay specification*⟩`>`

Only one ⟨*overlay specification*⟩ may be given. The default text is shown on the specified slides, otherwise the alternative text. The specification must always be present.

Example: `\alt<2>{On Slide 2}{Not on slide 2.}`

Once more, giving the overlay specification at the end is useful when the command is used inside other commands.

Example: Here is the definition of `\uncover`:

`\newcommand{\uncover}{\alt{\@firstofone}{\makeinvisible}}`

`\temporal<`⟨*overlay specification*⟩`>{`⟨*before slide text*⟩`}{`⟨*default text*⟩`}{`⟨*after slide text*⟩`}`

This command alternates between three different texts, depending on whether the current slide is temporally before the specified slides, is one of the specified slides, or comes after them. If the ⟨*overlay specification*⟩ is not an interval (that is, if it has a "hole"), the "hole" is considered to be part of the before slides.

Example:

```
\temporal<3-4>{Shown on 1, 2}{Shown on 3, 4}{Shown 5, 6, 7, ...}
\temporal<3,5>{Shown on 1, 2, 4}{Shown on 3, 5}{Shown 6, 7, 8, ...}
```

As a possible application of the `\temporal` command consider the following example:

Example:

```
\def\colorize<#1>{%
  \temporal<#1>{\color{red!50}}{\color{black}}{\color{black!50}}}

\begin{frame}
  \begin{itemize}
    \colorize<1> \item First item.
    \colorize<2> \item Second item.
    \colorize<3> \item Third item.
    \colorize<4> \item Fourth item.
  \end{itemize}
\end{frame}
```

`\item<`⟨*alert specification*⟩`>[`⟨*item label*⟩`]<`⟨*alert specification*⟩`>`

PRESEN-
TATION Only one ⟨*alert specification*⟩ may be given. The effect of ⟨*alert specification*⟩ is described in Section 9.6.3.

Example:

```
\begin{frame}
  \begin{itemize}
  \item<1-> First point, shown on all slides.
  \item<2-> Second point, shown on slide 2 and later.
  \item<2-> Third point, also shown on slide 2 and later.
  \item<3-> Fourth point, shown on slide 3.
  \end{itemize}
\end{frame}

\begin{frame}
  \begin{enumerate}
  \item<3-| alert@3>[0.] A zeroth point, shown at the very end.
  \item<1-| alert@1> The first and main point.
  \item<2-| alert@2> The second point.
  \end{enumerate}
\end{frame}
```

ARTICLE The ⟨*action specification*⟩ is currently completely ignored.

The related command `\bibitem` is also overlay specification-aware in the same way as `\item`.

`\label<`⟨*overlay specification*⟩`>{`⟨*label name*⟩`}`

If the ⟨*overlay specification*⟩ is present, the label is only inserted on the specified slide. Inserting a label on more than one slide will cause a 'multiple labels' warning. *However*, if no overlay specification is present, the specification is automatically set to just '1' and the label is thus inserted only on the first slide. This is typically the desired behavior since it does not really matter on which slide the label is inserted, *except* if you use an `\only` command and *except* if you wish to use that label as a hyperjump target. Then you need to specify a slide.

Labels can be used as target of hyperjumps. A convenient way of labelling a frame is to use the `label=`⟨*name*⟩ option of the `frame` environment. However, this will cause the whole frame to be kept in memory till the end of the compilation, which may pose a problem.

Example:

```
\begin{frame}
  \begin{align}
    a &= b + c   \label{first}\\ % no specification needed
    c &= d + e   \label{second}\\% no specification needed
  \end{align}
```

```
Blah blah, \uncover<2>{more blah blah.}

    \only<3>{Specification is needed now.\label<3>{mylabel}}
  \end{frame}
```

9.4 Environments with Overlay Specifications

Environments can also be equipped with overlay specifications. For most of the predefined environments, see Section 12.3, adding an overlay specification causes the whole environment to be uncovered only on the specified slides. This is useful for showing things incrementally as in the following example.

```
\begin{frame}
  \frametitle{A Theorem on Infinite Sets}

  \begin{theorem}<1->
    There exists an infinite set.
  \end{theorem}

  \begin{proof}<3->
    This follows from the axiom of infinity.
  \end{proof}

  \begin{example}<2->
    The set of natural numbers is infinite.
  \end{example}
\end{frame}
```

In the example, the first slide only contains the theorem, on the second slide an example is added, and on the third slide the proof is also shown.

For each of the basic commands \only, \alt, \visible, \uncover, and \invisible there exists "environment versions" onlyenv, altenv, visibleenv, uncoverenv, and invisibleenv. Except for altenv and onlyenv, these environments do the same as the commands.

\begin{onlyenv}<⟨*overlay specification*⟩>
  ⟨*environment contents*⟩
\end{onlyenv}

If the ⟨*overlay specification*⟩ is given, the contents of the environment is inserted into the text only on the specified slides. The difference to \only is, that the text is actually typeset inside a box that is then thrown away, whereas \only immediately throws away its contents. If the text is not "typesettable," the onlyenv may produce an error where \only would not.

Example:
```
\begin{frame}
  This line is always shown.
  \begin{onlyenv}<2>
    This line is inserted on slide 2.
  \end{onlyenv}
\end{frame}
```

\begin{altenv}<⟨*overlay specification*⟩>{⟨*begin text*⟩}{⟨*end text*⟩}{⟨*alternate begin text*⟩}{⟨*alternate end text*⟩}<⟨*over<sub>*specification*⟩>
  ⟨*environment contents*⟩
\end{altenv}

Only one ⟨*overlay specification*⟩ may be given. On the specified slides, ⟨*begin text*⟩ will be inserted at the beginning of the environment and ⟨*end text*⟩ will be inserted at the end. On all other slides, ⟨*alternate begin text*⟩ and ⟨*alternate end text*⟩ will be used.

Example:

```
\begin{frame}
  This
  \begin{altenv}<2>{(}{)}{[}{]}
    word
  \end{altenv}
  is in round brackets on slide 2 and in square brackets on slide 1.
\end{frame}
```

9.5 Dynamically Changing Text or Images

You may sometimes wish to have some part of a frame change dynamically from slide to slide. On each slide of the frame, something different should be shown inside this area. You could achieve the effect of dynamically changing text by giving a list of \only commands like this:

```
\only<1>{Initial text.}
\only<2>{Replaced by this on second slide.}
\only<3>{Replaced again by this on third slide.}
```

The trouble with this approach is that it may lead to slight, but annoying differences in the heights of the lines, which may cause the whole frame to "wobble" from slide to slide. This problem becomes much more severe if the replacement text is several lines long.

To solve this problem, you can use two environments: overlayarea and overprint. The first is more flexible, but less user-friendly.

\begin{overlayarea}{⟨*area width*⟩}{⟨*area height*⟩}
  ⟨*environment contents*⟩
\end{overlayarea}

Everything within the environment will be placed in a rectangular area of the specified size. The area will have the same size on all slides of a frame, regardless of its actual contents.

Example:

```
\begin{overlayarea}{\textwidth}{3cm}
  \only<1>{Some text for the first slide.\\Possibly several lines long.}
  \only<2>{Replacement on the second slide.}
\end{overlayarea}
```

\begin{overprint}[⟨*area width*⟩]
  ⟨*environment contents*⟩
\end{overprint}

The ⟨*area width*⟩ defaults to the text width. Inside the environment, use \onslide commands to specify different things that should be shown for this environment on different slides. The \onslide commands are used like \item commands. Everything within the environment will be placed in a rectangular area of the specified width. The height and depth of the area are chosen large enough to accommodate the largest contents of the area. The overlay specifications of the \onslide commands must be disjoint. This may be a problem for handouts, since, there, all overlay specifications default to 1. If you use the option handout, you can disable all but one \onslide by setting the others to 0.

Example:

```
\begin{overprint}
  \onslide<1| handout:1>
    Some text for the first slide.\\
    Possibly several lines long.
  \onslide<2| handout:0>
    Replacement on the second slide. Supressed for handout.
\end{overprint}
```

A similar need for dynamical changes arises when you have, say, a series of pictures named `first.pdf`, `second.pdf`, and `third.pdf` that show different stages of some process. To make a frame that shows these pictures on different slides, the following code might be used:

```
\begin{frame}
  \frametitle{The Three Process Stages}

  \includegraphics<1>{first.pdf}
  \includegraphics<2>{second.pdf}
  \includegraphics<3>{third.pdf}
\end{frame}
```

The above code uses the fact the BEAMER makes the `\includegraphics` command overlay specification-aware. It works nicely, but only if each `.pdf` file contains the complete graphic to be shown. However, some programs, like `xfig`, sometimes also produce series of graphics in which each file just contains the *additional* graphic elements to be shown on the next slide. In this case, the first graphic must be shown not on overlay 1, but from overlay 1 on, and so on. While this is easy to achieve by changing the overlay specification <1> to <1->, the graphics must also be shown *on top of each other*. An easy way to achieve this is to use TeX's `\llap` command like this:

```
\begin{frame}
  \frametitle{The Three Process Stages}

  \includegraphics<1->{first.pdf}%
  \llap{\includegraphics<2->{second.pdf}}%
  \llap{\includegraphics<3->{third.pdf}}
\end{frame}
```

or like this:

```
\begin{frame}
  \frametitle{The Three Process Stages}

  \includegraphics{first.pdf}%
  \pause%
  \llap{\includegraphics{second.pdf}}%
  \pause%
  \llap{\includegraphics{third.pdf}}
\end{frame}
```

A more convenient way is to use the `\multiinclude` command, see Section 14.1.3 for details.

9.6 Advanced Overlay Specifications

9.6.1 Making Commands and Environments Overlay Specification-Aware

This section explains how to define new commands that are overlay specification-aware. Also, it explains how to setup counters correctly that should be increased from frame to frame (like equation numbering), but not from slide to slide. You may wish to skip this section, unless you want to write your own extensions to the BEAMER class.

BEAMER extends the syntax of LaTeX's standard command `\newcommand`:

`\newcommand<>{`⟨*command name*⟩`}[`⟨*argument number*⟩`][`⟨*default optional value*⟩`]{`⟨*text*⟩`}`

Declares the new command named ⟨*command name*⟩. The ⟨*text*⟩ should contain the body of this command and it may contain occurrences of parameters like #⟨*number*⟩. Here ⟨*number*⟩ may be between 1 and ⟨*argument number*⟩ + 1. The additionally allowed argument is the overlay specification.

When ⟨*command name*⟩ is used, it will scan as many as ⟨*argument number*⟩ arguments. While scanning them, it will look for an overlay specification, which may be given between any two arguments, before the first argument, or after the last argument. If it finds an overlay specification like <3>, it will call

⟨*text*⟩ with arguments 1 to ⟨*argument number*⟩ set to the normal arguments and the argument number ⟨*argument number*⟩ + 1 set to <3> (including the pointed brackets). If no overlay specification is found, the extra argument is empty.

If the ⟨*default optional value*⟩ is provided, the first argument of ⟨*command name*⟩ is optional. If no optional argument is specified in square brackets, the ⟨*default optional value*⟩ is used.

Example: The following command will typeset its argument in red on the specified slides:

```
\newcommand<>{\makered}[1]{{\color#2{red}#1}}
```

Example: Here is BEAMER's definition of \emph:

```
\newcommand<>{\emph}[1]{{\only#2{\itshape}#1}}
```

Example: Here is BEAMER's definition of \transdissolve (the command \beamer@dotrans mainly passes its argument to hyperref):

```
\newcommand<>{\transdissolve}[1][]{\only#2{\beamer@dotrans[#1]{Dissolve}}}
```

\renewcommand<>{⟨*existing command name*⟩}[⟨*argument number*⟩][⟨*default optional value*⟩]{⟨*text*⟩}

Redeclares a command that already exists in the same way as \newcommand<>. Inside ⟨*text*⟩, you can still access to original definitions using the command \beameroriginal, see the example.

Example: This command is used in BEAMER to make \hyperlink overlay specification-aware:

```
\renewcommand<>{\hyperlink}[2]{\only#3{\beameroriginal{\hyperlink}{#1}{#2}}}
```

\newenvironment<>{⟨*environment name*⟩}[⟨*argument number*⟩][⟨*default optional value*⟩]
{⟨*begin text*⟩}{⟨*end text*⟩}

Declares a new environment that is overlay specification-aware. If this environment is encountered, the same algorithm as for \newcommand<> is used to parse the arguments and the overlay specification.

Note that, as always, the ⟨*end text*⟩ may not contain any arguments like #1. In particular, you do not have access to the overlay specification. In this case, it is usually a good idea to use altenv environment in the ⟨*begin text*⟩.

Example: Declare your own action block:

```
\newenvironment<>{myboldblock}[1]{%
  \begin{actionenv}#2%
    \textbf{#1}
    \par}
{\par%
\end{actionenv}}

\begin{frame}
  \begin{myboldblock}<2>
    This theorem is shown only on the second slide.
  \end{myboldblock}
\end{frame}
```

Example: Text in the following environment is normally bold and italic on non-specified slides:

```
\newenvironment<>{boldornormal}
  {\begin{altenv}#1
    {\begin{bfseries}}{\end{bfseries}}
    {}{}}
  {\end{altenv}}
```

Incidentally, since altenv also accepts its argument at the end, the same effect could have been achieved using just

```
\newenvironment{boldornormal}
  {\begin{altenv}
```

```
    {\begin{bfseries}}{\end{bfseries}}
    {}{}}
  {\end{altenv}}
```

\renewenvironment<>{⟨*existing environment name*⟩}[⟨*argument number*⟩][⟨*default optional value*⟩]
{⟨*begin text*⟩}{⟨*end text*⟩}

Redefines an existing environment. The original environment is still available under the name original⟨*existing environment name*⟩.

Example:

```
\renewenvironment<>{verse}
{\begin{actionenv}#1\begin{originalverse}}
{\end{originalverse}\end{actionenv}}
```

The following two commands can be used to ensure that a certain counter is automatically reset on subsequent slides of a frame. This is necessary for example for the equation count. You might want this count to be increased from frame to frame, but certainly not from overlay slide to overlay slide. For equation counters and footnote counters (you should not use footnotes), these commands have already been invoked.

\resetcounteronoverlays{⟨*counter name*⟩}

After you have invoked this command, the value of the specified counter will be the same on all slides of every frame.

Example: \resetcounteronoverlays{equation}

\resetcountonoverlays{⟨*count register name*⟩}

The same as \resetcounteronoverlays, except that this command should be used with counts that have been created using the TEX primitive \newcount instead of LATEX's \definecounter.

Example:

```
\newcount\mycount
\resetcountonoverlays{mycount}
```

9.6.2   Mode Specifications

This section is only important if you use BEAMER's mode mechanism to create different versions of your presentation. If you are not familiar with BEAMER's modes, please skip this section or read Section 21 first.

In certain cases you may wish to have different overlay specifications to apply to a command in different modes. For example, you might wish a certain text to appear only from the third slide on during your presentation, but in a handout for the audience there should be no third slide and the text should appear already on the second slide. In this case you could write

\only<3| handout:2>{Some text}

The vertical bar, which must be followed by a (white) space, separates the two different specifications 3 and handout:2. By writing a mode name before a colon, you specify that the following specification only applies to that mode. If no mode is given, as in 3, the mode beamer is automatically added. For this reason, if you write \only<3>{Text} and you are in handout mode, the text will be shown on all slides since there is no restriction specified for handouts and since the 3 is the same as beamer:3.

It is also possible to give an overlay specification that contains only a mode name (or several, separated by vertical bars):

\only<article>{This text is shown only in article mode.}

An overlay specification that does not contain any slide numbers is called a (pure) *mode specification*. If a mode specification is given, all modes that are not mentioned are automatically suppressed. Thus <beamer:1-> means "on all slides in beamer mode and also on all slides in all other modes, since nothing special is specified for them," whereas <beamer> means "on all slides in beamer mode and not on any other slide."

Mode specifications can also be used outside frames as in the following examples:

```
\section<presentation>{This section exists only in the presentation modes}
\section<article>{This section exists only in the article mode}
```

Presentation modes include `beamer`, `trans` and `handout`.

You can also mix pure mode specifications and overlay specifications, although this can get confusing:

```
\only<article| beamer:1>{Riddle}
```

This will cause the text `Riddle` to be inserted in `article` mode and on the first slide of a frame in `beamer` mode, but not at all in `handout` or `trans` mode. (Try to find out how `<beamer| beamer:1>` differs from `<beamer>` and from `<beamer:1>`.)

As if all this were not already complicated enough, there is another mode that behaves in a special way: the mode `second`. For this mode a special rule applies: An overlay specification for mode `beamer` also applies to mode `second` (but not the other way round). Thus, if we are in mode `second`, the specification `<second:2>` means "on slide 2" and `<beamer:2>` also means "on slide 2". To get a slide that is typeset in `beamer` mode, but not in `second` mode, you can use, `<second:0>`.

9.6.3 Action Specifications

This section also introduces a rather advanced concept. You may also wish to skip it on first reading.

Some overlay specification-aware commands cannot handle not only normal overlay specifications, but also so called *action specifications*. In an action specification, the list of slide numbers and ranges is prefixed by $\langle action \rangle$@, where $\langle action \rangle$ is the name of a certain action to be taken on the specified slides:

```
\item<3-| alert@3> Shown from slide 3 on, alerted on slide 3.
```

In the above example, the `\item` command, which allows actions to be specified, will uncover the item text from slide three on and it will, additionally, alert this item exactly on slide 3.

Not all commands can take an action specification. Currently, only `\item` (though not in `article` mode currently), `\action`, the environment `actionenv`, and the block environments (like `block` or `theorem`) handle them.

By default, the following actions are available:

- `alert` alters the item or block.

- `uncover` uncovers the item or block (this is the default, if no action is specified).

- `only` causes the whole item or block to be inserted only on the specified slides.

- `visible` causes the text to become visible only on the specified slides (the difference between `uncover` and `visible` is the same as between `\uncover` and `\visible`).

- `invisible` causes the text to become invisible on the specified slides.

The rest of this section explains how you can add your own actions and make commands action-specification-aware. You may wish to skip it upon first reading.

You can easily add your own actions: An action specification like $\langle action \rangle$@$\langle slide\ numbers \rangle$ simply inserts an environment called $\langle action \rangle$env around the `\item` or parameter of `\action` with <$\langle slide\ numbers \rangle$> as overlay specification. Thus, by defining a new overlay specification-aware environment named $\langle my\ action\ name \rangle$env, you can add your own action:

```
\newenvironment{checkenv}{\only{\setbeamertemplate{itemize item}{X}}}{}
```

You can then write

```
\item<beamer:check@2> Text.
```

This will change the itemization symbol before `Text.` to `X` on slide 2 in `beamer` mode. The definition of `checkenv` used the fact that `\only` also accepts an overlay specification given after its argument.

The whole action mechanism is based on the following environment:

`\begin{actionenv}<`⟨*action specification*⟩`>`
  ⟨*environment contents*⟩
`\end{actionenv}`

> This environment extracts all actions from the ⟨*action specification*⟩ for the current mode. For each action of the form ⟨*action*⟩@⟨*slide numbers*⟩, it inserts the following text: `\begin{`⟨*action*⟩`env}<`⟨*slide number*⟩`>` at the beginning of the environment and the text `\end{`⟨*action*⟩`env}` at the end. If there are several action specifications, several environments are opened (and closed in the appropriate order). An ⟨*overlay specification*⟩ without an action is promoted to `uncover@`⟨*overlay specification*⟩.

> If the so called *default overlay specification* is not empty, it will be used in case no ⟨*action specification*⟩ is given. The default overlay specification is usually just empty, but it may be set either by providing an additional optional argument to the command `\frame` or to the environments `itemize`, `enumerate`, or `description` (see these for details). Also, the default action specification can be set using the command `\beamerdefaultoverlayspecification`, see below.

> *Example:*
> ```
> \begin{frame}
>   \begin{actionenv}<2-| alert@3-4,6>
>     This text is shown the same way as the text below.
>   \end{actionenv}
>
>   \begin{uncoverenv}<2->
>     \begin{alertenv}<3-4,6>
>       This text is shown the same way as the text above.
>     \end{alertenv}
>   \end{uncoverenv}
> \end{frame}
> ```

`\action<`⟨*action specification*⟩`>{`⟨*text*⟩`}`

> This has the same effect as putting ⟨*text*⟩ in an `actionenv`.

> *Example:* `\action<alert@2>{Could also have used \texttt{\string\alert<2>\char`\{\char`\}}.}`

`\beamerdefaultoverlayspecification{`⟨*default overlay specification*⟩`}`

> Locally sets the default overlay specification to the given value. This overlay specification will be used in every `actionenv` environment and every `\item` that does not have its own overlay specification. The main use of this command is to install an incremental overlay specification like `<+->` or `<+-| alert@+>`, see Section 9.6.4.

> Usually, the default overlay specification is installed automatically by the optional arguments to `\frame`, `frame`, `itemize`, `enumerate`, and `description`. You will only have to use this command if you wish to do funny things.

> If given outside any frame, this command sets the default overlay specification for all following frames for which you do not override the default overlay specification.

> *Example:* `\beamerdefaultoverlayspecification{<+->}`

> *Example:* `\beamerdefaultoverlayspecification{}` clears the default overlay specification. (Actually, it installs the default overlay specification `<*>`, which just means "always," but the "portable" way of clearing the default overlay specification is this call.)

9.6.4 Incremental Specifications

This section is mostly important for people who have already used overlay specifications a lot and have grown tired of writing things like `<1->`, `<2->`, `<3->`, and so on again and again. You should skip this section on first reading.

Often you want to have overlay specifications that follow a pattern similar to the following:

```
\begin{itemize}
\item<1-> Apple
\item<2-> Peach
\item<3-> Plum
\item<4-> Orange
\end{itemize}
```

The problem starts if you decide to insert a new fruit, say, at the beginning. In this case, you would have to adjust all of the overlay specifications. Also, if you add a \pause command before the itemize, you would also have to update the overlay specifications.

BEAMER offers a special syntax to make creating lists as the one above more "robust." You can replace it by the following list of *incremental overlay specifications*:

```
\begin{itemize}
\item<+-> Apple
\item<+-> Peach
\item<+-> Plum
\item<+-> Orange
\end{itemize}
```

The effect of the +-sign is the following: You can use it in any overlay specification at any point where you would usually use a number. If a +-sign is encountered, it is replaced by the current value of the LATEX counter beamerpauses, which is 1 at the beginning of the frame. Then the counter is increased by 1, though it is only increased once for every overlay specification, even if the specification contains multiple +-signs (they are replaced by the same number).

In the above example, the first specification is replaced by <1->. Then the second is replaced by <2-> and so forth. We can now easily insert new entries, without having to change anything else. We might also write the following:

```
\begin{itemize}
\item<+-| alert@+> Apple
\item<+-| alert@+> Peach
\item<+-| alert@+> Plum
\item<+-| alert@+> Orange
\end{itemize}
```

This will alert the current item when it is uncovered. For example, the first specification <+-| alert@+> is replaced by <1-| alert@1>, the second is replaced by <2-| alert@2>, and so on. Since the itemize environment also allows you to specify a default overlay specification, see the documentation of that environment, the above example can be written even more economically as follows:

```
\begin{itemize}[<+-| alert@+>]
\item Apple
\item Peach
\item Plum
\item Orange
\end{itemize}
```

The \pause command also updates the counter beamerpauses. You can change this counter yourself using the normal LATEX commands \setcounter or \addtocounter.

Any occurence of a +-sign may be followed by an *offset* in round brackets. This offset will be added to the value of beamerpauses. Thus, if beamerpauses is 2, then <+(1)-> expands to <3-> and <+(-1)-+> expands to <1-2>. For example

```
\begin{frame}
\frametitle{Method 1}
\begin{itemize}
\item<2-> Apple
\item<3-> Peach
\item<4-> Plum
```

```
\item<5-> Orange
\end{itemize}
```

and

```
\begin{itemize}[<+(1)->]
\item Apple
\item Peach
\item Plum
\item Orange
\end{itemize}
```

are equivalent.

There is another special sign you can use in an overlay specification that behaves similarly to the +-sign: a dot. When you write `<.->`, a similar thing as in `<+->` happens *except* that the counter `beamerpauses` is *not* incremented and *except* that you get the value of `beamerpauses` decreased by one. Thus a dot, possibly followed by an offset, just expands to the current value of the counter `beamerpauses` minus one, possibly offset. This dot notation can be useful in case like the following:

```
\begin{itemize}[<+->]
\item Apple
\item<.-> Peach
\item Plum
\item Orange
\end{itemize}
```

In the example, the second item is shown at the same time as the first one since it does not update the counter.

In the following example, each time an item is uncovered, the specified text is alerted. When the next item is uncovered, this altering ends.

```
\begin{itemize}[<+->]
\item This is \alert<.>{important}.
\item We want to \alert<.>{highlight} this and \alert<.>{this}.
\item What is the \alert<.>{matrix}?
\end{itemize}
```

10 Structuring a Presentation: The Static Global Structure

This section lists the commands that are used for structuring a presentation "globally" using commands like \section or \part. These commands are used to create a *static* structure, meaning that the resulting presentation is normally presented one slide after the other in the order the slides occur. Section 11 explains which commands can be used to create the *interactive* structure. For the interactive structure, you must interact with the presentation program, typically by clicking on hyperlinks, to advance the presentation.

10.1 Adding a Title Page

You can use the \titlepage command to insert a title page into a frame. By default, it will arrange the following elements on the title page: the document title, the authors' names, their affiliation, a title graphic, and a date.

\titlepage

> Inserts the text of a title page into the current frame.
>
> *Example:* \frame{\titlepage}
>
> *Example:* \frame[plain]{\titlepage} for a titlepage that fills the whole frame.

Beamer-Template/-Color/-Font title page

> This template is invoked when the \titlepage command is used.
>
> The following template options are predefined:
>
> - [default][⟨*alignment*⟩] The title page is typeset showing the title, followed by the author, his or her affiliation, the date, and a titlegraphic. If any of these are missing, they are not shown. Except for the titlegraphic, if the BEAMER-color title, author, institute, or date is defined, respectively, it is used as textcolor for these entries. If a background color is defined for them, a colored bar in the corresponding color is drawn behind them, spanning the text width. The corresponding BEAMER-fonts are used for these entries.
>   The ⟨*alignment*⟩ option is passed on the beamercolorbox and can be used, for example, to flush the title page to the left by specifying left here.
>
> The following commands are useful for this template:
>
> - \insertauthor inserts a version of the author's name that is useful for the title page.
> - \insertdate inserts the date.
> - \insertinstitute inserts the institute.
> - \inserttitle inserts a version of the document title that is useful for the title page.
> - \insertsubtitle inserts a version of the document title that is useful for the title page.
> - \inserttitlegraphic inserts the title graphic into a template.

For compatibility with other classes, in article mode the following command is also provided:

\maketitle

PRESEN-
TATION
If used inside a frame, it has the same effect as \titlepage. If used outside a frame, it has the same effect as \frame{\titlepage}; in other words, a frame is added if necessary.

Before you invoke the title page command, you must specify all elements you wish to be shown. This is done using the following commands:

\title[⟨*short title*⟩]{⟨*title*⟩}

> The ⟨*short title*⟩ is used in headlines and footlines. Inside the ⟨*title*⟩ line breaks can be inserted using the double-backslash command.
>
> *Example:*
> ```
> \title{The Beamer Class}
> \title[Short Version]{A Very Long Title\\Over Several Lines}
> ```

ARTICLE The short form is ignored in `article` mode.

\subtitle[⟨*short subtitle*⟩]{⟨*subtitle*⟩}

The ⟨*short subtitle*⟩ is not used by default, but is available via the insert \insertshortsubtitle. The subtitle is shown below the title in a smaller font.

Example:

```
\title{The Beamer Class}
\subtitle{An easily paced introduction with many examples.}
```

ARTICLE This command causes the subtitle to be appended to the title with a linebreak and a \normalsize command issued before it. This may or may not be what you would like to happen.

\author[⟨*short author names*⟩]{⟨*author names*⟩}

The names should be separated using the command \and. In case authors have different affiliations, they should be suffixed by the command \inst with different parameters.

Example: \author[Hemaspaandra et al.]{L. Hemaspaandra\inst{1} \and T. Tantau\inst{2}}

ARTICLE The short form is ignored in `article` mode.

\institute[⟨*short institute*⟩]{⟨*institute*⟩}

If more than one institute is given, they should be separated using the command \and and they should be prefixed by the command \inst with different parameters.

Example:

```
\institute[Universities of Rijeka and Berlin]{
  \inst{1}Department of Informatics\\
  University of Rijeka
  \and
  \inst{2}Fakult\"at f\"ur Elektrotechnik und Informatik\\
  Technical University of Berlin}
```

ARTICLE The short form is ignored in `article` mode. The long form is also ignored, except if the document class (like `llncs`) defines it.

\date[⟨*short date*⟩]{⟨*date*⟩}

Example: \date{\today} or \date[STACS 2003]{STACS Conference, 2003}.

ARTICLE The short form is ignored in `article` mode.

\titlegraphic{⟨*text*⟩}

The ⟨*text*⟩ is shown as title graphic. Typically, a picture environment is used as ⟨*text*⟩.

Example: \titlegraphic{\pgfuseimage{titlegraphic}}

ARTICLE The command is ignored in `article` mode.

\subject{⟨*text*⟩}

Enters the ⟨*text*⟩ as the subject text in the PDF document info. It currently has no other effect.

\keywords{⟨*text*⟩}

Enters the ⟨*text*⟩ as keywords in the PDF document info. It currently has no other effect.

By default, the \title and \author commands will also insert their arguments into a resulting PDF-file in the document information fields. This may cause problems if you use complicated things like boxes as arguments to these commands. In this case, you might wish to switch off the automatic generation of these entries using the following class option:

\documentclass[usepdftitle=false]{beamer}

Suppresses the automatic generation of title and author entries in the PDF document information.

10.2   Adding Sections and Subsections

You can structure your text using the commands \section and \subsection. Unlike standard LaTeX, these commands will not create a heading at the position where you use them. Rather, they will add an entry to the table of contents and also to the navigation bars.

In order to create a line break in the table of contents (usually not a good idea), you can use the command \breakhere. Note that the standard command \\ does not work (actually, we do not really know why; comments would be appreciated).

\section<⟨*mode specification*⟩>[⟨*short section name*⟩]{⟨*section name*⟩}

> Starts a section. No heading is created. The ⟨*section name*⟩ is shown in the table of contents and in the navigation bars, except if ⟨*short section name*⟩ is specified. In this case, ⟨*short section name*⟩ is used in the navigation bars instead. If a ⟨*mode specification*⟩ is given, the command only has an effect for the specified modes.
>
> *Example:* \section[Summary]{Summary of Main Results}

ARTICLE   The ⟨*mode specification*⟩ allows you to provide an alternate section command in article mode. This is necessary for example if the ⟨*short section name*⟩ is unsuitable for the table of contents:

> *Example:*
>
> \section<presentation>[Results]{Results on the Main Problem}
> \section<article>{Results on the Main Problem}

> **Beamer-Template/-Color/-Font** section in toc
>
> This template is used when a section entry is to be typeset. For the permissible ⟨*options*⟩ see the parent template table of contents.
>
> The following commands are useful for this template:
>
> - \inserttocsection inserts the table of contents version of the current section name.
> - \inserttocsectionnumber inserts the number of the current section (in the table of contents).

> **Beamer-Template/-Color/-Font** section in toc shaded
>
> This template is used instead of the previous one if the section should be shown in a shaded way, because it is not the current section. For the permissible ⟨*options*⟩ see the parent template table of contents.

\section<⟨*mode specification*⟩>*{⟨*section name*⟩}

> Starts a section without an entry in the table of contents. No heading is created, but the ⟨*section name*⟩ is shown in the navigation bar.
>
> *Example:* \section*{Outline}
>
> *Example:* \section<beamer>*{Outline}

\subsection<⟨*mode specification*⟩>[⟨*short subsection name*⟩]{⟨*subsection name*⟩}

> This command works the same way as the \section command.
>
> *Example:* \subsection[Applications]{Applications to the Reduction of Pollution}

> **Beamer-Template/-Color/-Font** subsection in toc
>
> Like section in toc, only for subsection.
>
> In addition to the inserts for the section in toc template, the following commands are available for this template:
>
> - \inserttocsubsection inserts the table of contents version of the current subsection name.
> - \inserttocsubsectionnumber inserts the number of the current subsection (in the table of contents).

Beamer-Template/-Color/-Font `subsection in toc shaded`

Like `section in toc shaded`, only for subsections.

`\subsection<`⟨*mode specification*⟩`>*{`⟨*subsection name*⟩`}`

Starts a subsection without an entry in the table of contents. No heading is created, but the ⟨*subsection name*⟩ is shown in the navigation bar, *except* if ⟨*subsection name*⟩ is empty. In this case, neither a table of contents entry nor a navigation bar entry is created, *but* any frames in this "empty" subsection are shown in the navigation bar.

Example:

```
\section{Summary}

  \frame{This frame is not shown in the navigation bar}

  \subsection*{}

  \frame{This frame is shown in the navigation bar, but no subsection
    entry is shown.}

  \subsection*{A subsection}

  \frame{Normal frame, shown in navigation bar. The subsection name is
    also shown in the navigation bar, but not in the table of contents.}
```

`\subsubsection<`⟨*mode specification*⟩`>[`⟨*short subsubsection name*⟩`]{`⟨*subsubsection name*⟩`}`

This command works the like `\subsection`. However, subsubsections are supported less well than subsections. For example, in the table of contents subsubsections are always shown with the same shading/hiding parameters as the subsection.

We *strongly* discourage the use of subsubsections in presentations. If you do not use them, you will give a better presentation.

Example: `\subsubsection[Applications]{Applications to the Reduction of Pollution}`

Beamer-Template/-Color/-Font `subsubsection in toc`

Like `subsection in toc`, only for subsection.

In addition to the inserts for the `subsection in toc` template, the following commands are available for this template:

- `\inserttocsubsubsection` inserts the table of contents version of the current subsubsection name.
- `\inserttocsubsubsectionnumber` inserts the number of the current subsubsection (in the table of contents).

Beamer-Template/-Color/-Font `subsubsection in toc shaded`

Like `subsection in toc shaded`, only for subsubsections.

`\subsubsection<`⟨*mode specification*⟩`>*{`⟨*subsubsection name*⟩`}`

Starts a subsubsection without an entry in the table of contents. No heading is created, but the ⟨*subsubsection name*⟩ is shown in a possible sidebar.

Often, you may want a certain type of frame to be shown directly after a section or subsection starts. For example, you may wish every subsection to start with a frame showing the table of contents with the current subsection highlighted. To facilitate this, you can use the following commands.

`\AtBeginSection[`⟨*special star text*⟩`]{`⟨*text*⟩`}`

The given text will be inserted at the beginning of every section. If the ⟨*special star text*⟩ parameter is specified, this text will be used for starred sections instead. Different calls of this command will not "add up" the given texts (like the `\AtBeginDocument` command does), but will overwrite any previous text.

Example:

```
\AtBeginSection[] % Do nothing for \section*
{
  \begin{frame}<beamer>
    \frametitle{Outline}
    \tableofcontents[currentsection]
  \end{frame}
}
```

ARTICLE This command has no effect in `article` mode.

`\AtBeginSubsection[`⟨*special star text*⟩`]{`⟨*text*⟩`}`

The given text will be inserted at the beginning of every subsection. If the ⟨*special star text*⟩ parameter is specified, this text will be used for starred subsections instead. Different calls of this command will not "add up" the given texts.

Example:

```
\AtBeginSubsection[] % Do nothing for \subsection*
{
  \begin{frame}<beamer>
    \frametitle{Outline}
    \tableofcontents[currentsection,currentsubsection]
  \end{frame}
}
```

`\AtBeginSubsubsection[`⟨*special star text*⟩`]{`⟨*text*⟩`}`

Like `\AtBeginSubsection`, only for subsubsections.

BEAMER also provides `\sectionpage` and `\subsectionpage` commands, which are used to fill a frame with section or subsection number and title in a stylish way. They are very similar to `\partpage` command described below.

Example:

```
\section{A section}

  \frame{\sectionpage}

  \frame{Some text.}
```

If you enable TRANSLATOR as described in Section 25.3.1, you will also get translated strings for "Section", "Subsection" and others.

10.3 Adding Parts

If you give a long talk (like a lecture), you may wish to break up your talk into several parts. Each such part acts like a little "talk of its own" with its own table of contents, its own navigation bars, and so on. Inside one part, the sections and subsections of the other parts are not shown at all.

To create a new part, use the `\part` command. All sections and subsections following this command will be "local" to that part. Like the `\section` and `\subsection` command, the `\part` command does not cause any frame or special text to be produced. However, it is often advisable for the start of a new part to use the command `\partpage` to insert some text into a frame that "advertises" the beginning of a new part.

`\part<`⟨*mode specification*⟩`>[`⟨*short part name*⟩`]{`⟨*part name*⟩`}`

Starts a part. The ⟨*part name*⟩ will be shown when the `\partpage` command is used. The ⟨*short part name*⟩ is not shown anywhere by default, but it is accessible via the command `\insertshortpart`.

Example:

```
\begin{document}
  \frame{\titlepage}

  \section*{Outlines}
  \subsection{Part I: Review of Previous Lecture}
  \frame{
    \frametitle{Outline of Part I}
    \tableofcontents[part=1]}
  \subsection{Part II: Today's Lecture}
  \frame{
    \frametitle{Outline of Part II}
    \tableofcontents[part=2]}

  \part{Review of Previous Lecture}
  \frame{\partpage}
  \section[Previous Lecture]{Summary of the Previous Lecture}
  \subsection{Topics}
  \frame{...}
  \subsection{Learning Objectives}
  \frame{...}

  \part{Today's Lecture}
  \frame{\partpage}
  \section{Topic A}
  \frame{\tableofcontents[currentsection]}
  \subsection{Foo}
  \frame{...}
  \section{Topic B}
  \frame{\tableofcontents[currentsection]}
  \subsection{bar}
  \frame{...}
\end{document}
```

\partpage

> Works like \titlepage, only that the current part, not the current presentation is "advertised."
>
> *Example:* \frame{\partpage}

Beamer-Template/-Color/-Font part page

> This template is invoked when the \partpage command is used.
>
> The following template options are predefined:
>
> - [default] [⟨*alignment*⟩] The part page is typeset showing the current part number and, below, the current part title. The BEAMER-color and -font part page are used, including the background color of part page. As for the title page template, the ⟨*alignment*⟩ option is passed on the beamercolorbox.
>
> The following commands are useful for this template:
>
> - \insertpart inserts the current part name.
> - \insertpartnumber inserts the current part number as an Arabic number into a template.
> - \insertpartromannumber inserts the current part number as a Roman number into a template.

\AtBeginPart{⟨*text*⟩}

> The given text will be inserted at the beginning of every part.
>
> *Example:*
>
> \AtBeginPart{\frame{\partpage}}

10.4 Splitting a Course Into Lectures

When using BEAMER with the `article` mode, you may wish to have the lecture notes of a whole course reside in one file. In this case, only a few frames are actually part of any particular lecture.

The `\lecture` command makes it easy to select only a certain set of frames from a file to be presented. This command takes (among other things) a label name. If you say `\includeonlylecture` with this label name, then only the frames following the corresponding `\lecture` command are shown. The frames following other `\lecture` commands are suppressed.

By default, the `\lecture` command has no other effect. It does not create any frames or introduce entries in the table of contents. However, you can use `\AtBeginLecture` to have BEAMER insert, say, a title page at the beginning of (each) lecture.

`\lecture[`⟨*short lecture name*⟩`]{`⟨*lecture name*⟩`}{`⟨*lecture label*⟩`}`

> Starts a lecture. The ⟨*lecture name*⟩ will be available via the `\insertlecture` command. The ⟨*short lecture name*⟩ is available via the `\insertshortlecture` command.
>
> *Example:*
> ```
> \begin{document}
> \lecture{Vector Spaces}{week 1}
>
> \section{Introduction}
> ...
> \section{Summary}
>
> \lecture{Scalar Products}{week 2}
>
> \section{Introduction}
> ...
> \section{Summary}
>
> \end{document}
> ```

ARTICLE This command has no effect in `article` mode.

`\includeonlylecture`⟨*lecture label*⟩

> Causes all `\frame`, `frame`, `\section`, `\subsection`, and `\part` commands following a `\lecture` command to be suppressed, except if the lecture's label matches the ⟨*lecture label*⟩. Frames before any `\lecture` commands are always included. This command should be given in the preamble.
>
> *Example:* `\includeonlylecture{week 1}`

ARTICLE This command has no effect in `article` mode.

`\AtBeginLecture{`⟨*text*⟩`}`

> The given text will be inserted at the beginning of every lecture.
>
> *Example:*
>
> `\AtBeginLecture{\frame{\Large Today's Lecture: \insertlecture}}`

ARTICLE This command has no effect in `article` mode.

10.5 Adding a Table of Contents

You can create a table of contents using the command `\tableofcontents`. Unlike the normal LaTeX table of contents command, this command takes an optional parameter in square brackets that can be used to create certain special effects.

`\tableofcontents[`⟨*comma-separated option list*⟩`]`

Inserts a table of contents into the current frame.

Example:

```
\section*{Outline}
\frame{\tableofcontents}

\section{Introduction}
\frame{\tableofcontents[currentsection]}
\subsection{Why?}
\frame{...}
\frame{...}
\subsection{Where?}
\frame{...}

\section{Results}
\frame{\tableofcontents[currentsection]}
\subsection{Because}
\frame{...}
\subsection{Here}
\frame{...}
```

The following options can be given:

- `currentsection` causes all sections but the current to be shown in a semi-transparent way. Also, all subsections but those in the current section are shown in the semi-transparent way. This command is a shorthand for specifying the following options:

  `sectionstyle=show/shaded,subsectionstyle=show/show/shaded`

- `currentsubsection` causes all subsections but the current subsection in the current section to be shown in a semi-transparent way. This command is a shorthand for specifying the option `subsectionstyle=show/shaded`.

- `firstsection=`⟨*section number*⟩ specifies which section should be numbered as section "1." This is useful if you have a first section (like an overview section) that should not receive a number. Section numbers are not shown by default. To show them, you must install a different table of contents templates.

- `hideallsubsections` causes all subsections to be hidden. This command is a shorthand for specifying the option `subsectionstyle=hide`.

- `hideothersubsections` causes the subsections of sections other than the current one to be hidden. This command is a shorthand for specifying the option `subsectionstyle=show/show/hide`.

- `part=`⟨*part number*⟩ causes the table of contents of part ⟨*part number*⟩ to be shown, instead of the table of contents of the current part (which is the default). This option can be combined with the other options, although combining it with the `current` option obviously makes no sense.

- `pausesections` causes a `\pause` command to be issued before each section. This is useful if you wish to show the table of contents in an incremental way.

- `pausesubsections` causes a `\pause` command to be issued before each subsection.

- `sections={`⟨*overlay specification*⟩`}` causes only the sections mentioned in the ⟨*overlay specification*⟩ to be shown. For example, `sections={<2-4| handout:0>}` causes only the second, third, and fourth section to be shown in the normal version, nothing to be shown in the handout version, and everything to be shown in all other versions. For convenience, if you omit the pointed brackets, the specification is assumed to apply to all versions. Thus `sections={2-4}` causes sections two, three, and four to be shown in all versions.

- `sectionstyle=⟨style for current section⟩/⟨style for other sections⟩` specifies how sections should be displayed. Allowed ⟨styles⟩ are `show`, `shaded`, and `hide`. The first will show the section title normally, the second will show it in a semi-transparent way, and the third will completely suppress it. You can also omit the second style, in which case the first is used for all sections (this is not really useful).

- `subsectionstyle=⟨style for current subsection⟩/⟨style for other subsections in current section⟩/` ⟨*style for subsections in other sections*⟩ specifies how subsections should be displayed. The same styles as for the `sectionstyle` option may be given. You can omit the last style, in which case the second also applies to the last, and you can omit the last two, in which case the first applies to all.

  Example: `subsectionstyle=shaded` causes all subsections to be shaded.

  Example: `subsectionstyle=hide` causes all subsections to be hidden.

  Example: `subsectionstyle=show/shaded` causes all subsections but the current subsection in the current section to be shown in a semi-transparent way.

  Example: `subsectionstyle=show/show/hide` causes all subsections outside the current section to be suppressed.

  Example: `subsectionstyle=show/shaded/hide` causes all subsections outside the current section to be suppressed and only the current subsection in the current section to be highlighted.

- `subsubsectionstyle=⟨style for current subsubsection⟩/⟨style for other subsubsections in current subsection⟩/`
  ⟨*style for subsubsections in other subsections in current section*⟩/⟨*style for subsubsections in other subsections in other sections*⟩ specifies how subsubsections should be displayed. The same styles as for the `sectionstyle` option may be given. You can omit the last style, in which case the second also applies to the last, and you can omit the last two, in which case the first applies to all. This option operates in an analogous manner to `subsectionstyle`.

The last examples are useful if you do not wish to show too many details when presenting the talk outline.

ARTICLE The options are ignored in `article` mode.

Parent Beamer-Template `section/subsection in toc`

This is a parent template, whose children are `section in toc` and `subsection in toc`. This means that if you use the `\setbeamertemplate` command on this template, the command is instead called for both of these children (with the same arguments).

The following template options are predefined:

- [`default`] In the default setting, the sections and subsections are typeset using the fonts and colors `section in toc` and `subsection in toc`, though the background colors are ignored. The subsections are indented.

- [`sections numbered`] Similar to the default setting, but the section numbers are also shown. The subsections are not numbered.

- [`subsections numbered`] This time, the subsections are numbered, but not the sections. Nevertheless, since the subsections are "fully numbered" as in "1.2" or "3.2," if every section has at least one subsection, the section numbered will not really be missed.

- [`circle`] Draws little circles before the sections. Inside the circles the section number is shown. The BEAMER-font and color `section number projected` is used for typesetting the circles, that is, the circle gets the background color and the text inside the circle the foreground color.

- [`square`] Similar to the `circle` option, except that small squares are used instead of circles. Small, unnumbered squares are shown in front of the subsections.

- [`ball`] Like `square`, the only difference being the balls are used instead of squares.

- [`ball unnumbered`] Similar to `ball`, except that no numbering is used. This option makes the table of contents look more like an `itemize`.

If none of the above options suits you, you have to change the templates `section in toc` and `subsection in toc` directly.

Parent Beamer-Template `section/subsection in toc shaded`

A parent template with children `section in toc shaded` and `subsection in toc shaded`. They are used to render section and subsection entries when they are currently shaded; like all non-current subsections in `\tableofcontents[currentsubsection]`.

The following template options are predefined:

- [`default`] [⟨*opaqueness*⟩] In the default setting, the templates `section in toc shaded` and `subsection in toc shaded` just show whatever the nonshaded versions of these templates show, but only ⟨*opaqueness*⟩% opaque. The default is 20%.

  Example: `\setbeamertemplate{section in toc shaded}[default][50]` makes dimmed entries 50% transparent.

10.6 Adding a Bibliography

You can use the bibliography environment and the `\cite` commands of LaTeX in a BEAMER presentation. You will typically have to typeset your bibliography items partly "by hand." Nevertheless, you *can* use `bibtex` to create a "first approximation" of the bibliography. Copy the content of the file `main.bbl` into your presentation. If you are not familiar with `bibtex`, you may wish to consult its documentation. It is a powerful tool for creating high-quality citations.

Using `bibtex` or your editor, place your bibliographic references in the environment `thebibliography`. This (standard LaTeX) environment takes one parameter, which should be the longest `\bibitem` label in the following list of bibliographic entries.

`\begin{thebibliography}{`⟨*longest label text*⟩`}`
  ⟨*environment contents*⟩
`\end{thebibliography}`

Inserts a bibliography into the current frame. The ⟨*longest label text*⟩ is used to determine the indentation of the list. However, several predefined options for the typesetting of the bibliography ignore this parameter since they replace the references by a symbol.

Inside the environment, use a (standard LaTeX) `\bibitem` command for each reference item. Inside each item, use a (standard LaTeX) `\newblock` command to separate the authors' names, the title, the book/journal reference, and any notes. Each of these commands may introduce a new line or color or other formatting, as specified by the template for bibliographies.

The environment must be placed inside a frame. If the bibliography does not fit on one frame, you should split it (create a new frame and a second `thebibliography` environment) or use the `allowframebreaks` option. Even better, you should reconsider whether it is a good idea to present so many references.

Example:
```
\begin{frame}
  \frametitle{For Further Reading}

  \begin{thebibliography}{Dijkstra, 1982}
  \bibitem[Salomaa, 1973]{Salomaa1973}
    A.~Salomaa.
    \newblock {\em Formal Languages}.
    \newblock Academic Press, 1973.

  \bibitem[Dijkstra, 1982]{Dijkstra1982}
    E.~Dijkstra.
    \newblock Smoothsort, an alternative for sorting in situ.
    \newblock {\em Science of Computer Programming}, 1(3):223--233, 1982.
  \end{thebibliography}
\end{frame}
```

Four templates govern the appearance of the author, title, journal, and note text. These author templates are inserted before the first block of the entry (the first block is all text before the first occurrence of a

`\newblock` command). The title template is inserted before the second block (the text between the first and second occurrence of `\newblock`). Likewise for the journal and note templates.

The templates are inserted *before* the blocks and you do not have access to the blocks themselves via insert commands. The corresponding BEAMER-color and -font are also installed before the blocks.

Beamer-Template/-Color/-Font `bibliography entry author`

This template is inserted before the author of a bibliography entry. The color and font are also installed. Note that the effect of this template will persist until the end of the bibliography item or until one of the following templates undo the effect.

By default, this template does nothing. The default color is the structure color.

Beamer-Template/-Color/-Font `bibliography entry title`

This template is inserted before the title of a bibliography entry (more precisely, it is inserted after the first occurrence of the `\newblock` command). By default, this template starts a new paragraph, causing a line break. The default color is the normal text color.

Beamer-Template/-Color/-Font `bibliography entry location`

This template is inserted before the journal of a bibliography entry (the second `\newblock`). By default, this template starts a new paragraph. The default color is a slightly transparent version of the structure color.

Beamer-Template/-Color/-Font `bibliography entry note`

This template is inserted before any note text at the end of a bibliography entry (it is inserted before the third `\newblock`). By default, this template starts a new paragraph. The default color is the same as for the journal.

`\bibitem<`⟨*overlay specification*⟩`>[`⟨*citation text*⟩`]{`⟨*label name*⟩`}`

The ⟨*citation text*⟩ is inserted into the text when the item is cited using `\cite{`⟨*label name*⟩`}` in the main presentation text. For a BEAMER presentation, this should usually be as long as possible.

Use `\newblock` commands to separate the authors's names, the title, the book/journal reference, and any notes. If the ⟨*overlay specification*⟩ is present, the entry will only be shown on the specified slides.

Example:

```
\bibitem[Dijkstra, 1982]{Dijkstra1982}
  E.~Dijkstra.
  \newblock Smoothsort, an alternative for sorting in situ.
  \newblock {\em Science of Computer Programming}, 1(3):223--233, 1982.
```

Beamer-Template/-Color/-Font `bibliography item`

Color/font parents: `item`

This template is used to render the bibliography item. Unlike normal LaTeX, the default template for the bibliography does not repeat the citation text (like "[Dijkstra, 1982]") before each item in the bibliography. Instead, a cute, small article symbol is drawn. The rationale is that the audience will not be able to remember any abbreviated citation texts till the end of the talk.

The following template options are predefined:

- [default] Draws a cute little article icon as the reference. Use this for journal articles, parts of books (like conference proceedings), or technical reports.
- [article] Alias for the default.
- [book] Draws a cute little book icon as the reference. Use this for, well, books.
- [online] Draws a cute little globe icon as the reference. Use this for websites and the like.
- [triangle] Draws a triangle as the reference. This is more in keeping with the standard itemize items.

- [text] Uses the reference text (like "[Dijkstra, 1982]") as the reference text. Be sure you know what you are doing if you use this.

The following insert is useful for the template:

- \insertbiblabel inserts the current citation label.

10.7 Adding an Appendix

You can add an appendix to your talk by using the \appendix command. You should put frames and perhaps whole subsections into the appendix that you do not intend to show during your presentation, but which might be useful to answer a question. The \appendix command essentially just starts a new part named \appendixname. However, it also sets up certain hyperlinks. Like other parts, the appendix is kept separate from your actual talk.

\appendix<⟨mode specification⟩>

Starts the appendix in the specified modes. All frames, all \subsection commands, and all \section commands used after this command will not be shown as part of the normal navigation bars.

Example:

```
\begin{document}
\frame{\titlepage}
\section*{Outline}
\frame{\tableofcontents}
\section{Main Text}
\frame{Some text}
\section*{Summary}
\frame{Summary text}

\appendix
\section{\appendixname}
\frame{\tableofcontents}
\subsection{Additional material}
\frame{Details}
\frame{Text omitted in main talk.}
\subsection{Even more additional material}
\frame{More details}
\end{document}
```

11 Structuring a Presentation: The Interactive Global Structure

11.1 Adding Hyperlinks and Buttons

To create anticipated nonlinear jumps in your talk structure, you can add hyperlinks to your presentation. A hyperlink is a text (usually rendered as a button) that, when you click on it, jumps the presentation to some other slide. Creating such a button is a three-step process:

1. You specify a target using the command \hypertarget or (easier) the command \label. In some cases, see below, this step may be skipped.

2. You render the button using \beamerbutton or a similar command. This will *render* the button, but clicking it will not yet have any effect.

3. You put the button inside a \hyperlink command. Now clicking it will jump to the target of the link.

\hypertarget<⟨*overlay specification*⟩>{⟨*target name*⟩}{⟨*text*⟩}

> If the ⟨*overlay specification*⟩ is present, the ⟨*text*⟩ is the target for hyper jumps to ⟨*target name*⟩ only on the specified slide. On all other slides, the text is shown normally. Note that you *must* add an overlay specification to the \hypertarget command whenever you use it on frames that have multiple slides (otherwise pdflatex rightfully complains that you have defined the same target on different slides).
>
> *Example:*
>
> ```
> \begin{frame}
>   \begin{itemize}
>   \item<1-> First item.
>   \item<2-> Second item.
>   \item<3-> Third item.
>   \end{itemize}
>
>   \hyperlink{jumptosecond}{\beamergotobutton{Jump to second slide}}
>   \hypertarget<2>{jumptosecond}{}
> \end{frame}
> ```

ARTICLE You must say \usepackage[hyperref]{beamerarticle} or \usepackage{hyperref} in your preamble to use this command in article mode.

The \label command creates a hypertarget as a side-effect and the label=⟨*name*⟩ option of the \frame command creates a label named ⟨*name*⟩<⟨*slide number*⟩> for each slide of the frame as a side-effect. Thus the above example could be written more easily as:

```
\begin{frame}[label=threeitems]
  \begin{itemize}
  \item<1-> First item.
  \item<2-> Second item.
  \item<3-> Third item.
  \end{itemize}

  \hyperlink{threeitems<2>}{\beamergotobutton{Jump to second slide}}
\end{frame}
```

The following commands can be used to specify in an abstract way what a button will be used for.

\beamerbutton{⟨*button text*⟩}

> Draws a button with the given ⟨*button text*⟩.
>
> *Example:* \hyperlink{somewhere}{\beamerbutton{Go somewhere}}

ARTICLE This command (and the following) just insert their argument in article mode.

Beamer-Template/-Color/-Font `button`

When the `\beamerbutton` command is called, this template is used to render the button. Inside the template you can use the command `\insertbuttontext` to insert the argument that was passed to `\beamerbutton`.

The following template options are predefined:

- [`default`] Typesets the button with rounded corners. The fore- and background of the BEAMER-color `button` are used and also the BEAMER-font `button`. The border of the button gets the foreground of the BEAMER-color `button border`.

The following inserts are useful for this element:

- `\insertbuttontext` inserts the text of the current button. Inside "Goto-Buttons" (see below) this text is prefixed by the insert `\insertgotosymbol` and similarly for skip and return buttons.
- `\insertgotosymbol` This text is inserted at the beginning of goto buttons. Redefine this command to change the symbol.

  Example: `\renewcommand{\insertgotosymbol}{\somearrowcommand}`
- `\insertskipsymbol` This text is inserted at the beginning of skip buttons.
- `\insertreturnsymbol` This text is inserted at the beginning of return buttons.

Beamer-Color `button border`

The foreground of this color is used to render the border of buttons.

`\beamergotobutton{`⟨*button text*⟩`}`

Draws a button with the given ⟨*button text*⟩. Before the text, a small symbol (usually a right-pointing arrow) is inserted that indicates that pressing this button will jump to another "area" of the presentation.

Example: `\hyperlink{detour}{\beamergotobutton{Go to detour}}`

`\beamerskipbutton{`⟨*button text*⟩`}`

The symbol drawn for this button is usually a double right arrow. Use this button if pressing it will skip over a well-defined part of your talk.

Example:

```
\frame{
  \begin{theorem}
    ...
  \end{theorem}

  \begin{overprint}
  \onslide<1>
    \hfill\hyperlinkframestartnext{\beamerskipbutton{Skip proof}}
  \onslide<2>
    \begin{proof}
      ...
    \end{proof}
  \end{overprint}
}
```

`\beamerreturnbutton{`⟨*button text*⟩`}`

The symbol drawn for this button is usually a left-pointing arrow. Use this button if pressing it will return from a detour.

Example:

```
\frame<1>[label=mytheorem]
{
  \begin{theorem}
```

```
        ...
      \end{theorem}

      \begin{overprint}
      \onslide<1>
        \hfill\hyperlink{mytheorem<2>}{\beamergotobutton{Go to proof details}}
      \onslide<2>
        \begin{proof}
          ...
        \end{proof}
        \hfill\hyperlink{mytheorem<1>}{\beamerreturnbutton{Return}}
      \end{overprint}
    }
    \appendix
    \againframe<2>{mytheorem}
```

To make a button "clickable" you must place it in a command like \hyperlink. The command \hyperlink is a standard command of the hyperref package. The BEAMER class defines a whole bunch of other hyperlink commands that you can also use.

\hyperlink<⟨*overlay specification*⟩>{⟨*target name*⟩}{⟨*link text*⟩}<⟨*overlay specification*⟩>

> Only one ⟨*overlay specification*⟩ may be given. The ⟨*link text*⟩ is typeset in the usual way. If you click anywhere on this text, you will jump to the slide on which the \hypertarget command was used with the parameter ⟨*target name*⟩. If an ⟨*overlay specification*⟩ is present, the hyperlink (including the ⟨*link text*⟩) is completely suppressed on the non-specified slides.

The following commands have a predefined target; otherwise they behave exactly like \hyperlink. In particular, they all also accept an overlay specification and they also accept it at the end, rather than at the beginning.

\hyperlinkslideprev<⟨*overlay specification*⟩>{⟨*link text*⟩}

> Clicking the text jumps one slide back.

\hyperlinkslidenext<⟨*overlay specification*⟩>{⟨*link text*⟩}

> Clicking the text jumps one slide forward.

\hyperlinkframestart<⟨*overlay specification*⟩>{⟨*link text*⟩}

> Clicking the text jumps to the first slide of the current frame.

\hyperlinkframeend<⟨*overlay specification*⟩>{⟨*link text*⟩}

> Clicking the text jumps to the last slide of the current frame.

\hyperlinkframestartnext<⟨*overlay specification*⟩>{⟨*link text*⟩}

> Clicking the text jumps to the first slide of the next frame.

\hyperlinkframeendprev<⟨*overlay specification*⟩>{⟨*link text*⟩}

> Clicking the text jumps to the last slide of the previous frame.

The previous four command exist also with "frame" replaced by "subsection" everywhere, and also again with "frame" replaced by "section".

\hyperlinkpresentationstart<⟨*overlay specification*⟩>{⟨*link text*⟩}

> Clicking the text jumps to the first slide of the presentation.

\hyperlinkpresentationend<⟨*overlay specification*⟩>{⟨*link text*⟩}

> Clicking the text jumps to the last slide of the presentation. This *excludes* the appendix.

106

\hyperlinkappendixstart<⟨*overlay specification*⟩>{⟨*link text*⟩}

> Clicking the text jumps to the first slide of the appendix. If there is no appendix, this will jump to the last slide of the document.

\hyperlinkappendixend<⟨*overlay specification*⟩>{⟨*link text*⟩}

> Clicking the text jumps to the last slide of the appendix.

\hyperlinkdocumentstart<⟨*overlay specification*⟩>{⟨*link text*⟩}

> Clicking the text jumps to the first slide of the presentation.

\hyperlinkdocumentend<⟨*overlay specification*⟩>{⟨*link text*⟩}

> Clicking the text jumps to the last slide of the presentation or, if an appendix is present, to the last slide of the appendix.

11.2 Repeating a Frame at a Later Point

Sometimes you may wish some slides of a frame to be shown in your main talk, but wish some "supplementary" slides of the frame to be shown only in the appendix. In this case, the \againframe command is useful.

\againframe<⟨*overlay specification*⟩>[<⟨*default overlay specification*⟩>] [⟨*options*⟩]{⟨*name*⟩}

PRESEN-
TATION
Resumes a frame that was previously created using \frame with the option label=⟨*name*⟩. You must have used this option, just placing a label inside a frame "by hand" is not enough. You can use this command to "continue" a frame that has been interrupted by another frame. The effect of this command is to call the \frame command with the given ⟨*overlay specification*⟩, ⟨*default overlay specification*⟩ (if present), and ⟨*options*⟩ (if present) and with the original frame's contents.

Example:

```
\frame<1-2>[label=myframe]
{
  \begin{itemize}
  \item<alert@1> First subject.
  \item<alert@2> Second subject.
  \item<alert@3> Third subject.
  \end{itemize}
}

\frame
{
  Some stuff explaining more on the second matter.
}

\againframe<3>{myframe}
```

The effect of the above code is to create four slides. In the first two, the items 1 and 2 are highlighted. The third slide contains the text "Some stuff explaining more on the second matter." The fourth slide is identical to the first two slides, except that the third point is now highlighted.

Example:

```
\frame<1>[label=Cantor]
{
  \frametitle{Main Theorem}

  \begin{Theorem}
    $\alpha < 2^\alpha$ for all ordinals~$\alpha$.
  \end{Theorem}
```

```
\begin{overprint}
\onslide<1>
  \hyperlink{Cantor<2>}{\beamergotobutton{Proof details}}

\onslide<2->
   % this is only shown in the appendix, where this frame is resumed.
   \begin{proof}
     As shown by Cantor, ...
   \end{proof}

   \hfill\hyperlink{Cantor<1>}{\beamerreturnbutton{Return}}
  \end{overprint}
}


...
\appendix

\againframe<2>{Cantor}
```

In this example, the proof details are deferred to a slide in the appendix. Hyperlinks are setup, so that one can jump to the proof and go back.

ARTICLE This command is ignored in `article` mode.

11.3 Adding Anticipated Zooming

Anticipated zooming is necessary when you have a very complicated graphic that you are not willing to simplify since, indeed, all the complex details merit an explanation. In this case, use the command \framezoom. It allows you to specify that clicking on a certain area of a frame should zoom out this area. You can then explain the details. Clicking on the zoomed out picture will take you back to the original one.

\framezoom<⟨*button overlay specification*⟩><⟨*zoomed overlay specification*⟩>[⟨*options*⟩]
(⟨*upper left x*⟩,⟨*upper left y*⟩)(⟨*zoom area width*⟩,⟨*zoom area depth*⟩)

This command should be given somewhere at the beginning of a frame. When given, two different things will happen, depending on whether the ⟨*button overlay specification*⟩ applies to the current slide of the frame or whether the ⟨*zoomed overlay specification*⟩ applies. These overlay specifications should not overlap.

If the ⟨*button overlay specification*⟩ applies, a clickable area is created inside the frame. The size of this area is given by ⟨*zoom area width*⟩ and ⟨*zoom area depth*⟩, which are two normal TEX dimensions (like 1cm or 20pt). The upper left corner of this area is given by ⟨*upper left x*⟩ and ⟨*upper left y*⟩, which are also TEX dimensions. They are measures *relative to the place where the first normal text of a frame would go*. Thus, the location (0pt,0pt) is at the beginning of the normal text (which excludes the headline and also the frame title).

By default, the button is clickable, but it will not be indicated in any special way. You can draw a border around the button by using the following ⟨*option*⟩:

- border=⟨*width in pixels*⟩ will draw a border around the specified button area. The default width is 1 pixel. The color of this button is the `linkbordercolor` of `hyperref`. BEAMER sets this color to a 50% gray by default. To change this, you can use the command \hypersetup{linkbordercolor={⟨*red*⟩ ⟨*green*⟩ ⟨*b* where ⟨*red*⟩, ⟨*green*⟩, and ⟨*blue*⟩ are values between 0 and 1.

When you press the button created in this way, the viewer application will hyperjump to the first of the frames specified by the ⟨*zoomed overlay specification*⟩. For the slides to which this overlay specification applies, the following happens:

The exact same area as the one specified before is "zoomed out" to fill the whole normal text area of the frame. Everything else, including the sidebars, the headlines and footlines, and even the frame title retain their normal size. The zooming is performed in such a way that the whole specified area is completely shown. The aspect ratio is kept correct and the zoomed area will possibly show more than just the specified area if the aspect ratio of this area and the aspect ratio of the available text area do not agree.

Behind the whole text area (which contains the zoomed area) a big invisible "Back" button is put. Thus clicking anywhere on the text area will jump back to the original (unzoomed) picture.

You can specify several zoom areas for a single frame. In this case, you should specify different ⟨zoomed overlay specification⟩, but you can specify the same ⟨button overlay specification⟩. You cannot nest zoomings in the sense that you cannot have a zoom button on a slide that is in some ⟨zoomed overlay specification⟩. However, you can have overlapping and even nested ⟨button overlay specification⟩. When clicking on an area that belongs to several buttons, the one given last will "win" (it should hence be the smallest one).

If you do not wish to have the frame title shown on a zoomed slide, you can add an overlay specification to the \frametitle command that simply suppresses the title for the slide. Also, by using the plain option, you can have the zoomed slide fill the whole page.

Example: A simple case

```
\begin{frame}
  \frametitle{A Complicated Picture}

  \framezoom<1><2>(0cm,0cm)(2cm,1.5cm)
  \framezoom<1><3>(1cm,3cm)(2cm,1.5cm)
  \framezoom<1><4>(3cm,2cm)(3cm,2cm)

  \pgfimage[height=8cm]{complicatedimagefilename}
\end{frame}
```

Example: A more complicate case in which the zoomed parts completely fill the frames.

```
\begin{frame}<1>[label=zooms]
  \frametitle<1>{A Complicated Picture}

  \framezoom<1><2>[border](0cm,0cm)(2cm,1.5cm)
  \framezoom<1><3>[border](1cm,3cm)(2cm,1.5cm)
  \framezoom<1><4>[border](3cm,2cm)(3cm,2cm)

  \pgfimage[height=8cm]{complicatedimagefilename}
\end{frame}
\againframe<2->[plain]{zooms}
```

12 Structuring a Presentation: The Local Structure

LaTeX provides different commands for structuring text "locally," for example, via the itemize environment. These environments are also available in the BEAMER class, although their appearance has been slightly changed. Furthermore, the BEAMER class also defines some new commands and environments, see below, that may help you to structure your text.

12.1 Itemizations, Enumerations, and Descriptions

There are three predefined environments for creating lists, namely enumerate, itemize, and description. The first two can be nested to depth three, but nesting them to this depth creates totally unreadable slides.

The \item command is overlay specification-aware. If an overlay specification is provided, the item will only be shown on the specified slides, see the following example. If the \item command is to take an optional argument and an overlay specification, the overlay specification can either come first as in \item<1>[Cat] or come last as in \item[Cat]<1>.

```
\begin{frame}
  There are three important points:
  \begin{enumerate}
  \item<1-> A first one,
  \item<2-> a second one with a bunch of subpoints,
    \begin{itemize}
    \item first subpoint. (Only shown from second slide on!).
    \item<3-> second subpoint added on third slide.
    \item<4-> third subpoint added on fourth slide.
    \end{itemize}
  \item<5-> and a third one.
  \end{enumerate}
\end{frame}
```

\begin{itemize}[<⟨default overlay specification⟩>]
  ⟨environment contents⟩
\end{itemize}

Used to display a list of items that do not have a special ordering. Inside the environment, use an \item command for each topic.

If the optional parameter ⟨default overlay specification⟩ is given, in every occurrence of an \item command that does not have an overlay specification attached to it, the ⟨default overlay specification⟩ is used. By setting this specification to be an incremental overlay specification, see Section 9.6.4, you can implement, for example, a step-wise uncovering of the items. The ⟨default overlay specification⟩ is inherited by subenvironments. Naturally, in a subenvironment you can reset it locally by setting it to <1->.

Example:

```
\begin{itemize}
\item This is important.
\item This is also important.
\end{itemize}
```

Example:

```
\begin{itemize}[<+->]
\item This is shown from the first slide on.
\item This is shown from the second slide on.
\item This is shown from the third slide on.
\item<1-> This is shown from the first slide on.
\item This is shown from the fourth slide on.
\end{itemize}
```

Example:

```
\begin{itemize}[<+-| alert@+>]
```

```
\item This is shown from the first slide on and alerted on the first slide.
\item This is shown from the second slide on and alerted on the second slide.
\item This is shown from the third slide on and alerted on the third slide.
\end{itemize}
```

Example:

```
\newenvironment{mystepwiseitemize}{\begin{itemize}[<+-| alert@+>]}{\end{itemize}}
```

The appearance of an `itemize` list is governed by several templates. The first template concerns the way the little marker introducing each item is typeset:

Parent Beamer-Template `itemize items`

This template is a parent template, whose children are `itemize item`, `itemize subitem`, and `itemize subsubitem`. This means that if you use the `\setbeamertemplate` command on this template, the command is instead called for all of these children (with the same arguments).

The following template options are predefined:

- [default] The default item marker is a small triangle colored with the foreground of the BEAMER-color `itemize item` (or, for subitems, `itemize subitem` etc.). Note that these colors will automatically change under certain circumstances such as inside an example block or inside an `alertenv` environment.
- [triangle] Alias for the default.
- [circle] Uses little circles (or dots) as item markers.
- [square] Uses little squares as item markers.
- [ball] Uses little balls as item markers.

Beamer-Template/-Color/-Font `itemize item`

Color/font parents: `item`

This template (with `item` instead of `items`) governs how the marker in front of a first-level item is typeset. "First-level" refers to the level of nesting. See the `itemize items` template for the ⟨*options*⟩ that may be given.

When the template is inserted, the BEAMER-font and -color `itemize item` is installed. Typically, the font is ignored by the template as some special symbol is drawn anyway, by the font may be important if an optional argument is given to the `\item` command as in `\item[First]`.

The font and color inherit from the `item` font and color, which are explained at the end of this section.

Beamer-Template/-Color/-Font `itemize subitem`

Color/font parents: `subitem`

Like `itemize item`, only for second-level items. An item of an itemize inside an enumerate counts as a second-level item.

Beamer-Template/-Color/-Font `itemize subsubitem`

Color/font parents: `subsubitem`

Like `itemize item`, only for third-level items.

`\begin{enumerate}`[<⟨*default overlay specification*⟩>] [⟨*mini template*⟩]
  ⟨*environment contents*⟩
`\end{enumerate}`

Used to display a list of items that are ordered. Inside the environment, use an `\item` command for each topic. By default, before each item increasing Arabic numbers followed by a dot are printed (as in "1." and "2."). This can be changed by specifying a different template, see below.

The first optional argument ⟨*default overlay specification*⟩ has exactly the same effect as for the `itemize` environment. It is "detected" by the opening `<`-sign in the ⟨*default overlay specification*⟩. Thus, if there is only one optional argument and if this argument does not start with `<`, then it is considered to be a ⟨*mini template*⟩.

The syntax of the ⟨mini template⟩ is the same as the syntax of mini templates in the enumerate package (you do not need to include the enumerate package, this is done automatically). Roughly spoken, the text of the ⟨mini template⟩ is printed before each item, but any occurrence of a 1 in the mini template is replaced by the current item number, an occurrence of the letter A is replaced by the i-th letter of the alphabet (in uppercase) for the i-th item, and the letters a, i, and I are replaced by the corresponding lowercase letters, lowercase Roman letters, and uppercase Roman letters, respectively. So the mini template (i) would yield the items (i), (ii), (iii), (iv), and so on. The mini template A.) would yield the items A.), B.), C.), D.) and so on. For more details on the possible mini templates, see the documentation of the enumerate package. Note that there is also a template that governs the appearance of the mini template.

Example:
```
\begin{enumerate}
\item This is important.
\item This is also important.
\end{enumerate}

\begin{enumerate}[(i)]
\item First Roman point.
\item Second Roman point.
\end{enumerate}

\begin{enumerate}[<+->][(i)]
\item First Roman point.
\item Second Roman point, uncovered on second slide.
\end{enumerate}
```

ARTICLE   To use the ⟨mini template⟩, you have to include the package enumerate.

Parent Beamer-Template enumerate items

Similar to itemize items, this template is a parent template, whose children are enumerate item, enumerate subitem, enumerate subsubitem, and enumerate mini template. These templates govern how the text (the number) of an enumeration is typeset.

The following template options are predefined:

- [default] The default enumeration marker uses the scheme 1., 2., 3. for the first level, 1.1, 1.2, 1.3 for the second level and 1.1.1, 1.1.2, 1.1.3 for the third level.
- [circle] Places the numbers inside little circles. The colors are taken from item projected or subitem projected or subsubitem projected.
- [square] Places the numbers on little squares.
- [ball] "Projects" the numbers onto little balls.

Beamer-Template/-Color/-Font enumerate item

This template governs how the number in front of a first-level item is typeset. The level here refers to the level of enumeration nesting only. Thus an enumerate inside an itemize is a first-level enumerate (but it uses the second-level itemize/enumerate body).

When the template is inserted, the BEAMER-font and -color enumerate item are installed.

The following command is useful for this template:

- \insertenumlabel inserts the current number of the top-level enumeration (as an Arabic number). This insert is also available in the next two templates.

Beamer-Template/-Color/-Font enumerate subitem

Like enumerate item, only for second-level items.

- \insertsubenumlabel inserts the current number of the second-level enumeration (as an Arabic number).

Example:
```
\setbeamertemplate{enumerate subitem}{\insertenumlabel-\insertsubenumlabel}
```

Beamer-Template/-Color/-Font `enumerate subsubitem`

Like `enumerate item`, only for third-level items.

- `\insertsubsubenumlabel` inserts the current number of the second-level enumeration (as an Arabic number).

Beamer-Template/-Color/-Font `enumerate mini template`

This template is used to typeset the number that arises from a mini template.

- `\insertenumlabel` inserts the current number rendered by this mini template. For example, if the ⟨*mini template*⟩ is (i) and this command is used in the fourth item, `\insertenumlabel` would yield (iv).

The following templates govern how the *body* of an `itemize` or an `enumerate` is typeset.

Beamer-Template `itemize/enumerate body begin`

This template is inserted at the beginning of a first-level `itemize` or `enumerate` environment. Furthermore, before this template is inserted, the BEAMER-font and -color `itemize/enumerate body` is used.

Beamer-Template `itemize/enumerate body end`

This template is inserted at the end of a first-level `itemize` or `enumerate` environment.

There exist corresponding templates like `itemize/enumerate subbody begin` for second- and third-level itemize or enumerates.

Parent Beamer-Template `items`

This template is a parent template of `itemize items` and `enumerate items`.

Example: `\setbeamertemplate{items}[circle]` will cause all items in `itemize` or `enumerate` environments to become circles (of the appropriate size, color, and font).

`\begin{description}`[<⟨*default overlay specification*⟩>] [⟨*long text*⟩]
  ⟨*environment contents*⟩
`\end{description}`

Like `itemize`, but used to display a list that explains or defines labels. The width of ⟨*long text*⟩ is used to set the indentation. Normally, you choose the widest label in the description and copy it here. If you do not give this argument, the default width is used, which can be changed using `\setbeamersize` with the argument `description width=`⟨*width*⟩.

As for `enumerate`, the ⟨*default overlay specification*⟩ is detected by an opening <. The effect is the same as for `enumerate` and `itemize`.

Example:
```
\begin{description}
\item[Lion] King of the savanna.
\item[Tiger] King of the jungle.
\end{description}
```

```
\begin{description}[longest label]
\item<1->[short] Some text.
\item<2->[longest label] Some text.
\item<3->[long label] Some text.
\end{description}
```

Example: The following has the same effect as the previous example:
```
\begin{description}[<+->][longest label]
\item[short] Some text.
\item[longest label] Some text.
\item[long label] Some text.
\end{description}
```

Beamer-Template/-Color/-Font `description item`

> This template is used to typeset the description items. When this template is called, the BEAMER-font and -color `description item` are installed.
>
> The following template options are predefined:
>
> - [default] By default, the description item text is just inserted without any modification.
>
> The main insert that is useful inside this template is:
>
> - `\insertdescriptionitem` inserts the text of the current description item.

In order to simplify changing the color or font of items, the different kinds of items inherit from or just use the following "general" BEAMER-color and fonts:

Beamer-Color/-Font `item`

> Color parents: `local structure`
>
> Font parents: `structure`
>
> This color/font serves as a parent for the individual items of `itemize` and `enumerate` environments, but also for items in the table of contents. Since its color parent is the `local structure`, a change of that color causes the color of items to change accordingly.

Beamer-Color/-Font `item projected`

> Color/font parents: `item`
>
> This is a special "version" of the `item` color and font that should be used by templates that render items with text (as in an enumeration) and which "project" this text onto something like a ball or a square or whatever. While the normal `item` color typically has a transparent background, the `item projected` typically has a colored background and, say, a white foreground.

Beamer-Color/-Font `subitem`

> Color/font parents: `item`
>
> Same as `item` for subitems, that is, for items on the second level of indentation.

Beamer-Color/-Font `subitem projected`

> Color/font parents: `item projected`
>
> Same as `item projected` for subitems, that is, for items on the second level of indentation.

Beamer-Color/-Font `subsubitem`

> Color/font parents: `subitem`
>
> Same as `subitem` for subsubitems, that is, for items on the third level of indentation.

Beamer-Color/-Font `subsubitem projected`

> Color/font parents: `subitem projected`
>
> Same as `subitem projected` for subsubitems, that is, for items on the third level of indentation.

12.2 Highlighting

The BEAMER class predefines commands and environments for highlighting text. Using these commands makes it easy to change the appearance of a document by changing the theme.

`\structure<`⟨*overlay specification*⟩`>{`⟨*text*⟩`}`

> The given text is marked as part of the structure, that is, it is supposed to help the audience see the structure of your presentation. If the ⟨*overlay specification*⟩ is present, the command only has an effect on the specified slides.
>
> *Example:* `\structure{Paragraph Heading.}`
>
> Internally, this command just puts the *text* inside a `structureenv` environment.

ARTICLE Structure text is typeset as bold text. This can be changed by modifying the templates.

Beamer-Color/-Font `structure`

> This color/font is used when structured text is typeset, but it is also widely used as a base for many other colors including the headings of blocks, item buttons, and titles. In most color themes, the colors for navigational elements in the headline or the footline are derived from the foreground color of `structure`. By changing the structure color you can easily change the "basic color" of your presentation, other than the color of normal text. See also the related color `local structure` and the related font `tiny structure`.
>
> Inside the `\structure` command, the background of the color is ignored, but this is not necessarily true for elements that inherit their color from `structure`. There is no template `structure`, use `structure begin` and `structure end` instead.

Beamer-Color `local structure`

> This color should be used to typeset structural elements that change their color according to the "local environment." For example, an item "button" in an `itemize` environment changes its color according to circumstances. If it is used inside an example block, it should have the `example text` color; if it is currently "alerted" it should have the `alerted text` color. This color is setup by certain environments to have the color that should be used to typset things like item buttons. Since the color used for items, `item`, inherits from this color by default, items automatically change their color according to the current situation.
>
> If you write your own environment in which the item buttons and similar structural elements should have a different color, you should change the color `local structure` inside these environments.

Beamer-Font `tiny structure`

> This special font is used for "tiny" structural text. Basically, this font should be used whenever a structural element uses a tiny font. The idea is that the tiny versions of the `structure` font often are not suitable. For example, it is often necessary to use a boldface version for them. Also, one might wish to have serif smallcaps structural text, but still retain normal sans-serif tiny structural text.

`\begin{structureenv}<`*⟨overlay specification⟩*`>`
  ⟨environment contents⟩
`\end{structureenv}`

> Environment version of the `\structure` command.

Beamer-Template `structure begin`

> This text is inserted at the beginning of a `structureenv` environment.
>
> The following template options are predefined:
>
> - `[default]`
>
> ARTICLE The text is typeset in boldface.

Beamer-Template `structure end`

> This text is inserted at the end of a `structureenv` environment.

`\alert<`*⟨overlay specification⟩*`>{`*⟨highlighted text⟩*`}`

> The given text is highlighted, typically by coloring the text red. If the *⟨overlay specification⟩* is present, the command only has an effect on the specified slides.
>
> *Example:* `This is \alert{important}.`
>
> Internally, this command just puts the *highlighted text* inside an `alertenv`.

ARTICLE Alerted text is typeset as emphasized text. This can be changed by modifying the templates, see below.

Beamer-Color/-Font `alerted text`

> This color/font is used when alerted text is typeset. The background is currently ignored. There is no template `alerted text`, rather there are templates `alerted text begin` and `alerted text end` that are inserted before and after alerted text.

`\begin{alertenv}<`*⟨overlay specification⟩*`>`
    ⟨environment contents⟩
`\end{alertenv}`

Environment version of the `\alert` command.

Beamer-Template `alerted text begin`

This text is inserted at the beginning of a an `alertenv` environment.

The following template options are predefined:

- [`default`]

PRESEN-
TATION
This changes the color `local structure` to `alerted text`. This causes things like buttons or items to be colored in the same color as the alerted text, which is often visually pleasing. See also the `\structure` command.

ARTICLE The text is emphasized.

Beamer-Template `alerted text end`

This text is inserted at the end of an `alertenv` environment.

12.3 Block Environments

The BEAMER class predefines an environment for typesetting a "block" of text that has a heading. The appearance of blocks can easily be changed using the following template:

Parent Beamer-Template `blocks`

Changing this parent template changes the templates of normal blocks, alerted blocks, and example blocks.

Example: `\setbeamertemplate{blocks}[default]`

Example: `\setbeamertemplate{blocks}[rounded][shadow=true]`

The following template options are predefined:

- [`default`] The default setting typesets the block title on its own line. If a background is specified either for the `block title` or for the `block body`, this background color is used as background of the title or body, respectively. For alerted and example blocks, the corresponding BEAMER-colors and -fonts are used, instead.

- [`rounded`] [*⟨shadow=true⟩*] Makes the blocks "rounded." This means that the corners of the backgrounds of the blocks are "rounded off." If the `shadow=true` option is given, a "shadow" is drawn behind the block.

`\begin{block}<`*⟨action specification⟩*`>{`*⟨block title⟩*`}<`*⟨action specification⟩*`>`
    ⟨environment contents⟩
`\end{block}`

Only one *⟨action specification⟩* may be given. Inserts a block, like a definition or a theorem, with the title *⟨block title⟩*. If the *⟨action specification⟩* is present, the given actions are taken on the specified slides, see Section 9.6.3. In the example, the definition is shown only from slide 3 onward.

Example:
```
\begin{block}<3->{Definition}
  A \alert{set} consists of elements.
\end{block}
```

ARTICLE The block name is typeset in bold.

Beamer-Template `block begin`

This template is inserted at the beginning of a block before the *⟨environment contents⟩*. Inside this template, the block title can be accessed via the following insert:

116

- \insertblocktitle Inserts the ⟨*block title*⟩ into the template.

When the template starts, no special color or font is installed (for somewhat complicated reasons). Thus, this template should install the correct colors and fonts for the title and the body itself.

Beamer-Template `block end`

This template is inserted at the end of a block.

Beamer-Color/-Font `block title`

This BEAMER-color/-font should be used to typeset the title of the block. Since neither the color nor the font are setup automatically, the template `block begin` must do so itself.

The default block template and also the `rounded` version honor the background of this color.

Beamer-Color/-Font `block body`

This BEAMER-color/-font should be used to typeset the body of the block, that is, the ⟨*environment contents*⟩. As for `block title`, the color and font must be setup by the template `block begin`.

\begin{alertblock}<⟨*action specification*⟩>{⟨*block title*⟩}<⟨*action specification*⟩>
  ⟨*environment contents*⟩
\end{alertblock}

Inserts a block whose title is highlighting. Behaves like the `block` environment otherwise.

Example:

```
\begin{alertblock}{Wrong Theorem}
$1=2$.
\end{alertblock}
```

ARTICLE The block name is typeset in bold and is emphasized.

Beamer-Template `block alerted begin`
Same applies as for normal blocks.

Beamer-Template `block alerted end`
Same applies as for normal blocks.

Beamer-Color/-Font `block title alerted`
Same applies as for normal blocks.

Beamer-Color/-Font `block body alerted`
Same applies as for normal blocks.

\begin{exampleblock}<⟨*action specification*⟩>{⟨*block title*⟩}<⟨*overlay specification*⟩>
  ⟨*environment contents*⟩
\end{exampleblock}

Inserts a block that is supposed to be an example. Behaves like the `block` environment otherwise.

Example: In the following example, the block is completely suppressed on the first slide (it does not even occupy any space).

```
\begin{exampleblock}{Example}<only@2->
The set $\{1,2,3,5\}$ has four elements.
\end{exampleblock}
```

ARTICLE The block name is typeset in italics.

Beamer-Template `block example begin`
Same applies as for normal blocks.

Beamer-Template `block example end`
Same applies as for normal blocks.

Beamer-Color/-Font `block title example`

Same applies as for normal blocks.

Beamer-Color/-Font `block body example`

Same applies as for normal blocks.

12.4 Theorem Environments

The BEAMER class predefines several environments, like `theorem` or `definition` or `proof`, that you can use to typeset things like, well, theorems, definitions, or proofs. The complete list is the following: `theorem`, `corollary`, `definition`, `definitions`, `fact`, `example`, and `examples`. The following German block environments are also predefined: `Problem`, `Loesung`, `Definition`, `Satz`, `Beweis`, `Folgerung`, `Lemma`, `Fakt`, `Beispiel`, and `Beispiele`.

Here is a typical example on how to use them:

```
\begin{frame}
  \frametitle{A Theorem on Infinite Sets}

  \begin{theorem}<1->
    There exists an infinite set.
  \end{theorem}

  \begin{proof}<2->
    This follows from the axiom of infinity.
  \end{proof}

  \begin{example}<3->[Natural Numbers]
    The set of natural numbers is infinite.
  \end{example}
\end{frame}
```

In the following, only the English versions are discussed. The German ones behave analogously.

`\begin{theorem}`<⟨*action specification*⟩>[⟨*additional text*⟩]<⟨*action specification*⟩>
⟨*environment contents*⟩
`\end{theorem}`

Inserts a theorem. Only one ⟨*action specification*⟩ may be given. If present, the ⟨*additional text*⟩ is shown behind the word "Theorem" in rounded brackets (although this can be changed by the template).

The appearance of the theorem is governed by the templates `theorem begin` and `theorem end`, see their description later on for details on how to change these. Every theorem is put into a `block` environment, thus the templates for blocks also apply.

The theorem style (a concept from `amsthm`) used for this environment is `plain`. In this style, the body of a theorem should be typeset in italics. The head of the theorem should be typeset in a bold font, but this is usually overruled by the templates.

If the option `envcountsect` is given either as class option in one of the `presentation` modes or as an option to the package `beamerarticle` in `article` mode, then the numbering of the theorems is local to each section with the section number prefixing the theorem number; otherwise they are numbered consecutively throughout the presentation or article. We recommend using this option in `article` mode.

By default, no theorem numbers are shown in the `presentation` modes.

Example:

```
\begin{theorem}[Kummer, 1992]
  If $\#^_A^n$ is $n$-enumerable, then $A$ is recursive.
\end{theorem}

\begin{theorem}<2->[Tantau, 2002]
  If $\#_A^2$ is $2$-fa-enumerable, then $A$ is regular.
\end{theorem}
```

The environments `corollary`, `fact`, and `lemma` behave exactly the same way.

`\documentclass[envcountsect]{beamer}`

Causes theorems, definitions, and so on to be numbered locally to each section. Thus, the first theorem of the second section would be Theorem 2.1 (assuming that there are no definitions, lemmas, or corollaries earlier in the section).

`\begin{definition}<`⟨*action specification*⟩`>[`⟨*additional text*⟩`]<`⟨*action specification*⟩`>`
⟨*environment contents*⟩
`\end{definition}`

Behaves like the `theorem` environment, except that the theorem style `definition` is used. In this style, the body of a theorem is typeset in an upright font.

The environment `definitions` behaves exactly the same way.

`\begin{example}<`⟨*action specification*⟩`>[`⟨*additional text*⟩`]<`⟨*action specification*⟩`>`
⟨*environment contents*⟩
`\end{example}`

Behaves like the `theorem` environment, except that the theorem style `example` is used. A side-effect of using this theorem style is that the ⟨*environment contents*⟩ is put in an `exampleblock` instead of a `block`.

The environment `examples` behaves exactly the same way.

The default template for typesetting theorems suppresses the theorem number, even if this number is "available" for typesetting (which it is by default in all predefined environments; but if you define your own environment using `\newtheorem*` no number will be available).

In `article` mode, theorems are automatically numbered. By specifying the class option `envcountsect`, theorems will be numbered locally to each section, which is usually a good idea, except for very short articles.

`\begin{proof}<`⟨*action specification*⟩`>[`⟨*proof name*⟩`]<`⟨*action specification*⟩`>`
⟨*environment contents*⟩
`\end{proof}`

Typesets a proof. If the optional ⟨*proof name*⟩ is given, it completely replaces the word "Proof." This is different from normal theorems, where the optional argument is shown in brackets.

At the end of the theorem, a `\qed` symbol is shown, except if you say `\qedhere` earlier in the proof (this is exactly as in `amsthm`). The default `\qed` symbol is an open circle. To completely suppress the symbol, write `\def\qedsymbol{}` in your preamble. To get a closed square, say

`\setbeamertemplate{qed symbol}{\vrule width1.5ex height1.5ex depth0pt}`

If you use `babel` and a different language, the text "Proof" is replaced by whatever is appropriate in the selected language.

Example:
```
\begin{proof}<2->[Sketch of proof]
  Suppose ...
\end{proof}
```

Beamer-Template/-Color/-Font `qed symbol`

The symbol is shown at the end of every proof.

You can define new environments using the following command:

`\newtheorem*{`⟨*environment name*⟩`}[`⟨*numbered same as*⟩`]{`⟨*head text*⟩`}[`⟨*number within*⟩`]`

This command is used exactly the same way as in the `amsthm` package (as a matter of fact, it is the command from that package), see its documentation. The only difference is that environments declared using this

119

command are overlay specification-aware in BEAMER and that, when typeset, are typeset according to BEAMER's templates.

ARTICLE Environments declared using this command are also overlay specification-aware in `article` mode.

Example: `\newtheorem{observation}[theorem]{Observation}`

You can also use `amsthm`'s command `\newtheoremstyle` to define new theorem styles. Note that the default template for theorems will ignore any head font setting, but will honor the body font setting.

If you wish to define the environments like `theorem` differently (for example, have it numbered within each subsection), you can use the following class option to disable the definition of the predefined environments:

`\documentclass[notheorems]{beamer}`

Switches off the definition of default blocks like `theorem`, but still loads `amsthm` and makes theorems overlay specification-aware.

The option is also available as a package option for `beamerarticle` and has the same effect.

ICLE In the `article` version, the package `amsthm` sometimes clashes with the document class. In this case you can use the following option, which is once more available as a class option for BEAMER and as a package option for `beamerarticle`, to switch off the loading of `amsthm` altogether.

`\documentclass[noamsthm]{beamer}`

Does not load `amsthm` and also not `amsmath`. Environments like `theorem` or `proof` will not be available.

`\documentclass[noamssymb]{beamer}`

Does not load `amssymb`. This option is mainly intended for users who are loading specialist font packages. Note that `\blacktriangleright` needs to be defined if `itemize` environments are in use.

Parent Beamer-Template theorems

This template is a parent of `theorem begin` and `theorem end`, see the first for a detailed discussion of how the theorem templates are set.

Example: `\setbeamertemplate{theorems}[numbered]`

The following template options are predefined:

- [default] By default, theorems are typeset as follows: The font specification for the body is honored, the font specification for the head is ignored. No theorem number is printed.

- [normal font] Like the default, except all font specifications for the body are ignored. Thus, the fonts are used that are normally used for blocks.

- [numbered] This option is like the default, except that the theorem number is printed for environments that are numbered.

- [ams style] This causes theorems to be put in a `block` or `exampleblock`, but to be otherwise typeset as is normally done in `amsthm`. Thus the head font and body font depend on the setting for the theorem to be typeset and theorems are numbered.

Beamer-Template theorem begin

Whenever an environment declared using the command `\newtheorem` is to be typeset, this template is inserted at the beginning and the template `theorem end` at the end. If there is an overlay specification when an environment like `theorem` is used, this overlay specification will directly follow the ⟨*block beginning template*⟩ upon invocation. This is even true if there was an optional argument to the `theorem` environment. This optional argument is available via the insert `\inserttheoremaddition`.

Numerous inserts are available in this template, see below.

Before the template starts, the font is set to the body font prescribed by the environment to be typeset.

Example: The following typesets theorems like `amsthm`:

```
\setbeamertemplate{theorem begin}
{%
  \begin{\inserttheoremblockenv}
  {%
    \inserttheoremheadfont
    \inserttheoremname
    \inserttheoremnumber
    \ifx\inserttheoremaddition\@empty\else\ (\inserttheoremaddition)\fi%
    \inserttheorempunctuation
  }%
}
\setbeamertemplate{theorem end}{\end{\inserttheoremblockenv}}
```

Example: In the following example, all font "suggestions" for the environment are suppressed or ignored; and the theorem number is suppressed.

```
\setbeamertemplate{theorem begin}
{%
  \normalfont% ignore body font
  \begin{\inserttheoremblockenv}
  {%
    \inserttheoremname
    \ifx\inserttheoremaddition\@empty\else\ (\inserttheoremaddition)\fi%
  }%
}
\setbeamertemplate{theorem end}{\end{\inserttheoremblockenv}}
```

The following inserts are available inside this template:

- `\inserttheoremblockenv` This will normally expand to `block`, but if a theorem that has theorem style `example` is typeset, it will expand to `exampleblock`. Thus you can use this insert to decide which environment should be used when typesetting the theorem.

- `\inserttheoremheadfont` This will expand to a font changing command that switches to the font to be used in the head of the theorem. By not inserting it, you can ignore the head font.

- `\inserttheoremname` This will expand to the name of the environment to be typeset (like "Theorem" or "Corollary").

- `\inserttheoremnumber` This will expand to the number of the current theorem preceeded by a space or to nothing, if the current theorem does not have a number.

- `\inserttheoremaddition` This will expand to the optional argument given to the environment or will be empty, if there was no optional argument.

- `\inserttheorempunctuation` This will expand to the punctuation character for the current environment. This is usually a period.

Beamer-Template `theorem end`

Inserted at the end of a theorem.

12.5   Framed and Boxed Text

In order to draw a frame (a rectangle) around some text, you can use LaTeX's standard command `\fbox` and also `\frame` (inside a BEAMER frame, the `\frame` command changes its meaning to the normal LaTeX `\frame` command). More frame types are offered by the package `fancybox`, which defines the following commands: `\shadowbox`, `\doublebox`, `\ovalbox`, and `\Ovalbox`. Please consult the LaTeX Companion for details on how to use these commands.

The BEAMER class also defines two environments for creating colored boxes.

`\begin{beamercolorbox}[⟨options⟩]{⟨beamer color⟩}`

⟨*environment contents*⟩
\end{beamercolorbox}

This environment can be used to conveniently typeset some text using some BEAMER-color. Basically, the following two command blocks do the same:

```
\begin{beamercolorbox}{beamer color}
  Text
\end{beamercolorbox}
```

```
{
  \usebeamercolor{beamer color}
  \colorbox{bg}{
    \color{fg}
    Text
  }
}
```

In other words, the environment installs the ⟨*beamer color*⟩ and uses the background for the background of the box and the foreground for the text inside the box. However, in reality, numerous ⟨*options*⟩ can be given to specify in much greater detail how the box is rendered.

If the background color of ⟨*beamer color*⟩ is empty, no background is drawn behind the text, that is, the background is "transparent."

This command is used extensively by the default inner and outer themes for typesetting the headlines and footlines. It is not really intended to be used in normal frames (for example, it is not available inside `article` mode). You should prefer using structuring elements like blocks or theorems that automatically insert colored boxes as needed.

Example: The following example could be used to typeset a headline with two lines, the first showing the document title, the second showing the author's name:

```
\begin{beamercolorbox}[ht=2.5ex,dp=1ex,center]{title in head/foot}
  \usebeamerfont{title in head/foot}
  \insertshorttitle
\end{beamercolorbox}%
\begin{beamercolorbox}[ht=2.5ex,dp=1ex,center]{author in head/foot}
  \usebeamerfont{author in head/foot}
  \insertshortauthor
\end{beamercolorbox}
```

Example: Typesetting a postit:

```
\setbeamercolor{postit}{fg=black,bg=yellow}
\begin{beamercolorbox}[sep=1em,wd=5cm]{postit}
  Place me somewhere!
\end{beamercolorbox}
```

The following ⟨*options*⟩ can be given:

- wd={⟨*width*⟩} sets the width of the box. This command has two effects: First, TEX's \hsize is set to ⟨*width*⟩. Second, after the box has been typeset, its width is set to ⟨*width*⟩ (no matter what it actually turned out to be). Since setting the \hsize does not automatically change some of LATEX's linewidth dimensions, you should consider using a minipage inside this environment if you fool around with the width.

  If the width is larger than the normal text width, as specified by the value of \textwidth, the width of the resulting box is reset to the width \textwidth, but intelligent negative skips are inserted at the left and right end of the box. The net effect of this is that you can use a width larger than the text width for a box and can insert the resulting box directly into normal text without getting annoying warnings and having the box positioned sensibly.

- dp={⟨*depth*⟩} sets the depth of the box, overriding the real depth of the box. The box is first typeset normally, then the depth is changed afterwards. This option is useful for creating boxes that have guaranteed size.

If the option is not given, the box has its "natural" depth, which results from the typesetting. For example, a box containing only the letter "a" will have a different depth from a box containing only the letter "g."

- `ht=`⟨*height*⟩ sets the height of the box, overriding the real height. Note that the "height" does not include the depth (see, for example, the TEX-book for details). If you want a one-line box that always has the same size, setting the height to 2.25ex and the depth to 1ex is usually a good option.

- `left` causes the text inside the box to be typeset left-aligned and with a (radically) ragged right border. This is the default. To get a better ragged right border, use the `rightskip` option. Note that this will override any `leftskip` or `rightskip` setting.

- `right` causes the text to be right-aligned with a (radically) ragged left border. Note that this will override any `leftskip` or `rightskip` setting.

- `center` centers the text inside the box. Note that this will override any `leftskip` or `rightskip` setting.

- `leftskip=`⟨*left skip*⟩ installs the ⟨*left skip*⟩ inside the box as the left skip. TEX's left skip is a glue that is inserted at the left end of every line. See the TEX-book for details. Note that this will override any `left`, `center` or `right` setting.

- `rightskip=`⟨*right skip*⟩ install the ⟨*right skip*⟩. To get a good ragged right border, try, say, `\rightskip=0pt plus 4em`. Note that this will override any `left`, `center` or `right` setting.

- `sep=`⟨*dimension*⟩ sets the size of extra space around the text. This space is added "inside the box," which means that if you specify a `sep` of 1cm and insert the box normally into the vertical list, then the left border of the box will be aligned with the left border of the slide text, while the left border of the text inside the box will be 1cm to the right of this left border. Likewise, the text inside the box will stop 1cm before the right border of the normal text.

- `colsep=`⟨*dimension*⟩ sets the extra "color separation space" around the text. This space behaves the same way as the space added by `sep`, only this space is only inserted if the box has a colored background, that is, if the background of the ⟨*beamer color*⟩ is not empty. This command can be used together with `sep`, the effects accumulate.

- `colsep*=`⟨*dimension*⟩ sets an extra color separation space around the text that is *horizontally outside the box*. This means that if the box has a background, this background will protrude by ⟨*dimension*⟩ to the left and right of the text, but this protruding background will not be taken into consideration by TEX for typesetting purposes.

  A typical example usage of this option arises when you insert a box with a colored background in the middle of normal text. In this case, if the background color is set, you would like a background to be drawn behind the text *and* you would like a certain extra space around this text (the background should not stop immediately at the borders of the text, this looks silly) *and* you would like the normal text always to be at the same horizontal position, independently of whether a background is present or not. In this case, using `colsep*=4pt` is a good option.

- `shadow=`⟨*true or false*⟩ draws a shadow behind the box. Currently, this option only has an effect if used together with the `rounded` option, but that may change.

- `rounded=`⟨*true or false*⟩ causes the borders of the box to be rounded off if there is a background installed. This command internally calls `beamerboxesrounded`.

- `ignorebg` causes the background color of the ⟨*beamer color*⟩ to be ignored, that is, to be treated as if it were set to "transparent" or "empty."

- `vmode` causes TEX to be in vertical mode when the box starts. Normally, TEX will be in horizontal mode at the start of the box (a `\leavevmode` is inserted automatically at the beginning of the box unless this option is given). Only TEXperts need this option, so, if you use it, you will probably know what you are doing anyway.

`\begin{beamerboxesrounded}[`⟨*options*⟩`]{`⟨*head*⟩`}`
  ⟨*environment contents*⟩

123

`\end{beamerboxesrounded}`

The text inside the environment is framed by a rectangular area with rounded corners. For the large rectangular area, the BEAMER-color specified with the `lower` option is used. Its background is used for the background, its foreground for the foreground. If the ⟨*head*⟩ is not empty, ⟨*head*⟩ is drawn in the upper part of the box using the BEAMER-color specified with the `upper` option for the fore- and background. The following options can be given:

- `lower`=⟨*beamer color*⟩ sets the BEAMER-color to be used for the lower (main) part of the box. Its background is used for the background, its foreground for the foreground of the main part of the box. If either is empty, the current background or foreground is used. The box will never be transparent.

- `upper`=⟨*beamer color*⟩ sets the BEAMER-color used for the upper (head) part of the box. It is only used if the ⟨*head*⟩ is not empty.

- `width`=⟨*dimension*⟩ causes the width of the text inside the box to be the specified ⟨*dimension*⟩. By default, the `\textwidth` is used. Note that the box will protrude 4pt to the left and right.

- `shadow`=⟨*true or false*⟩. If set to `true`, a shadow will be drawn.

If no ⟨*head*⟩ is given, the head part is completely suppressed.

Example:

```
\begin{beamerboxesrounded}[upper=block head,lower=block body,shadow=true]{Theorem}
  $A = B$.
\end{beamerboxesrounded}
```

ARTICLE This environment is not available in `article` mode.

12.6 Figures and Tables

You can use the standard LaTeX environments `figure` and `table` much the same way you would normally use them. However, any placement specification will be ignored. Figures and tables are immediately inserted where the environments start. If there are too many of them to fit on the frame, you must manually split them among additional frames or use the `allowframebreaks` option.

Example:

```
\begin{frame}
  \begin{figure}
    \pgfuseimage{myfigure}
    \caption{This caption is placed below the figure.}
  \end{figure}

  \begin{figure}
    \caption{This caption is placed above the figure.}
    \pgfuseimage{myotherfigure}
  \end{figure}
\end{frame}
```

Beamer-Template/-Color/-Font `caption`

This template is used to render the caption.

The following template options are predefined:

- [`default`] typesets the caption name (a word like "Figure" or "Abbildung" or "Table," depending on whether a table or figure is typeset and depending on the currently installed language) before the caption text. No number is printed, since these make little sense in a normal presentation.

- [`numbered`] adds the figure or table number to the caption. Use this option only if your audience has a printed handout or printed lecture notes that follow the same numbering.

- [`caption name own line`] As the name suggests, this options puts the caption name (like "Figure") on its own line.

124

Inside the template, you can use the following inserts:

- \insertcaption Inserts the text of the current caption.
- \insertcaptionname Inserts the name of the current caption. This word is either "Table" or "Figure" or, if the babel package is used, some translation thereof.
- \insertcaptionnumber Inserts the number of the current figure or table.

Beamer-Color/-Font `caption name`

These BEAMER-color and -font are used to typeset the caption name (a word like "Figure"). The `caption` template must directly "use" them, they are not installed automatically by the \insertcaptionname command.

Beamer-Template `caption label separator`

This template is inserted between caption name and caption text.

The following template options are predefined:

- [default] Typesets the colon followed by the space.
- [none] Typesets no separator.
- [colon] Alias for the default.
- [period] Typesets the period followed by the space.
- [space] Typesets the space.
- [quad] Typesets the \quad followed by the space.
- [endash] Typesets the en-dash surrounded by spaces (--).

12.7   Splitting a Frame into Multiple Columns

The BEAMER class offers several commands and environments for splitting (perhaps only part of) a frame into multiple columns. These commands have nothing to do with LaTeX's commands for creating columns. Columns are especially useful for placing a graphic next to a description/explanation.

The main environment for creating columns is called columns. Inside this environment, you can either place several column environments, each of which creates a new column, or use the \column command to create new columns.

\begin{columns}[⟨options⟩]
  ⟨environment contents⟩
\end{columns}

A multi-column area. Inside the environment you should place only column environments or \column commands (see below). The following ⟨options⟩ may be given:

- b will cause the bottom lines of the columns to be vertically aligned.
- c will cause the columns to be centered vertically relative to each other. Default, unless the global option t is used.
- onlytextwidth is the same as totalwidth=\textwidth.
- t will cause the first lines of the columns to be aligned. Default if global option t is used.
- T is similar to the t option, but T aligns the tops of the first lines while t aligns the so-called baselines of the first lines. If strange things seem to happen in conjunction with the t option (for example if a graphic suddenly "drops down" with the t option instead of "going up,"), try using this option instead.
- totalwidth=⟨width⟩ will cause the columns to occupy not the whole page width, but only ⟨width⟩, all told. Note that this means that any margins are ignored.

Example:

```
\begin{columns}[t]
  \begin{column}{5cm}
    Two\\lines.
  \end{column}
  \begin{column}{5cm}
    One line (but aligned).
  \end{column}
\end{columns}
```

Example:

```
\begin{columns}[t]
  \column{5cm}
    Two\\lines.

  \column[T]{5cm}
    \includegraphis[height=3cm]{mygraphic.jpg}
\end{columns}
```

ARTICLE This environment is ignored in `article` mode.

To create a column, you can either use the `column` environment or the `\column` command.

`\begin{column}[⟨placement⟩]{⟨column width⟩}`
  ⟨environment contents⟩
`\end{column}`

Creates a single column of width ⟨*column width*⟩. The vertical placement of the enclosing `columns` environment can be overruled by specifying a specific ⟨*placement*⟩ (`t` and `T` for the two top modes, `c` for centered, and `b` for bottom).

Example: The following code has the same effect as the above examples:

```
\begin{columns}
  \begin{column}[t]{5cm}
    Two\\lines.
  \end{column}
  \begin{column}[t]{5cm}
    One line (but aligned).
  \end{column}
\end{columns}
```

ARTICLE This command is ignored in `article` mode.

`\column[⟨placement⟩]{⟨column width⟩}`

Starts a single column. The parameters and options are the same as for the `column` environment. The column automatically ends with the next occurrence of `\column` or of a `column` environment or of the end of the current `columns` environment.

Example:

```
\begin{columns}
  \column[t]{5cm}
    Two\\lines.
  \column[t]{5cm}
    One line (but aligned).
\end{columns}
```

ARTICLE This command is ignored in `article` mode.

12.8   Positioning Text and Graphics Absolutely

Normally, BEAMER uses TeX's normal typesetting mechanism to position text and graphics on the page. In certain situation you may instead wish a certain text or graphic to appear at a page position that is specified *absolutely*. This means that the position is specified relative to the upper left corner of the slide.

The package `textpos` provides several commands for positioning text absolutely and it works together with BEAMER. When using this package, you will typically have to specify the options `overlay` and perhaps `absolute`. For details on how to use the package, please see its documentation.

12.9   Verbatim and Fragile Text

If you wish to use a `{verbatim}` environment in a frame, you have to add the option `[fragile]` to the `{frame}` environment. In this case, you really have to use the `{frame}` environment (not the `\frame` command) and the `\end{frame}` must be alone on a single line. Using this option will cause the frame contents to be written to an external file and then read back. See the description of the `{frame}` environment for more details.

You must also use the `[fragile]` option for frames that include any "fragile" text, which is any text that is not "interpreted the way text is usually interpreted by TeX." For example, if you use a package that (locally) redefined the meaning of, say, the character &, you must use this option.

Inside `{verbatim}` environments you obviously cannot use commands like `\alert<2>` to highlight part of code since the text is written in, well, verbatim. There are several good packages like `alltt` or `listings` that allow you to circumvent this problem. For simple cases, the following environment can be used, which is defined by BEAMER:

`\begin{semiverbatim}`
  ⟨*environment contents*⟩
`\end{semiverbatim}`

> The text inside this environment is typeset like verbatim text. However, the characters \, {, and } retain their meaning. Thus, you can say things like
>
> `\alert<1->{std::cout << "AT&T likes 100% performance";}`
>
> To typeset the three characters \, {, and } you can use the commands \\ (which is redefined inside this environment—you do not need it anyway), \{, and \}. Thus in order to get typeset "\alert<1>{X}" you can write \\alert<1>\{X\}.

12.10   Abstract

The `{abstract}` environment is overlay specificiation-aware in BEAMER:

`\begin{abstract}<`⟨*action specification*⟩`>`
  ⟨*environment contents*⟩
`\end{abstract}`

> You can use this environment to typeset an abstract.

> **Beamer-Color/-Font** `abstract`
>
> > These BEAMER-color and -font are used to typeset the abstract. If a background color is set, this background color is used as background for the whole abstract by default.

> **Beamer-Template/-Color/-Font** `abstract title`
>
> > Color parents: `titlelike`
> >
> > This template is used for the title. By default, this inserts the word `\abstractname`, centered. The background color is ignored.

> **Beamer-Template** `abstract begin`
>
> > This template is inserted at the very beginning of the abstract, before the abstract title and the ⟨*environment contents*⟩ is inserted.

Beamer-Template `abstract end`

    This template is inserted at the end of the abstract, after the ⟨*environment contents*⟩.

12.11 Verse, Quotations, Quotes

LaTeX defines three environments for typesetting quotations and verses: `verse`, `quotation`, and `quote`. These environments are also available in the BEAMER class, where they are overlay specification-aware. If an overlay specification is given, the verse or quotation is shown only on the specified slides and is covered otherwise. The difference between a `quotation` and a `quote` is that the first has paragraph indentation, whereas the second hasn't.

    You can change the font and color used for these by changing the BEAMER-colors and -fonts listed below. Unlike the standard LaTeX environments, the default font theme typesets a verse in an italic serif font, quotations and quotes are typeset using an italic font (whether serif or sans-serif depends on the standard document font).

`\begin{verse}<`⟨*action specification*⟩`>`
  ⟨*environment contents*⟩
`\end{verse}`

    You can use this environment to typeset a verse.

    Beamer-Color/-Font `verse`

        These BEAMER-color and -font are used to typeset the verse. If a background color is set, this background color is used as background for the whole abstract. The default font is italic serif.

    Beamer-Template `verse begin`

        This template is inserted at the beginning of the verse.

    Beamer-Template `verse end`

        This template is inserted at the end of the verse.

`\begin{quotation}<`⟨*action specification*⟩`>`
  ⟨*environment contents*⟩
`\end{quotation}`

    Use this environment to typeset multi-paragraph quotations. Think again, before presenting multi-paragraph quotations.

    Beamer-Color/-Font `quotation`

        These BEAMER-color and -font are used to typeset the quotation.

    Beamer-Template `quotation begin`

        This template is inserted at the beginning of the quotation.

    Beamer-Template `quotation end`

        This template is inserted at the end of the quotation.

`\begin{quote}<`⟨*action specification*⟩`>`
  ⟨*environment contents*⟩
`\end{quote}`

    Use this environment to typeset a single-paragraph quotation.

    Beamer-Color/-Font `quote`

        These BEAMER-color and -font are used to typeset the quote.

    Beamer-Template `quote begin`

        This template is inserted at the beginning of the quote.

    Beamer-Template `quote end`

        This template is inserted at the end of the quote.

12.12 Footnotes

First a word of warning: Using footnotes is usually not a good idea. They disrupt the flow of reading.

You can use the usual \footnote command. It has been augmented to take an additional option, for placing footnotes at the frame bottom instead of at the bottom of the current minipage.

\footnote<⟨*overlay specification*⟩>[⟨*options*⟩]{⟨*text*⟩}

Inserts a footnote into the current frame. Footnotes will always be shown at the bottom of the current frame; they will never be "moved" to other frames. As usual, one can give a number as ⟨*options*⟩, which will cause the footnote to use that number. The BEAMER class adds one additional option:

- frame causes the footnote to be shown at the bottom of the frame. This is normally the default behavior anyway, but in minipages and certain blocks it makes a difference. In a minipage, the footnote is usually shown as part of the minipage rather than as part of the frame.

If an ⟨*overlay specification*⟩ is given, this causes the footnote ⟨*text*⟩ to be shown only on the specified slides. The footnote symbol in the text is shown on all slides.

Example: \footnote{On a fast machine.}

Example: \footnote[frame,2]{Not proved.}

Example: \footnote<.->{Der Spiegel, 4/04, S.~90.}

Beamer-Template/-Color/-Font footnote

This template will be used to render the footnote. Inside this template, the following two inserts can be used:

- \insertfootnotetext Inserts the current footnote text.
- \insertfootnotemark Inserts the current footnote mark (like a raised number). This mark is computed automatically.

Beamer-Color/-Font footnote mark

This BEAMER-color/-font is used when rendering the footnote mark, both in the text and at the beginning of the footnote itself.

13 Graphics

In the following, the advantages and disadvantages of different possible ways of creating graphics for BEAMER presentations are discussed. Much of the information presented in the following is not really special to BEAMER, but applies to any other document class as well.

13.1 Including External Graphic Files Versus Inlines Graphics

There are two principal ways of creating TEX-documents that include graphics: Either the graphic resides in an external file that is *included* or the graphic is *inlined*, which means that TEX-file contains a bunch of commands like "draw a red line from here to there." In the following, the advantages and disadvantages of these two approaches are discussed.

You can use an external program, like `xfig`, GIMP or Inkscape, to create a graphic. These programs have an option to *export* graphic files in a format that can then be inserted into the presentation.

The main advantage is:

- You can use a powerful program to create a high-quality graphic.

The main disadvantages are:

- You have to worry about many files. Typically there are at least two for each presentation, namely the program's graphic data file and the exported graphic file in a format that can be read by TEX.

- Changing the graphic using the program does not automatically change the graphic in the presentation. Rather, you must reexport the graphic and rerun LATEX.

- It may be difficult to get the line width, fonts, and font sizes right.

- Creating formulas as part of graphics is often difficult or impossible.

You can use all the standard LATEX commands for inserting graphics, like `\includegraphics` (be sure to include the package `graphics` or `graphicx`). Also, the `pgf` package offers commands for including graphics. Either will work fine in most situations, so choose whichever you like. Like `\pgfdeclareimage`, `\includegraphics` also includes an image only once in a `.pdf` file, even if it used several times (as a matter of fact, the `graphics` package is even a bit smarter about this than `pgf`). However, currently only `pgf` offers the ability to include images that are partly transparent.

At the end of this section you will find notes on how to include specific graphic formats like `.eps` or `.jpg`.

The commands `\includegraphics`, `\pgfuseimage`, and `\pgfimage` are overlay-specification-aware in BEAMER. If the overlay specification does not apply, the command has no effect. This is useful for creating a simple animation where each picture of the animation resides in a different file:

```
\begin{frame}
  \includegraphics<1>[height=2cm]{step1.pdf}%
  \includegraphics<2>[height=2cm]{step2.pdf}%
  \includegraphics<3>[height=2cm]{step3.pdf}%
\end{frame}
```

A different way of creating graphics is to insert graphic drawing commands directly into your LATEX file. There are numerous packages that help you do this. They have various degrees of sophistication. Inlining graphics suffers from none of the disadvantages mentioned above for including external graphic files, but the main disadvantage is that it is often hard to use these packages. In some sense, you "program" your graphics, which requires a bit of practice.

When choosing a graphic package, there are a few things to keep in mind:

- Many packages produce poor quality graphics. This is especially true of the standard `picture` environment of LATEX.

- Powerful packages that produce high-quality graphics often do not work together with `pdflatex`, `lualatex` or `xelatex`.

- The most powerful and easiest-to-use package around, namely `pstricks`, does not work together with `pdflatex`, `lualatex` or `xelatex` and this is a fundamental problem. Due to the fundamental differences between PDF and PostScript, it is not possible to write a "pdflatex back-end for `pstricks`." (Situation with `lualatex` and `xelatex` is very similar.) Regardless, PST-PDF, XETEX-PSTRICKS and PDFTRICKS package can help here and simplify things from user's perspective.

There are three possible solutions to the above problem, each with it's own advantages and disadvantages.

- Use the PGF package. It produces high-quality graphics and works together with `pdflatex`, `lualatex`, `xelatex` and also with normal `latex`. It is not as powerful as `pstricks` (as pointed out above, this is because of rather fundamental reasons) and not as easy to use, but it should be sufficient in most cases.

- Use LUAMPLIB package and `lualatex`. It provides you with an environment using which you can type MetaPost code directly in your document.

- Use `pstricks` and stick to `latex` and `dvips` or use some of the workarounds mentioned above.

13.2 Including Graphic Files Ending `.eps` or `.ps`

External graphic files ending with the extension `.eps` (Encapsulated PostScript) or `.ps` (PostScript) can be included if you use `latex` and `dvips`, but *not* when using `pdflatex`. This is true both for the normal `graphics` package and for `pgf`. When using `pgf`, do *not* add the extension `.eps`. When using `graphics`, do add the extension.

If you have a `.eps` graphic and wish to use `pdflatex`, you can use the program `ps2pdf` to convert the graphic to a `.pdf` file. Some modern distributions enable `write18` which allows `pdflatex` to do that automatically. Note, however, that it is often a better idea to directly generate a `.pdf` if the program that produced the `.eps` supports this.

13.3 Including Graphic Files Ending `.pdf`, `.jpg`, `.jpeg` or `.png`

The four formats `.pdf`, `.jpg`, `.jpeg`, and `.png` can only be included by `pdflatex`. As before, do not add these extension when using `pgf`, but do add them when using `graphics`. If your graphic file has any of these formats and you wish/must use `latex` and `dvips`, you have to convert your graphic to `.eps` first.

13.4 Including Graphic Files Ending `.mps`

A graphic file ending `.mps` (MetaPost PostScript) is a special kind of Encapsulated PostScript file. Files in this format are produced by the MetaPost program. As you know, TeX is a program that converts simple plain text into beautifully typeset documents. The MetaPost program is similar, only it converts simple plain text into beautiful graphics.

The MetaPost program converts a plain text file ending `.mp` into an `.mps` file (although for some unfathomable reason the extension is not added). The `.mp` file must contain text written in the MetaFont programming language. Since `.mps` files are actually also `.eps` files, you can use the normal `\includegraphics` command to include them.

However, as a special bonus, you can *also* include such a file when using `pdflatex`. Normally, `pdflatex` cannot handle `.eps` files, but the `.mps` files produced by MetaPost have such a simple and special structure that this is possible. The `graphics` package implements some filters to convert such PostScript output to PDF on-the-fly. For this to work, the file should end `.mps` instead of `.eps`. The following command can be used to make the `graphics` package just *assume* the extension `.mps` for any file it knows nothing about (like files ending with `.1`, which is what MetaPost loves to produce):

```
\DeclareGraphicsRule{*}{mps}{*}{}
```

This special feature currently only works with the `graphics` package, not with `pgf`.

13.5 Including Graphic Files Ending `.mmp`

The format `.mmp` (Multi-MetaPost) is actually not a format that can be included directly in a TEX-file. Rather, like a `.mp` file, it first has to be converted using the MetaPost program. The crucial difference between `.mp` and `.mmp` is that in the latter multiple graphics can reside in a single `.mmp` file (actually, multiple graphics can also reside in a `.mp` file, but by convention such a file is called `.mmp`). When running MetaPost on a `.mmp` file, it will create not a single encapsulated PostScript file, but several, ending `.0`, `.1`, `.2`, and so on. The idea is that `.0` might contain a main graphic and the following pictures contain overlay material that should be incrementally added to this graphic.

To include the series of resulting files, you can use the command `\multiinclude` from the `mpmulti` or from the `xmpmulti` package. How this program works is explained in Section 14.1.3.

14 Animations, Sounds, and Slide Transitions

14.1 Animations

14.1.1 Including External Animation Files

If you have created an animation using some external program (like a renderer), you can use the capabilities of the presentation program (like the Acrobat Reader) to show the animation. Unfortunately, currently there is no portable way of doing this and even the Acrobat Reader does not support this feature on all platforms.

To include an animation in a presentation, you can use, for example, the package `multimedia.sty` which is part of the BEAMER package. You have to include this package explicitly. Despite being distributed as part of the BEAMER distribution, this package is perfectly self-sufficient and can be used independently of BEAMER.

`\usepackage{multimedia}`

> A stand-alone package that implements several commands for including external animation and sound files in a PDF document. The package can be used together with both `dvips` plus `ps2pdf` and `pdflatex`, though the special sound support is available only in `pdflatex`.

> When including this package, you must also include the `hyperref` package. Since you will typically want to include `hyperref` only at the very end of the preamble, `multimedia` will not include `hyperref` itself. However, `multimedia` can be included both before and after `hyperref`. Since BEAMER includes `hyperref` automatically, you need not worry about this when creating a presentation using BEAMER.

For including an animation in a PDF file, you can use the command `\movie`, which is explained below. Depending on the used options, this command will either setup the PDF file such that the viewer application (like the Acrobat Reader) itself will try to play the movie or that an external program will be called. The latter approach, though much less flexible, must be taken if the viewer application is unable to display the movie itself.

`\movie[⟨options⟩]{⟨poster text⟩}{⟨movie filename⟩}`

> This command will insert the movie with the filename ⟨movie filename⟩ into the PDF file. The movie file must reside at some place where the viewer application will be able to find it, which is typically only the directory in which the final PDF file resides. The movie file will *not* be embedded into the PDF file in the sense that the actual movie data is part of the `main.pdf` file. The movie file must hence be copied and passed along with the PDF file. (Nevertheless, one often says that the movie is "embedded" in the document, but that just means that one can click on the movie when viewing the document and the movie will start to play.)

> The movie will use a rectangular area whose size is determined either by the `width=` and `height=` options or by the size of the ⟨poster text⟩. The ⟨poster text⟩ can be any TEX text; for example, it might be a `\pgfuseimage` command or an `\includegraphics` command or a `pgfpicture` environment or just plain text. The ⟨poster text⟩ is typeset in a box, the box is inserted into the normal text, and the movie rectangle is put exactly over this box. Thus, if the ⟨poster text⟩ is an image from the movie, this image will be shown until the movie is started, when it will be exactly replaced by the movie itself. However, there is also a different, sometimes better, way of creating a poster image, namely by using the `poster` option as explained later on.

> The aspect ratio of the movie will *not* be corrected automatically if the dimension of the ⟨poster text⟩ box does not have the same aspect ratio. Most movies have an aspect ratio of 4:3 or 16:9.

> Despite the name, a movie may consist only of sound with no images. In this case, the ⟨poster text⟩ might be a symbol representing the sound. There is also a different, dedicated command for including sounds in a PDF file, see the `\sound` command in Section 14.2.

> Unless further options are given, the movie will start only when the user clicks on it. Whether the viewer application can actually display the movie depends on the application and the version. For example, the Acrobat Reader up to version 5 does not seem to be able to display any movies or sounds on Linux. On the other hand, the Acrobat Reader Version 6 on MacOS is able to display anything that QuickTime can display, which is just about everything. Embedding movies in a PDF document is provided for by the PDF

standard and is not a peculiarity of the Acrobat Reader. In particular, one might expect other viewers like xpdf and poppler-based viewers (Okular, Evince) to support embedded movies in the future.

Example: \movie{\pgfuseimage{myposterimage}}{mymovie.avi}

Example: \movie[width=3cm,height=2cm,poster]{}{mymovie.mpg}

If your viewer application is not able to render your movie, but some external application is, you must use the externalviewer option. This will ask the viewer application to launch an application for showing the movie instead of displaying it itself. Since this application is started in a new window, this is not nearly as nice as having the movie displayed directly by the viewer (unless you use evil trickery to suppress the frame of the viewer application). Which application is chosen is left to the discretion of the viewer application, which tries to make its choice according to the extension of the ⟨*movie filename*⟩ and according to some mapping table for mapping extensions to viewer applications. How this mapping table can be modified depends on the viewer application, please see the release notes of your viewer.

The following ⟨*options*⟩ may be given:

- autostart. Causes the movie to start playing immediately when the page is shown. At most one movie can be started in this way. The viewer application will typically be able to show at most one movie at the same time anyway. When the page is no longer shown, the movie immediately stops. This can be a problem if you use the \movie command to include a sound that should be played on after the page has been closed. In this case, the \sound command must be used.

- borderwidth=⟨*TEX dimension*⟩. Causes a border of thickness ⟨*TEX dimension*⟩ to be drawn around the movie. Some versions of the Acrobat Reader seem to have a bug and do not display this border if is smaller than 0.5bp (about 0.51pt).

- depth=⟨*TEX dimension*⟩. Overrides the depth of the ⟨*poster text*⟩ box and sets it to the given dimension.

- duration=⟨*time*⟩s. Specifies in seconds how long the movie should be shown. The ⟨*time*⟩ may be a fractional value and must be followed by the letter s. For example, duration=1.5s will show the movie for one and a half seconds. In conjunction with the start option, you can "cut out" a part of a movie for display.

- externalviewer. As explained above, this causes an external application to be launched for displaying the movie in a separate window. Most options, like duration or loop, have no effect since they are not passed along to the viewer application.

- height=⟨*TEX dimension*⟩. Overrides the height of the ⟨*poster text*⟩ box and sets it to the given dimension.

- label=⟨*movie label*⟩. Assigns a label to the movie such that it can later be referenced by the command \hyperlinkmovie, which can be used to stop the movie or to show a different part of it. The ⟨*movie label*⟩ is not a normal label. It should not be too fancy, since it is inserted literally into the PDF code. In particular, it should not contain closing parentheses.

- loop. Causes the movie to start again when the end has been reached. Normally, the movie just stops at the end.

- once. Causes the movie to just stop at the end. This is the default.

- open. Causes the player to stay open when the movie has finished.

- palindrome. Causes the movie to start playing backwards when the end has been reached, and to start playing forward once more when the beginning is reached, and so on.

- poster. Asks the viewer application to show the first image of the movie when the movie is not playing. Normally, nothing is shown when the movie is not playing (and thus the box containing the ⟨*poster text*⟩ is shown). For a movie that does not have any images (but sound) or for movies with an uninformative first image this option is not so useful.

- repeat is the same as loop.

- showcontrols=⟨*true or false*⟩. Causes a control bar to be displayed below the movie while it is playing. Instead of showcontrols=true you can also just say showcontrols. By default, no control bar is shown.

- `start=⟨time⟩s`. Causes the first ⟨time⟩ seconds of the movie to be skipped. For example, `start=10s,duration=5s` will show seconds 10 to 15 of the movie, when you play the movie.
- `width=⟨TₑXdimension⟩` works like the `height` option, only for the width of the poster box.

Example: The following example creates a "background sound" for the slide.

`\movie[autostart]{}{test.wav}`

Example: A movie with two extra buttons for showing different parts of the movie.

`\movie[label=cells,width=4cm,height=3cm,poster,showcontrols,duration=5s]{}{cells.avi}`

`\hyperlinkmovie[start=5s,duration=7s]{cells}{\beamerbutton{Show the middle stage}}`

`\hyperlinkmovie[start=12s,duration=5s]{cells}{\beamerbutton{Show the late stage}}`

A movie can serve as the destination of a special kind of hyperlink, namely a hyperlink introduced using the following command:

`\hyperlinkmovie[⟨options⟩]{⟨movie label⟩}{⟨text⟩}`

Causes the ⟨text⟩ to become a movie hyperlink. When you click on the ⟨text⟩, the movie with the label ⟨movie label⟩ will start to play (or stop or pause or resume, depending on the ⟨options⟩). The movie must be on the same page as the hyperlink.

The following ⟨options⟩ may be given, many of which are the same as for the `\movie` command; if a different option is given for the link than for the movie itself, the option for the link takes precedence:

- `duration=⟨time⟩s`. As for `\movie`, this causes the movie to be played only for the given number of seconds.
- `loop` and `repeat`. As for `\movie`, this causes the movie to loop.
- `once`. As for `\movie`, this causes the movie to played only once.
- `palindrome`. As for `\movie`, this causes the movie to be played forth and back.
- `pause`. Causes the playback of the movie to be paused, if the movie was currently playing. If not, nothing happens.
- `play`. Causes the movie to be played from whatever start position is specified. If the movie is already playing, it will be stopped and restarted at the starting position. This is the default.
- `resume`. Resumes playback of the movie, if it has previously been paused. If has not been paused, but not started or is already playing, nothing happens.
- `showcontrols=⟨true or false⟩`. As for `\movie`, this causes a control bar to be shown or not shown during playback.
- `start=⟨time⟩s`. As for `\movie`, this causes the given number of seconds to be skipped at the beginning of the movie if `play` is used to start the movie.
- `stop`. Causes the playback of the movie to be stopped.

14.1.2 Animations Created by Showing Slides in Rapid Succession

You can create an animation in a portable way by using the overlay commands of the BEAMER package to create a series of slides that, when shown in rapid succession, present an animation. This is a flexible approach, but such animations will typically be rather static since it will take some time to advance from one slide to the next. This approach is mostly useful for animations where you want to explain each "picture" of the animation. When you advance slides "by hand," that is, by pressing a forward button, it typically takes at least a second for the next slide to show.

More "lively" animations can be created by relying on a capability of the viewer program. Some programs support showing slides only for a certain number of seconds during a presentation (for the Acrobat Reader this works only in full-screen mode). By setting the number of seconds to zero, you can create a rapid succession of slides.

To facilitate the creation of animations using this feature, the following commands can be used: \animate and \animatevalue.

\animate<⟨overlay specification⟩>

The slides specified by ⟨overlay specification⟩ will be shown as quickly as possible.

Example:
```
\begin{frame}
  \frametitle{A Five Slide Animation}
  \animate<2-4>

  The first slide is shown normally. When the second slide is shown
  (presumably after pressing a forward key), the second, third, and
  fourth slides ''flash by.'' At the end, the content of the fifth
  slide is shown.

  ... code for creating an animation with five slides ...
\end{frame}
```

ARTICLE This command is ignored in article mode.

\animatevalue<⟨start slide⟩-⟨end slide⟩> {⟨name⟩}{⟨start value⟩}{⟨end value⟩}

The ⟨name⟩ must be the name of a counter or a dimension. It will be varied between two values. For the slides in the specified range, the counter or dimension is set to an interpolated value that depends on the current slide number. On slides before the ⟨start slide⟩, the counter or dimension is set to ⟨start value⟩; on the slides after the ⟨end slide⟩ it is set to ⟨end value⟩.

Example:
```
\newcount\opaqueness
\begin{frame}
  \animate<2-10>
  \animatevalue<1-10>{\opaqueness}{100}{0}
  \begin{colormixin}{\the\opaqueness!averagebackgroundcolor}
    \frametitle{Fadeout Frame}

    This text (and all other frame content) will fade out when the
    second slide is shown. This even works with
    {\color{green!90!black}colored} \alert{text}.
  \end{colormixin}
\end{frame}

\newcount\opaqueness
\newdimen\offset
\begin{frame}
  \frametitle{Flying Theorems (You Really Shouldn't!)}

  \animate<2-14>

  \animatevalue<1-15>{\opaqueness}{100}{0}
  \animatevalue<1-15>{\offset}{0cm}{-5cm}
  \begin{colormixin}{\the\opaqueness!averagebackgroundcolor}
  \hskip\offset
    \begin{minipage}{\textwidth}
      \begin{theorem}
        This theorem flies out.
      \end{theorem}
```

```
    \end{minipage}
  \end{colormixin}

  \animatevalue<1-15>{\opaqueness}{0}{100}
  \animatevalue<1-15>{\offset}{-5cm}{0cm}
  \begin{colormixin}{\the\opaqueness!averagebackgroundcolor}
  \hskip\offset
    \begin{minipage}{\textwidth}
      \begin{theorem}
        This theorem flies in.
      \end{theorem}
    \end{minipage}
  \end{colormixin}
\end{frame}
```

ARTICLE This command is ignored in `article` mode.

If your animation "graphics" reside in individual external graphic files, you might also consider using the `\multiinclude` command, which is explained in Section 14.1.3, together with `\animate`. For example, you might create an animation like this, assuming you have created graphic files named `animation.1` through to `animation.10`:

```
\begin{frame}
  \animate<2-9>
  \multiinclude[start=1]{animation}
\end{frame}
```

14.1.3 Including External Animations Residing in Multiple Image Files

Some animations reside in external files in the following way: For each stage of the animation there is an image file containing an image for this stage. You can include such a series of images conveniently by using the style `mpmulti.sty` from the ppower4 package. This style, written by Klaus Guntermann, introduces a command called `\multiinclude` that takes the base name of a graphic file like `mygraphic` and will then search for files called `mygraphic.0`, `mygraphic.1`, and so on, till no more files are found. It will then include these graphics files using the `\includegraphics` command, but will put these graphics "on top of each other." Furthermore, and this is the important part, it inserts a `\pause` command after each graphic. This command is defined in the ppower4 package and has the same effect as the `\pause` command of BEAMER. For this reason, both ppower4 and also BEAMER will first display the basic graphic and will then additionally show the next graphic on each slide.

If you try to use `mpmulti.sty` directly, you will run into the problem that it includes a file called `pause.sty`, which is part of the ppower4 package.

You might also consider using the style `xmpmulti.sty` that comes with BEAMER. This file is mainly identical to `mpmulti`, except for two differences: First, it does not include `pause.sty`, a style that conceptually clashes with BEAMER, although BEAMER contains a workaround that sidesteps the problem. Second, it extends the `\multiinclude` command by allowing a special default overlay specification to be given. The effect of this is explained below.

`\usepackage{xmpmulti}`

Defines the command `\multiinclude`. The code of this package is due to Klaus Guntermann with some additions of mine. It can be used together with BEAMER and with ppower4, i.e., it can be used as a replacement for `mpmulti` if the `pause` package is also included in a ppower4-presentation.

`\multiinclude[<⟨default overlay specification⟩>] [⟨options⟩]{⟨base file name⟩}`

Except for the possibility of specifying a ⟨default overlay specification⟩, this command is identical to the `\multiinclude` command from the ppower4 package.

If no overlay specification is given, the command will search for files called ⟨base file name⟩.⟨number⟩ for increasing numbers ⟨number⟩, starting with zero. As long as it finds these files, it issues an `\includegraphics` command on them. The files following the first one are put "on top" of the first one. Between any two invocations of \includegraphics, a \pause command is inserted. You can modify this behavior in different ways by given suitable ⟨options⟩, see below.

Example: Assume that MetaPost has created files called gra.0, gra.1, and gra.2. You can then create frame consisting of three slides that incrementally show the graphic as follows:

```
\begin{frame}
  \multiinclude{gra}
\end{frame}
```

The effect of providing a ⟨*default overlay specification*⟩ is the following: First, no \pause command is inserted between graphics. Instead, each graphic is surrounded by an actionenv environment with the overlay specification set to ⟨*default overlay specification*⟩.

Example: You can create the same effect as in the previous example using \multiinclude[<+->]{gra}.

Example: For a more interesting usage of the ⟨*default overlay specification*⟩, consider the following usage:

```
\multiinclude[<alert@+| +->]{gra}
```

This will always paint the most recently added part of the graphic in red (assuming you do not use special colors in the graphic itself).

Example: In order to have each graphic completely *replace* the previous one, you could use \multiinclude[<+>]{g

The following ⟨options⟩ may be given (these are the same as for the original command from the ppower4 package):

- pause=⟨*command*⟩ replaces the default pausing command \pause by ⟨*command*⟩. If a ⟨*default overlay specification*⟩ is given, the default pausing command is empty; otherwise it is \pause. Note that commands like \pauselevel are not available in \beamer.
- graphics=⟨*options*⟩ passes the ⟨*options*⟩ to the \includegraphics command.

  Example: \multiinclude[graphics={height=5cm}]{gra}
- format=⟨*extension*⟩ will cause the file names for which we search change from ⟨*base file name*⟩.⟨*number*⟩ to ⟨*base file name*⟩-⟨*number*⟩.⟨*extension*⟩. Note the change from the dot to a hyphen. This option allows you to include, say, .jpg files.
- start=⟨*number*⟩ specifies the start ⟨*number*⟩. The default is zero.
- end=⟨*number*⟩ specifies the end ⟨*number*⟩. The default is infinity.

Note that, if you do not use the format= option, the \includegraphics command will be somewhat at a loss in which format your graphic file actually is. After all, it ends with the cryptic "format suffix" .0 or .1. You can tell \includegraphics that any file having a suffix it knows nothing about is actually in format, say, .mps, using the following command:

```
\DeclareGraphicsRule{*}{mps}{*}{}
```

14.2   Sounds

You can include sounds in a presentation. Such sound can be played when you open a slide or when a certain button is clicked. The commands for including sounds are defined in the package multimedia, which is introduced in Section 14.1.1.

As was already pointed out in Section 14.1.1, a sound can be included in a PDF presentation by treating it as a movie and using the \movie command. While this is perfectly sufficient in most cases, there are two cases where this approach is not satisfactory:

1. When a page is closed, any playing movie is immediately stopped. Thus, you cannot use the \movie command to create sounds that persist for a longer time.

2. You cannot play two movies at the same time.

The PDF specification introduces special sound objects, which are treated quite differently from movie objects. You can create a sound object using the command \sound, which is somewhat similar to \movie. There also exists a \hyperlinksound command, which is similar to \hyperlinkmovie. While it is conceptually better to use \sound for sounds, there are a number of things to consider before using it:

- Several sounds *can* be played at the same time. In particular, it is possible to play a general sound in parallel to a (hopefully silent) movie.

- A sound playback *can* persist after the current page is closed (though it need not).

- The data of a sound file *can* be completely embedded in a PDF file, obliterating the need to "carry around" other files.

- The sound objects do *not* work together with dvips and ps2pdf. They only work with pdflatex.

- There is much less control over what part of a sound should be played. In particular, no control bar is shown and you can specify neither the start time nor the duration.

- A bug in some versions of the Acrobat Reader makes it necessary to provide very exact details on the encoding of the sound file. You have to provide the sampling rate, the number of channels (mono or stereo), the number of bits per sample, and the sample encoding method (raw, signed, Alaw or μlaw). If you do not know this data or provide it incorrectly, the sound will be played incorrectly.

- It seems that you can only include uncompressed sound data, which can easily become huge. This is not required by the specification, but some versions of Acrobat Reader are unable to play any compressed data. Data formats that *do* work are .aif and .au.

\sound[⟨*options*⟩]{⟨*sound poster text*⟩}{⟨*sound filename*⟩}

This command will insert the sound with the filename ⟨*sound filename*⟩ into the PDF file. As for \movie, the file must be accessible when the sound is to be played. Unlike \movie, you can however use the option inlinesound to actually embed the sound data in the PDF file.

Also as for a movie, the ⟨*sound poster text*⟩ will be be put in a box that, when clicked on, will start playing the movie. However, you might also leave this box empty and only use the autostart option. Once playback of a sound has started, it can only be stopped by starting the playback of a different sound or by use of the \hyperlinkmute command.

The supported sound formats depend on the viewer application. Some versions of Acrobat Reader support .aif and .au. Sometimes you also need to specify information like the sampling rate, even though this information could be extracted from the sound file and even though the PDF standard specifies that the viewer application should do so. In this regard, some versions of Acrobat Reader seem to be non-standard-conforming.

This command only works together with pdflatex. If you use dvips, the poster is still shown, but clicking it has no effect and no sound is embedded in any way.

Example: \sound[autostart,samplingrate=22050]{}{applause.au}

The following ⟨*options*⟩ may be given:

- autostart. Causes the sound to start playing immediately when the page is shown.

- automute. Causes all sounds to be muted when the current page is left.

- bitspersample=⟨*8 or 16*⟩. Specifies the number of bits per sample in the sound file. If this number is 16, this option need not be specified.

- channels=⟨*1 or 2*⟩. Specifies whether the sound is mono or stereo. If the sound is mono, this option need not be specified.

- depth=⟨*TEX dimension*⟩. Overrides the depth of the ⟨*sound poster text*⟩ box and sets it to the given dimension.

- encoding=⟨*method*⟩. Specifies the encoding method, which may be `Raw`, `Signed`, `muLaw`, or `ALaw`. If the method is `muLaw`, this option need not be specified.

- height=⟨*TEX dimension*⟩. Overrides the height of the ⟨*sound poster text*⟩ box and sets it to the given dimension.

- `inlinesound` causes the sound data to be stored directly in the PDF-file.

- label=⟨*sound label*⟩. Assigns a label to the sound such that it can later be referenced by the command `\hyperlinksound`, which can be used to start a sound. The ⟨*sound label*⟩ is not a normal label.

- `loop` or `repeat`. Causes the sound to start again when the end has been reached.

- mixsound=⟨*true or false*⟩. If set to `true`, the sound is played in addition to any sound that is already playing. If set to `false` all other sounds (though not sound from movies) are stopped before the sound is played. The default is `false`.

- samplingrate=⟨*number*⟩. Specifies the number of samples per second in the sound file. If this number is 44100, this option need not be specified.

- width=⟨*TEX dimension*⟩ works like the `height` option, only for the width of the poster box.

Example: The following example creates a "background sound" for the slide, assuming that `applause.au` is encoded correctly (44100 samples per second, mono, μlaw encoded, 16 bits per sample).

`\sound[autostart]{}{applause.au}`

Just like movies, sounds can also serve as destinations of special sound hyperlinks.

\hyperlinksound[⟨*options*⟩]{⟨*sound label*⟩}{⟨*text*⟩}

Causes the ⟨*text*⟩ to become a sound hyperlink. When you click on the ⟨*text*⟩, the sound with the label ⟨*sound label*⟩ will start to play.

The following ⟨*options*⟩ may be given:

- `loop` or `repeat`. Causes the sound to start again when the end has been reached.

- mixsound=⟨*true or false*⟩. If set to `true`, the sound is played in addition to any sound that is already playing. If set to `false` all other sounds (though not sound from movies) are stopped before the sound is played. The default is `false`.

Since there is no direct way of stopping the playback of a sound, the following command is useful:

\hyperlinkmute{⟨*text*⟩}

Causes the ⟨*text*⟩ to become a hyperlink that, when clicked, stops the playback of all sounds.

14.3 Slide Transitions

PDF in general, and the Acrobat Reader in particular, offer a standardized way of defining *slide transitions*. Such a transition is a visual effect that is used to show the slide. For example, instead of just showing the slide immediately, whatever was shown before might slowly "dissolve" and be replaced by the slide's content.

There are a number of commands that can be used to specify what effect should be used when the current slide is presented. Consider the following example:

```
\frame{\pgfuseimage{youngboy}}
\frame{
  \transdissolve
  \pgfuseimage{man}
}
```

The command \transdissolve causes the slide of the second frame to be shown in a "dissolved way." Note that the dissolving is a property of the second frame, not of the first one. We could have placed the command anywhere on the frame.

The transition commands are overlay-specification-aware. We could collapse the two frames into one frame like this:

```
\begin{frame}
  \only<1>{\pgfuseimage{youngboy}}
  \only<2>{\pgfuseimage{man}}
  \transdissolve<2>
\end{frame}
```

This states that on the first slide the young boy should be shown, on the second slide the old man should be shown, and when the second slide is shown, it should be shown in a "dissolved way."

In the following, the different commands for creating transitional effects are listed. All of them take an optional argument that may contain a list of ⟨key⟩=⟨value⟩ pairs. The following options are possible:

- duration=⟨seconds⟩. Specifies the number of ⟨seconds⟩ the transition effect needs. Default is one second, but often a shorter one (like 0.2 seconds) is more appropriate. Viewer applications, especially Acrobat, may interpret this option in slightly strange ways.

- direction=⟨degree⟩. For "directed" effects, this option specifies the effect's direction. Allowed values are 0, 90, 180, 270, and for the glitter effect also 315.

ICLE All of these commands are ignored in article mode.

\transblindshorizontal<⟨overlay specification⟩>[⟨options⟩]

    Show the slide as if horizontal blinds were pulled away.

    Example: \transblindshorizontal

\transblindsvertical<⟨overlay specification⟩>[⟨options⟩]

    Show the slide as if vertical blinds were pulled away.

    Example: \transblindsvertical<2,3>

\transboxin<⟨overlay specification⟩>[⟨options⟩]

    Show the slide by moving to the center from all four sides.

    Example: \transboxin<1>

\transboxout<⟨overlay specification⟩>[⟨options⟩]

    Show the slide by showing more and more of a rectangular area that is centered on the slide center.

    Example: \transboxout

\transdissolve<⟨overlay specification⟩>[⟨options⟩]

    Show the slide by slowly dissolving what was shown before.

    Example: \transdissolve[duration=0.2]

\transglitter<⟨overlay specification⟩>[⟨options⟩]

    Show the slide with a glitter effect that sweeps in the specified direction.

    Example: \transglitter<2-3>[direction=90]

\transreplace<⟨overlay specification⟩>[⟨options⟩]

    Replace the previous slide directly (default behaviour).

\transssplitverticalin<⟨*overlay specification*⟩>[⟨*options*⟩]

> Show the slide by sweeping two vertical lines from the sides inward.
>
> *Example:* \transssplitverticalin

\transssplitverticalout<⟨*overlay specification*⟩>[⟨*options*⟩]

> Show the slide by sweeping two vertical lines from the center outward.
>
> *Example:* \transssplitverticalout

\transsplithorizontalin<⟨*overlay specification*⟩>[⟨*options*⟩]

> Show the slide by sweeping two horizontal lines from the sides inward.
>
> *Example:* \transsplithorizontalin

\transsplithorizontalout<⟨*overlay specification*⟩>[⟨*options*⟩]

> Show the slide by sweeping two horizontal lines from the center outward.
>
> *Example:* \transsplithorizontalout

\transwipe<⟨*overlay specification*⟩>[⟨*options*⟩]

> Show the slide by sweeping a single line in the specified direction, thereby "wiping out" the previous contents.
>
> *Example:* \transwipe[direction=90]

You can also specify how *long* a given slide should be shown, using the following overlay-specification-aware command:

\transduration<⟨*overlay specification*⟩>{⟨*number of seconds*⟩}

> In full screen mode, show the slide for ⟨*number of seconds*⟩. If zero is specified, the slide is shown as short as possible. This can be used to create interesting pseudo-animations.
>
> *Example:* \transduration<2>{1} Notice that the *duration* of a slide transition is entire separate from the *type* of transition which takes place. Most notably, to cancel an existing auto-advance you need to use
>
> *Example:* \transduration{} possibly with an overlay specification.

Part III
Changing the Way Things Look

BEAMER offers ways to change the appearance of a presentation at all levels of detail. On the top level, *themes* can be used to globally change the appearance conveniently. On the bottom level, *templates* allow you to specify the appearance of every minute detail individually.

Two important aspects of the "appearance" of a presentation are treated in extra sections: colors and fonts. Here, too, color and font themes can be used to globally change the colors or fonts used in a presentation, while you can still change the color or font of, say, block titles independently of everything else.

15 Themes

15.1 Five Flavors of Themes

Themes make it easy to change the appearance of a presentation. The BEAMER class uses five different kinds of themes:

Presentation Themes Conceptually, a presentation theme dictates for every single detail of a presentation what it looks like. Thus, choosing a particular presentation theme will setup for, say, the numbers in enumeration what color they have, what color their background has, what font is used to render them, whether a circle or ball or rectangle or whatever is drawn behind them, and so forth. Thus, when you choose a presentation theme, your presentation will look the way someone (the creator of the theme) thought that a presentation should look like. Presentation themes typically only choose a particular color theme, font theme, inner theme, and outer theme that go well together.

Color Themes A color theme only dictates which colors are used in a presentation. If you have chosen a particular presentation theme and then choose a color theme, only the colors of your presentation will change. A color theme can specify colors in a very detailed way: For example, a color theme can specifically change the colors used to render, say, the border of a button, the background of a button, and the text on a button.

Font Themes A font theme dictates which fonts or font attributes are used in a presentation. As for colors, the font of all text elements used in a presentation can be specified independently.

Inner Themes An inner theme specifies how certain elements of a presentation are typeset. This includes all elements that are at the "inside" of the frame, that is, that are not part of the headline, footline, or sidebars. This includes all enumerations, itemize environments, block environments, theorem environments, or the table of contents. For example, an inner theme might specify that in an enumeration the number should be typeset without a dot and that a small circle should be shown behind it. The inner theme would *not* specify what color should be used for the number or the circle (this is the job of the color theme) nor which font should be used (this is the job of the font theme).

Outer Themes An outer theme specifies what the "outside" or "border" of the presentation slides should look like. It specifies whether there are head- and footlines, what is shown in them, whether there is a sidebar, where the logo goes, where the navigation symbols and bars go, and so on. It also specifies where the frametitle is put and how it is typeset.

The different themes reside in the five subdirectories `theme`, `color`, `font`, `inner`, and `outer` of the directory `beamer/themes`. Internally, a theme is stored as a normal style file. However, to use a theme, the following special commands should be used:

`\usetheme[`⟨*options*⟩`]{`⟨*name list*⟩`}`

Installs the presentation theme named ⟨*name*⟩. Currently, the effect of this command is the same as saying `\usepackage` for the style file named `beamertheme`⟨*name*⟩`.sty` for each ⟨*name*⟩ in the ⟨*name list*⟩.

`\usecolortheme[`⟨*options*⟩`]{`⟨*name list*⟩`}`

Same as `\usetheme`, only for color themes. Color style files are named `beamercolortheme`⟨*name*⟩`.sty`.

`\usefonttheme[`⟨*options*⟩`]{`⟨*name*⟩`}`

Same as `\usetheme`, only for font themes. Font style files are named `beamerfonttheme`⟨*name*⟩`.sty`.

`\useinnertheme[`⟨*options*⟩`]{`⟨*name*⟩`}`

Same as `\usetheme`, only for inner themes. Inner style files are named `beamerinnertheme`⟨*name*⟩`.sty`.

`\useoutertheme[`⟨*options*⟩`]{`⟨*name*⟩`}`

Same as `\usetheme`, only for outer themes. Outer style files are named `beameroutertheme`⟨*name*⟩`.sty`.

If you do not use any of these commands, a sober *default* theme is used for all of them. In the following, the presentation themes that come with the BEAMER class are described. The element, layout, color, and font themes are presented in the following sections.

15.2   Presentation Themes without Navigation Bars

A presentation theme dictates for every single detail of a presentation what it looks like. Normally, having chosen a particular presentation theme, you do not need to specify anything else having to do with the appearance of your presentation—the creator of the theme should have taken care of that for you. However, you still *can* change things afterward either by using a different color, font, element, or even layout theme; or by changing specific colors, fonts, or templates directly.

When Till started naming the presentation themes, he soon ran out of ideas on how to call them. Instead of giving them more and more cumbersome names, he decided to switch to a different naming convention: Except for two special cases, all presentation themes are named after cities. These cities happen to be cities in which or near which there was a conference or workshop that he attended or that a co-author of his attended.

All themes listed without author mentioned were developed by Till. If a theme has not been developed by us (that is, if someone else is to blame), this is indicated with the theme. We have sometimes slightly changed or "corrected" submitted themes, but we still list the original authors.

`\usetheme{default}`

Example:

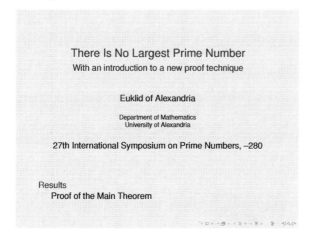
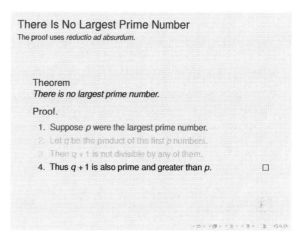

As the name suggests, this theme is installed by default. It is a sober no-nonsense theme that makes minimal use of color or font variations. This theme is useful for all kinds of talks, except for very long talks.

`\usetheme[headheight=⟨head height⟩,footheight=⟨foot height⟩]{boxes}`

Example:

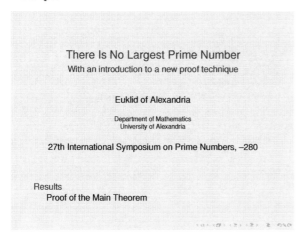
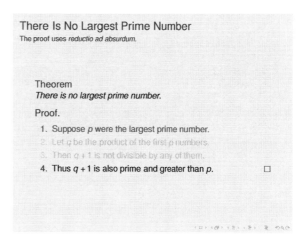

For this theme, you can specify an arbitrary number of templates for the boxes in the headline and in the footline. You can add a template for another box by using the following commands.

`\addheadbox{`⟨*beamer color*⟩`}{`⟨*box template*⟩`}`

Each time this command is invoked, a new box is added to the head line, with the first added box being shown on the left. All boxes will have the same size.

The ⟨*beamer color*⟩ will be used to setup the foreground and background colors of the box.

Example:

```
\addheadbox{section in head/foot}{\tiny\quad 1. Box}
\addheadbox{structure}{\tiny\quad 2. Box}
```

A similar effect as the above commands can be achieved by directly installing a head template that contains two `beamercolorboxes`:

```
\setbeamertemplate{headline}
{\leavevmode
\begin{beamercolorbox}[width=.5\paperwidth]{section in head/foot}
  \tiny\quad 1. Box
\end{beamercolorbox}%
\begin{beamercolorbox}[width=.5\paperwidth]{structure}
  \tiny\quad 2. Box
\end{beamercolorbox}
}
```

While being more complicated, the above commands offer more flexibility.

`\addfootbox{`⟨*beamer color*⟩`}{`⟨*box template*⟩`}`

Example:

```
\addfootbox{section in head/foot}{\tiny\quad 1. Box}
\addfootbox{structure}{\tiny\quad 2. Box}
```

`\usetheme[`⟨*options*⟩`]{Bergen}`

Example:

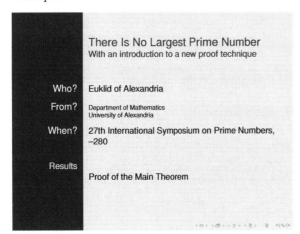 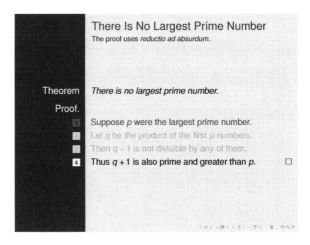

A theme based on the `inmargin` inner theme and the `rectangles` inner theme. Using this theme is not quite trivial since getting the spacing right can be trickier than with most other themes. Also, this theme goes badly with columns. You may wish to consult the remarks on the `inmargin` inner theme.

Bergen is a town in Norway. It hosted IWPEC 2004.

`\usetheme[`⟨*options*⟩`]{Boadilla}`

Example:

146

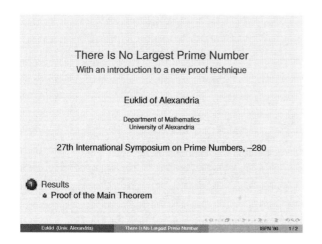 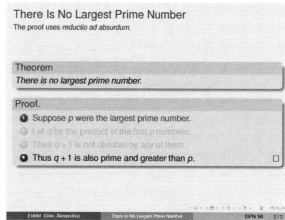

A theme giving much information in little space. The following ⟨options⟩ may be given:

- `secheader` causes a headline to be inserted showing the current section and subsection. By default, this headline is not shown.

Theme author: Manuel Carro. Boadilla is a village in the vicinity of Madrid, hosting the University's Computer Science department.

`\usetheme[`⟨*options*⟩`]{Madrid}`

Example:

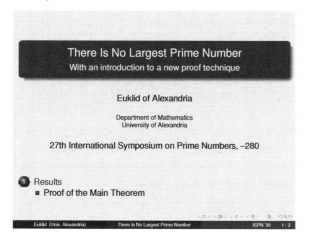 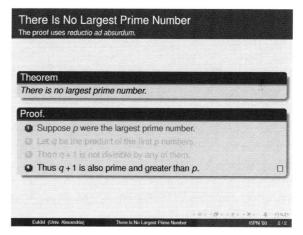

Like the `Boadilla` theme, except that stronger colors are used and that the itemize icons are not modified. The same ⟨options⟩ as for the `Boadilla` theme may be given.

Theme author: Manuel Carro. Madrid is the capital of Spain.

`\usetheme{AnnArbor}`

Example:

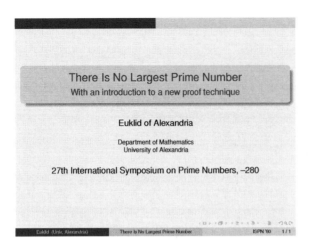
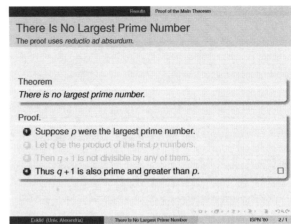

Like `Boadilla`, but using the colors of the University of Michigan.

Theme author: Madhusudan Singh. The University of Michigan is located at Ann Arbor.

\usetheme{CambridgeUS}

Example:

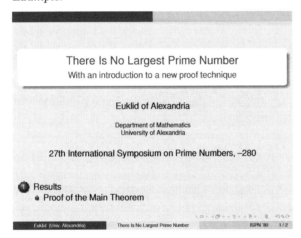
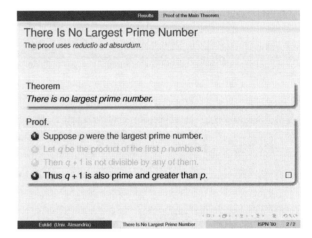

Like `Boadilla`, but using the colors of MIT.

Theme author: Madhusudan Singh.

\usetheme{EastLansing}

Example:

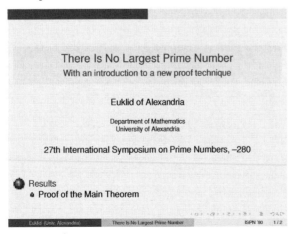
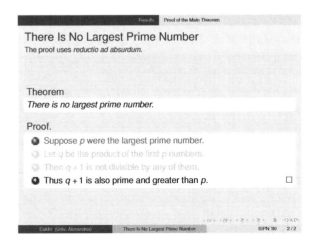

Like `Boadilla`, but using the colors of Michigan State University.

Theme author: Alan Munn. Michigan State University is located in East Lansing.

`\usetheme{Pittsburgh}`

Example:

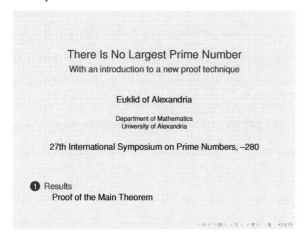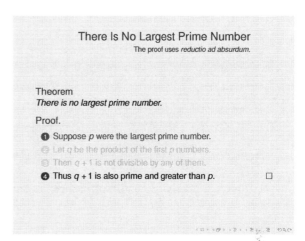

A sober theme. The right-flushed frame titles creates an interesting "tension" inside each frame.

Pittsburgh is a town in the eastern USA. It hosted the second RECOMB workshop of SNPs and haplotypes, 2004.

`\usetheme[`⟨*options*⟩`]{Rochester}`

Example:

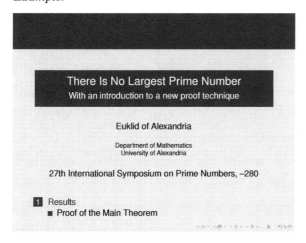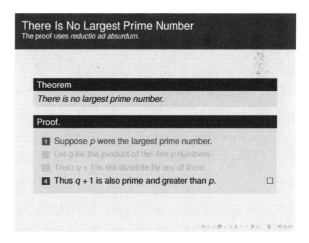

A dominant theme without any navigational elements. It can be made less dominant by using a different color theme.

The following ⟨*options*⟩ may be given:

- `height=`⟨*dimension*⟩ sets the height of the frame title bar.

Rochester is a town in upstate New York, USA. Till visited Rochester in 2001.

15.3   Presentation Themes with a Tree-Like Navigation Bar

`\usetheme{Antibes}`

Example:

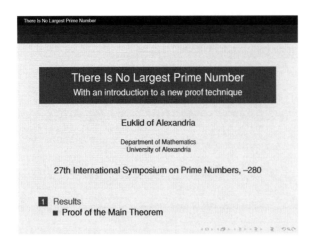 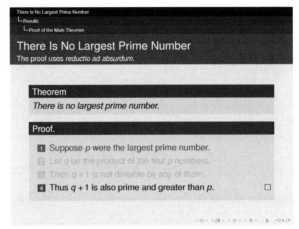

A dominant theme with a tree-like navigation at the top. The rectangular elements mirror the rectangular navigation at the top. The theme can be made less dominant by using a different color theme.

Antibes is a town in the south of France. It hosted STACS 2002.

\usetheme{JuanLesPins}

Example:

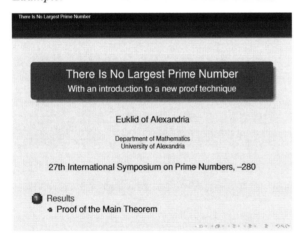 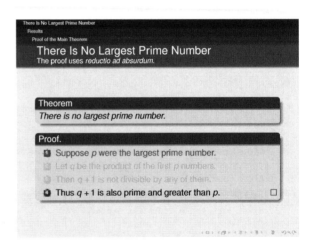

A variation on the **Antibes** theme that has a much "smoother" appearance. It can be made less dominant by choosing a different color theme.

Juan–Les–Pins is a cozy village near Antibes. It hosted STACS 2002.

\usetheme{Montpellier}

Example:

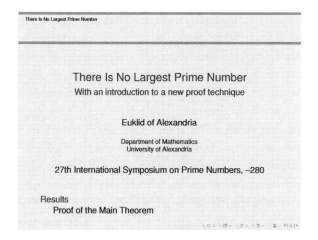
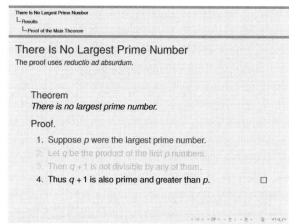

A sober theme giving basic navigational hints. The headline can be made more dominant by using a different color theme.

Montpellier is in the south of France. It hosted STACS 2004.

15.4 Presentation Themes with a Table of Contents Sidebar

\usetheme[⟨options⟩]{Berkeley}

Example:

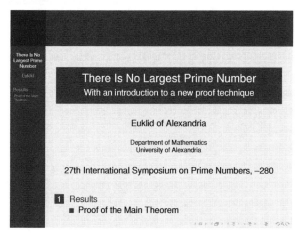
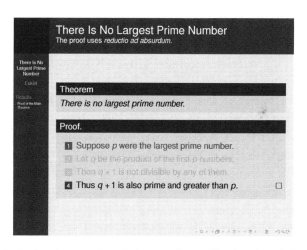

A dominant theme. If the navigation bar is on the left, it dominates since it is seen first. The height of the frame title is fixed to two and a half lines, thus you should be careful with overly long titles. A logo will be put in the corner area. Rectangular areas dominate the layout. The theme can be made less dominant by using a different color theme.

By default, the current entry of the table of contents in the sidebar will be highlighted by using a more vibrant color. A good alternative is to highlight the current entry by using a different color for the background of the current point. The color theme sidebartab installs the appropriate colors, so you just have to say

\usecolortheme{sidebartab}

This color theme works with all themes that show a table of contents in the sidebar.

This theme is useful for long talks like lectures that require a table of contents to be visible all the time.

The following ⟨options⟩ may be given:

- hideallsubsections causes only sections to be shown in the sidebar. This is useful, if you need to save space.

- `hideothersubsections` causes only the subsections of the current section to be shown. This is useful, if you need to save space.

- `left` puts the sidebar on the left (default).

- `right` puts the sidebar on the right.

- `width=⟨dimension⟩` sets the width of the sidebar. If set to zero, no sidebar is created.

Berkeley is on the western coast of the USA, near San Francisco. Till visited Berkeley for a year in 2004.

`\usetheme[⟨options⟩]{PaloAlto}`

Example:

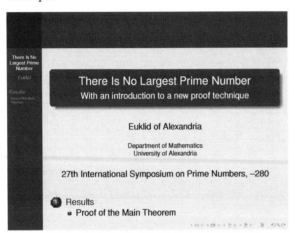 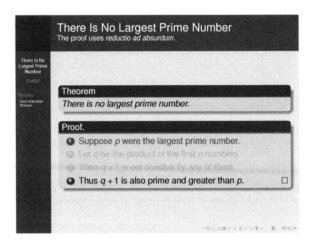

A variation on the `Berkeley` theme with less dominance of rectangular areas. The same ⟨options⟩ as for the `Berkeley` theme can be given.

Palo Alto is also near San Francisco. It hosted the Bay Area Theory Workshop 2004.

`\usetheme[⟨options⟩]{Goettingen}`

Example:

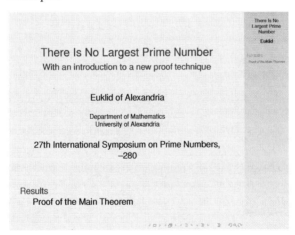 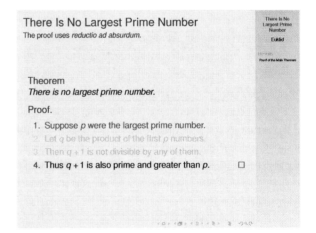

A relatively sober theme useful for a longer talk that demands a sidebar with a full table of contents. The same ⟨options⟩ as for the `Berkeley` theme can be given.

Göttingen is a town in Germany. It hosted the 42nd Theorietag.

`\usetheme[⟨options⟩]{Marburg}`

Example:

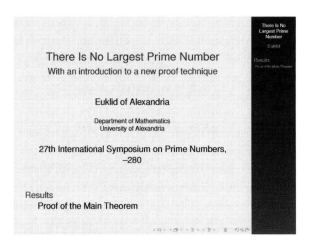 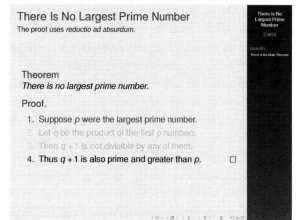

A very dominant variation of the `Goettingen` theme. The same ⟨*options*⟩ may be given.

Marburg is a town in Germany. It hosted the 46th Theorietag.

\usetheme[⟨*options*⟩]{Hannover}

Example:

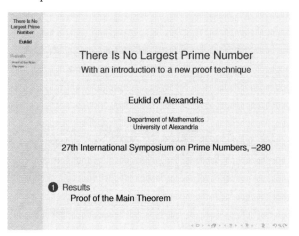 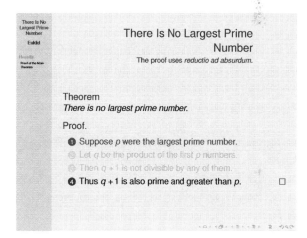

In this theme, the sidebar on the left is balanced by right-flushed frame titles.

The following ⟨*options*⟩ may be given:

- `hideallsubsections` causes only sections to be shown in the sidebar. This is useful, if you need to save space.
- `hideothersubsections` causes only the subsections of the current section to be shown. This is useful, if you need to save space.
- `width=`⟨*dimension*⟩ sets the width of the sidebar.

Hannover is a town in Germany. It hosted the 48th Theorietag.

15.5   Presentation Themes with a Mini Frame Navigation

\usetheme[⟨*options*⟩]{Berlin}

Example:

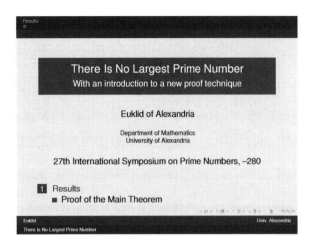
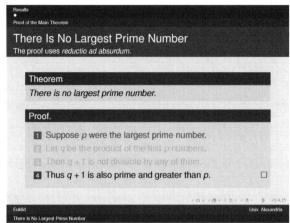

A dominant theme with strong colors and dominating rectangular areas. The head- and footlines give lots of information and leave little space for the actual slide contents. This theme is useful for conferences where the audience is not likely to know the title of the talk or who is presenting it. The theme can be made less dominant by using a different color theme.

The following ⟨*options*⟩ may be given:

- `compress` causes the mini frames in the headline to use only a single line. This is useful for saving space.

Berlin is the capital of Germany.

\usetheme[⟨*options*⟩]{Ilmenau}

Example:

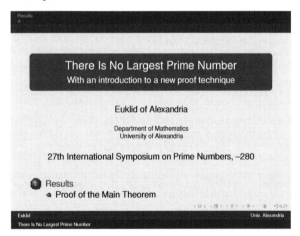
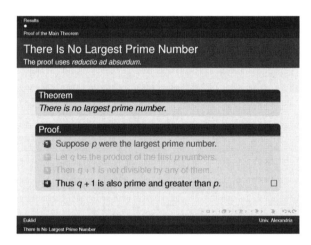

A variation on the `Berlin` theme. The same ⟨*options*⟩ may be given.

Ilmenau is a town in Germany. It hosted the 40th Theorietag.

\usetheme{Dresden}

Example:

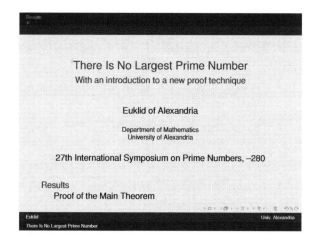 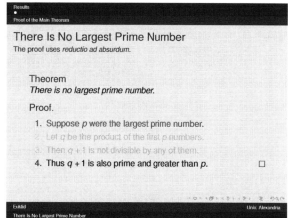

A variation on the `Berlin` theme with a strong separation into navigational stuff at the top/bottom and a sober main text. The same ⟨*options*⟩ may be given.

Dresden is a town in Germany. It hosted STACS 2001.

`\usetheme{Darmstadt}`

Example:

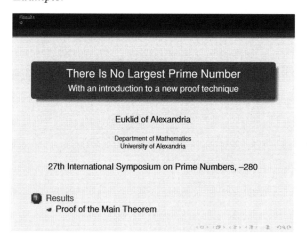 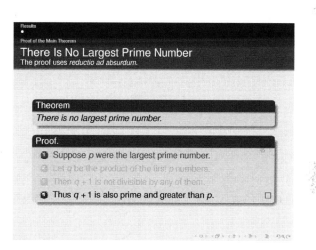

A theme with a strong separation into a navigational upper part and an informational main part. By using a different color theme, this separation can be lessened.

Darmstadt is a town in Germany.

`\usetheme{Frankfurt}`

Example:

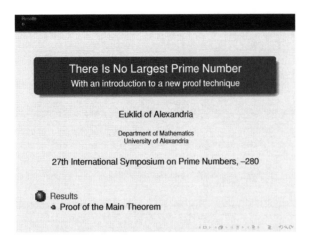 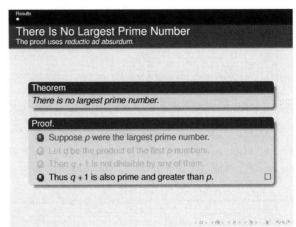

A variation on the `Darmstadt` theme that is slightly less cluttered by leaving out the subsection information. Frankfurt is a town in Germany.

`\usetheme{Singapore}`

Example:

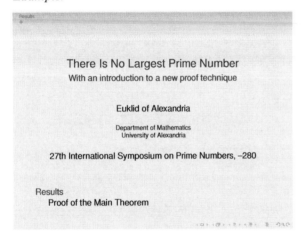 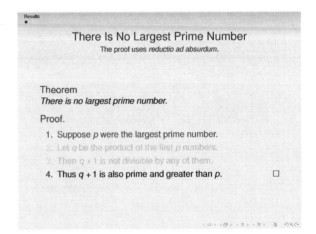

A not-too-sober theme with navigation that does not dominate.

Singapore is located in south-eastern Asia. It hosted COCOON 2002.

`\usetheme{Szeged}`

Example:

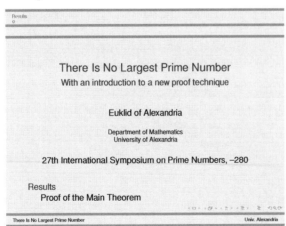 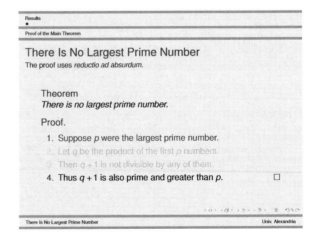

156

A sober theme with a strong dominance of horizontal lines.

Szeged is on the south border of Hungary. It hosted DLT 2003.

15.6 Presentation Themes with Section and Subsection Tables

\usetheme{Copenhagen}

Example:

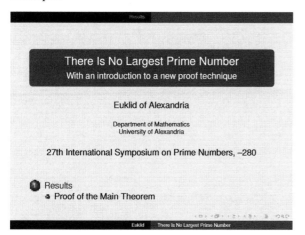 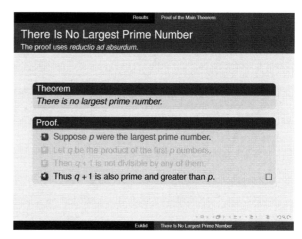

A not-quite-too-dominant theme. This theme gives compressed information about the current section and subsection at the top and about the title and the author at the bottom. No shadows are used, giving the presentation a "flat" look. The theme can be made less dominant by using a different color theme.

Copenhagen is the capital of Denmark. It is connected to Malmö by the Øresund bridge.

\usetheme{Luebeck}

Example:

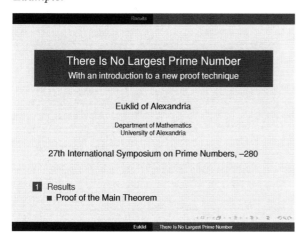 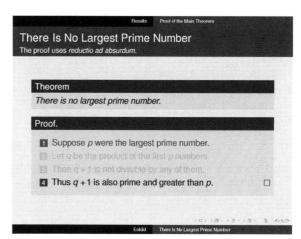

A variation on the Copenhagen theme.

Lübeck is a town in nothern Germany. It hosted the 41st Theorietag.

\usetheme{Malmoe}

Example:

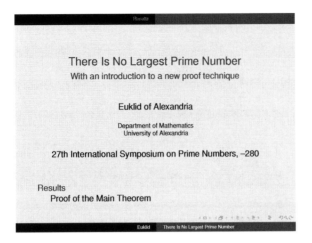 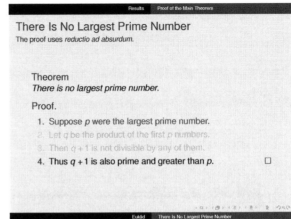

A more sober variation of the **Copenhagen** theme.

Malmö is a town in southern Sweden. It hosted FCT 2001.

\usetheme{Warsaw}

Example:

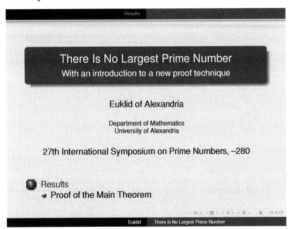 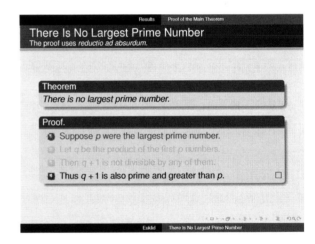

A dominant variation of the **Copenhagen** theme.

Warsaw is the capital of Poland. It hosted MFCS 2002.

15.7 Presentation Themes Included For Compatibility

Earlier versions of BEAMER included some further themes. These themes are still available for compatibility, though they are now implemented differently (they also mainly install appropriate color, font, inner, and outer themes). However, they may or may not honor color themes and they will not be supported in the future. The following list shows which of the new themes should be used instead of the old themes. (When switching, you may want to use the font theme `structurebold` with the option `onlysmall`.)

Old theme	Replacement options
none	Use `compatibility`.
bars	Try `Dresden` instead.
classic	Try `Singapore` instead.
lined	Try `Szeged` instead.
plain	Try `none` or `Pittsburgh` instead.
sidebar	Try `Goettingen` for the light version and `Marburg` for the dark version.
shadow	Try `Warsaw` instead.
split	Try `Malmoe` instead.
tree	Try `Montpellier` and, for the bars version, `Antibes` or `JuansLesPins`.

158

16 Inner Themes, Outer Themes, and Templates

This section discusses the inner and outer themes that are available in BEAMER. These themes install certain *templates* for the different elements of a presentation. The template mechanism is explained at the end of the section.

Before we plunge into the details, let us agree on some terminology for this section. In BEAMER, an *element* is part of a presentation that is potentially typeset in some special way. Examples of elements are frame titles, the author's name, or the footnote sign. The appearance of every element is governed by a *template* for this element. Appropriate templates are installed by inner and outer themes, where the *inner* themes only install templates for elements that are typically "inside the main text," while *outer* themes install templates for elements "around the main text." Thus, from the templates's point of view, there is no real difference between inner and outer themes.

16.1 Inner Themes

An inner theme installs templates that dictate how the following elements are typeset:

- Title and part pages.
- Itemize environments.
- Enumerate environments.
- Description environments.
- Block environments.
- Theorem and proof environments.
- Figures and tables.
- Footnotes.
- Bibliography entries.

In the following examples, the color themes `seahorse` and `rose` are used to show where and how background colors are honored. Furthermore, background colors have been specified for all elements that honor them in the default theme. In the default color theme, all of the large rectangular areas are transparent.

`\useinnertheme{default}`

Example:

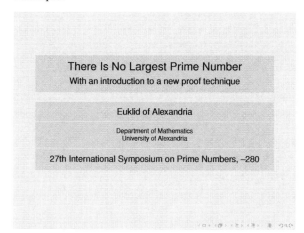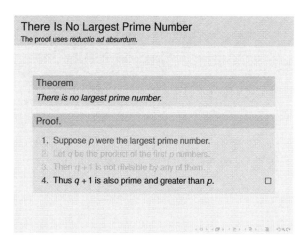

The default element theme is quite sober. The only extravagance is the fact that a little triangle is used in `itemize` environments instead of the usual dot.

In some cases the theme will honor background color specifications for elements. For example, if you set the background color for block titles to green, block titles will have a green background. The background specifications are currently honored for the following elements:

- Title, author, institute, and date fields in the title page.
- Block environments, both for the title and for the body.

This list may increase in the future.

`\useinnertheme{circles}`

Example:

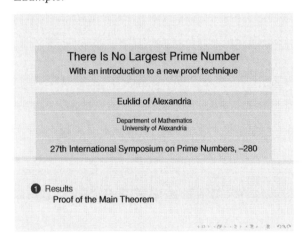
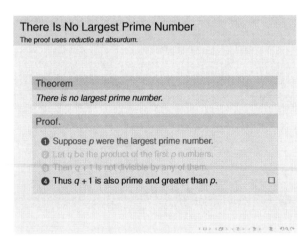

In this theme, `itemize` and `enumerate` items start with a small circle. Likewise, entries in the table of contents start with circles.

`\useinnertheme{rectangles}`

Example:

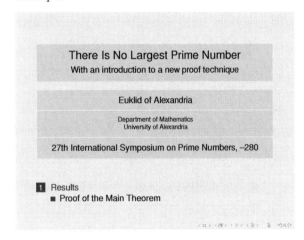
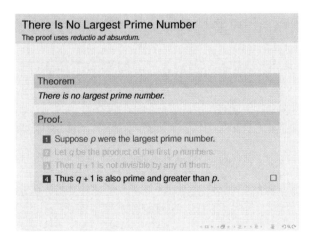

In this theme, `itemize` and `enumerate` items and table of contents entries start with small rectangles.

`\useinnertheme[⟨options⟩]{rounded}`

Example:

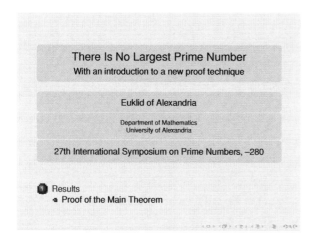
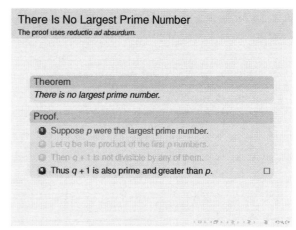

In this theme, `itemize` and `enumerate` items and table of contents entries start with small balls. If a background is specified for blocks, then the corners of the background rectangles will be rounded off. The following ⟨options⟩ may be given:

- `shadow` adds a shadow to all blocks.

`\useinnertheme{inmargin}`

Example:

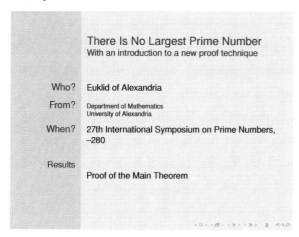
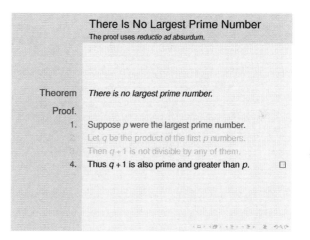

The idea behind this theme is to have "structuring" information on the left and "normal" information on the right. To this end, blocks are redefined such that the block title is shown on the left and the block body is shown on the right.

The code used to place text in the margin is a bit fragile. You may often need to adjust the spacing "by hand," so use at your own risk.

Itemize items are redefined such that they appear on the left. However, only the position is changed by changing some spacing parameters; the code used to draw the items is not changed otherwise. Because of this, you can load another inner theme first and then load this theme afterwards.

This theme is a "dirty" inner theme since it messes with things that an inner theme should not mess with. In particular, it changes the width of the left sidebar to a large value. However, you can still use it together with most outer themes.

Using columns inside this theme is problematic. Most of the time, the result will not be what you expect.

16.2 Outer Themes

An outer theme dictates (roughly) the overall layout of frames. It specifies where any navigational elements should go (like a mini table of contents or navigational mini frames) and what they should look like. Typically, an outer theme specifies how the following elements are rendered:

- The head- and footline.

- The sidebars.

- The logo.

- The frame title.

An outer theme will not specify how things like `itemize` environments should be rendered—that is the job of an inner theme.

In the following examples the color theme `seahorse` is used. Since the default color theme leaves most backgrounds empty, most of the outer themes look too unstructured with the default color theme.

`\useoutertheme{default}`

Example:

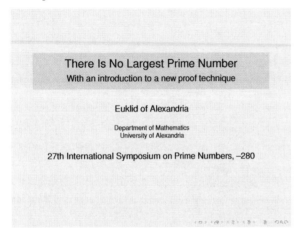
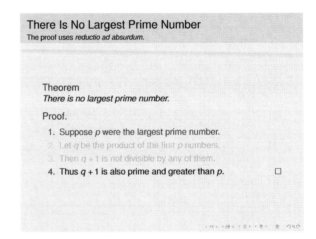

The default layout theme is the most sober and minimalistic theme around. It will flush left the frame title and it will not install any head- or footlines. However, even this theme honors the background color specified for the frame title. If a color is specified, a bar occupying the whole page width is put behind the frame title. A background color of the frame subtitle is ignored.

`\useoutertheme{infolines}`

Example:

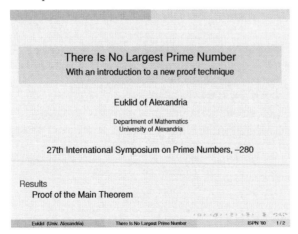
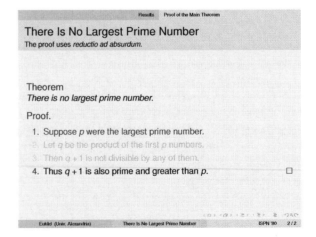

This theme installs a headline showing the current section and the current subsection. It installs a footline showing the author's name, the institution, the presentation's title, the current date, and a frame count. This theme uses only little space.

The colors used in the headline and footline are drawn from `palette primary`, `palette secondary`, and `primary tertiary` (see Section 17 for details on how to change these).

\useoutertheme[⟨*options*⟩]{miniframes}

Example:

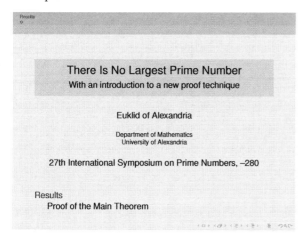 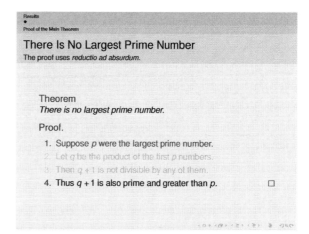

This theme installs a headline in which a horizontal navigational bar is shown. This bar contains one entry for each section of the presentation. Below each section entry, small circles are shown that represent the different frames in the section. The frames are arranged subsection-wise, that is, there is a line of frames for each subsection. If the class option `compress` is given, the frames will instead be arranged in a single row for each section. The navigation bars draws its color from `section in head/foot`.

Below the navigation bar, a line is put showing the title of the current subsection. The color is drawn from `subsection in head/foot`.

At the bottom, two lines are put that contain information such as the author's name, the institution, or the paper's title. What is shown exactly is influenced by the ⟨*options*⟩ given. The colors are drawn from the appropriate BEAMER-colors like `author in head/foot`.

At the top and bottom of both the head- and footline and between the navigation bar and the subsection name, separation lines are drawn *if* the background color of `separation line` is set. This separation line will have a height of 3pt. You can get even more fine-grained control over the colors of the separation lines by setting appropriate colors like `lower separation line head`.

The following ⟨*options*⟩ can be given:

- `footline=empty` suppresses the footline (default).
- `footline=authorinstitute` shows the author's name and the institute in the footline.
- `footline=authortitle` shows the author's name and the title in the footline.
- `footline=institutetitle` shows the institute and the title in the footline.
- `footline=authorinstitutetitle` shows the author's name, the institute, and the title in the footline.
- `subsection=`⟨*true or false*⟩ shows or suppresses line showing the subsection in the headline. It is shown by default. If the document does not use subsections, this option should be set `false`.

\useoutertheme[⟨*options*⟩]{smoothbars}

Example:

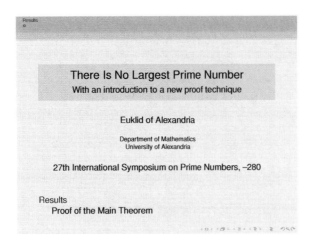 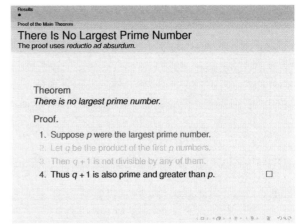

This theme behaves very much like the `miniframes` theme, at least with respect to the headline. The only differences are that smooth transitions are installed between the background colors of the navigation bar, the (optional) bar for the subsection name, and the background of the frame title. No footline is created. You can get the footlines of the `miniframes` theme by first loading that theme and then loading the `smoothbars` theme.

The following ⟨options⟩ can be given:

- `subsection=`⟨*true or false*⟩ shows or suppresses line showing the subsection in the headline. It is shown by default.

`\useoutertheme[`⟨*options*⟩`]{sidebar}`

Example:

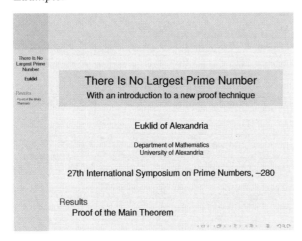 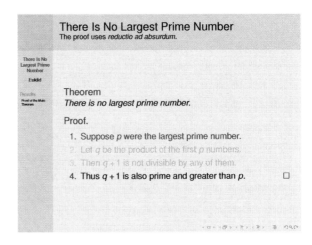

In this layout, a sidebar is shown that contains a small table of contents with the current section, subsection, or subsection highlighted. The frame title is vertically centered in a rectangular area at the top that always occupies the same amount of space in all frames. Finally, the logo is shown in the "corner" resulting from the sidebar and the frame title rectangle.

There are several ways of modifying the layout using the ⟨options⟩. If you set the width of the sidebar to 0pt, it is not shown, giving you a layout in which the frame title does not "wobble" since it always occupies the same amount of space on all slides. Conversely, if you set the height of the frame title rectangle to 0pt, the rectangular area is not used and the frame title is inserted normally (occupying as much space as needed on each slide).

The background color of the sidebar is taken from `sidebar`, the background color of the frame title from `frametitle`, and the background color of the logo corner from `logo`.

The colors of the entries in the table of contents are drawn from the BEAMER-color `section in sidebar` and `section in sidebar current` as well as the corresponding BEAMER-colors for subsections. If an entry does not fit on a single line it is automatically "linebroken."

The following ⟨*options*⟩ may be given:

- `height=`⟨*dimension*⟩ specifies the height of the frame title rectangle. If it is set to 0pt, no frame title rectangle is created. Instead, the frame title is inserted normally into the frame. The default is 2.5 base line heights of the frame title font. Thus, there is about enough space for a two-line frame title plus a one-line subtitle.

- `hideothersubsections` causes all subsections except those of the current section to be suppressed in the table of contents. This is useful if you have lots of subsections.

- `hideallsubsections` causes all subsections to be suppressed in the table of contents.

- `left` puts the sidebar on the left side. Note that in a left-to-right reading culture this is the side people look first. Note also that this table of contents is usually *not* the most important part of the frame, so you do not necessarily want people to look at it first. Nevertheless, it is the default.

- `right` puts the sidebar of the right side.

- `width=`⟨*dimension*⟩ specifies the width of the sidebar. If it is set to 0pt, it is completely suppressed. The default is 2.5 base line heights of the frame title font.

`\useoutertheme{split}`

Example:

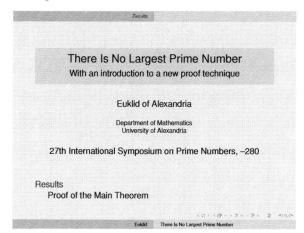 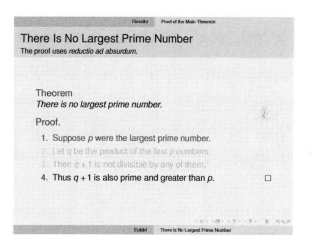

This theme installs a headline in which, on the left, the sections of the talk are shown and, on the right, the subsections of the current section. If the class option `compress` has been given, the sections and subsections will be put in one line; normally there is one line per section or subsection.

The footline shows the author on the left and the talk's title on the right.

The colors are taken from `palette primary` and `palette quaternary`.

`\useoutertheme{shadow}`

Example:

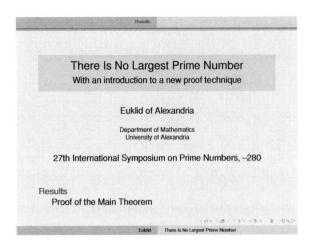
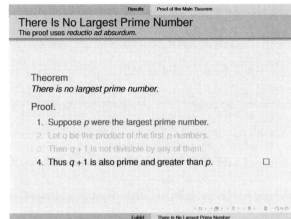

This layout theme extends the `split` theme by putting a horizontal shading behind the frame title and adding a little "shadow" at the bottom of the headline.

`\useoutertheme[⟨options⟩]{tree}`

Example:

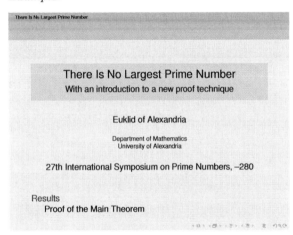
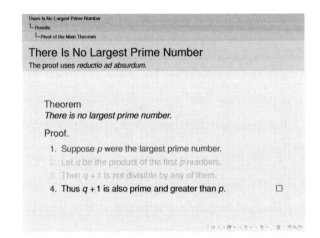

In this layout, the headline contains three lines that show the title of the current talk, the current section in this talk, and the current subsection in the section. The colors are drawn from `title in head/foot`, `section in head/foot`, and `subsection in head/foot`.

In addition, separation lines of height 3pt are shown above and below the three lines *if* the background of `separation line` is set. More fine-grained control of the colors of these lines can be gained by setting `upper separation line head` and `lower separation line head`.

The following ⟨*options*⟩ may be given:

- `hooks` causes little "hooks" to be drawn in front of the section and subsection entries. These are supposed to increase the tree-like appearance.

`\useoutertheme{smoothtree}`

Example:

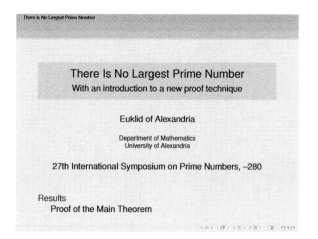 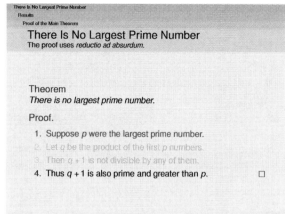

This layout is similar to the `tree` layout. The main difference is that the background colors change smoothly.

16.3 Changing the Templates Used for Different Elements of a Presentation

This section explains how BEAMER's template management works.

16.3.1 Overview of Beamer's Template Management

If you only wish to modify the appearance of a single or few elements, you do not need to create a whole new inner or outer theme. Instead, you can modify the appropriate template.

A template specifies how an element of a presentation is typeset. For example, the `frametitle` template dictates where the frame title is put, which font is used, and so on.

As the name suggests, you specify a template by writing the exact LaTeX code you would also use when typesetting a single frame title by hand. Only, instead of the actual title, you use the command `\insertframetitle`.

Example: Suppose we would like to have the frame title typeset in red, centered, and boldface. If we were to typeset a single frame title by hand, it might be done like this:

```
\begin{frame}
  \begin{centering}
    \color{red}
    \textbf{The Title of This Frame.}
    \par
  \end{centering}

  Blah, blah.
\end{frame}
```

In order to typeset the frame title in this way on all slides, in the simplest case we can change the frame title template as follows:

```
\setbeamertemplate{frametitle}
{
  \begin{centering}
    \color{red}
    \textbf{\insertframetitle}
    \par
  \end{centering}
}
```

We can then use the following code to get the desired effect:

```
\begin{frame}
  \frametitle{The Title of This Frame.}
```

167

```
Blah, blah.
\end{frame}
```

When rendering the frame, BEAMER will use the code of the frame title template to typeset the frame title and it will replace every occurrence of \insertframetitle by the current frame title.

We can take this example a step further. It would be nicer if we did not have to "hardwire" the color of the frametitle, but if this color could be specified independently of the code for the template. This way, a color theme could change this color. Since this is a problem that is common to most templates, BEAMER will automatically setup the BEAMER-color frametitle when the template frametitle is used. Thus, we can remove the \color{red} command if we set the BEAMER-color frametitle to red at some point.

```
\setbeamercolor{frametitle}{fg=red}
\setbeamertemplate{frametitle}
{
  \begin{centering}
    \textbf{\insertframetitle}
    \par
  \end{centering}
}
```

Next, we can also make the font "themable." Just like the color, the BEAMER-font frametitle is installed before the frametitle template is typeset. Thus, we should rewrite the code as follows:

```
\setbeamercolor{frametitle}{fg=red}
\setbeamerfont{frametitle}{series=\bfseries}
\setbeamertemplate{frametitle}
{
  \begin{centering}
    \insertframetitle\par
  \end{centering}
}
```

Users, themes, or whoever can now easily change the color or font of the frametitle without having to mess with the code used to typeset it.

ICLE In article mode, most of the template mechanism is switched off and has no effect. However, a few templates are also available. If this is the case, it is specially indicated.

Here are a few hints that might be helpful when you wish to set a template:

- Usually, you might wish to copy code from an existing template. The code often takes care of some things that you may not yet have thought about. The default inner and outer themes might be useful starting points. Also, the file beamerbaseauxtemplates.sty contains interesting "auxilliary" templates.

- When copying code from another template and when inserting this code in the preamble of your document (not in another style file), you may have to "switch on" the at-character (@). To do so, add the command \makeatletter before the \setbeamertemplate command and the command \makeatother afterward.

- Most templates having to do with the frame components (headlines, sidebars, etc.) can only be changed in the preamble. Other templates can be changed during the document.

- The height of the headline and footline templates is calculated automatically. This is done by typesetting the templates and then "having a look" at their heights. This recalculation is done right at the beginning of the document, *after* all packages have been loaded and even *after* these have executed their \AtBeginDocument initialization.

- Getting the boxes right inside any template is often a bit of a hassle. You may wish to consult the TEX book for the glorious details on "Making Boxes." If your headline is simple, you might also try putting everything into a pgfpicture environment, which makes the placement easier.

16.3.2 Using Beamer's Templates

As a user of the BEAMER class you typically do not "use" or "invoke" templates yourself, directly. For example, the frame title template is automatically invoked by BEAMER somewhere deep inside the frame typesetting process. The same is true of most other templates. However, if, for whatever reason, you wish to invoke a template yourself, you can use the following command.

`\usebeamertemplate***{⟨element name⟩}`

> If none of the stars is given, the text of the ⟨element name⟩ is directly inserted at the current position. This text should previously have been specified using the `\setbeamertemplate` command. No text is inserted if this command has not been called before.
>
> *Example:*
>
> `\setbeamertemplate{my template}{correct}`
> `...`
> `Your answer is \usebeamertemplate{my template}.`
>
> If you add one star, three things happen. First, the template is put inside a TEX-group, thereby limiting most side effects of commands used inside the template. Second, inside this group the BEAMER-color named ⟨element name⟩ is used and the foreground color is selected. Third, the BEAMER-font ⟨element name⟩ is also used. This one-starred version is usually the best version to use.
>
> If you add a second star, nearly the same happens as with only one star. However, in addition, the color is used with the command `\setbeamercolor*`. This causes the colors to be reset to the normal text color if no special foreground or background is specified by the BEAMER-color ⟨element name⟩. Thus, in this twice-starred version, the color used for the template is guaranteed to be independent of the color that was currently in use when the template is used.
>
> Finally, adding a third star will also cause a star to be added to the `\setbeamerfont*` command. This causes the font used for the template also to be reset to normal text, unless the BEAMER-font ⟨element name⟩ specifies things differently. This three-star version is the "most protected" version available.

`\ifbeamertemplateempty{⟨beamer template name⟩}{⟨executed if empty⟩}{⟨executed otherwise⟩}`

> This command checks whether a template is defined and set to a non-empty text. If the text is empty or the template is not defined at all, ⟨executed if empty⟩ is executed. Otherwise, ⟨executed otherwise⟩ is executed.

`\expandbeamertemplate{⟨beamer template name⟩}`

> This command does the same as `\usebeamertemplate{⟨beamer template name⟩}`. The difference is that this command performs a direct expansion and does not scan for a star. This is important inside, for example, an `\edef`. If you don't know the difference between `\def` and `\edef`, you won't need this command.

16.3.3 Setting Beamer's Templates

To set a BEAMER-template, you can use the following command:

`\setbeamertemplate{⟨element name⟩}[⟨predefined option⟩]⟨args⟩`

> In the simplest case, if no ⟨predefined option⟩ is given, the ⟨args⟩ must be a single argument and the text of the template ⟨element name⟩ is setup to be this text. Upon later invocation of the template by the command `\usebeamertemplate` this text is used.
>
> *Example:*
>
> `\setbeamertemplate{answer}{correct}`
> `...`
> `Your answer is \usebeamertemplate*{answer}.`
>
> If you specify a ⟨predefined option⟩, this command behaves slightly differently. In this case, someone has used the command `\defbeamertemplate` to predefine a template for you. By giving the name of this

predefined template as the optional parameter ⟨*predefined option*⟩, you cause the template ⟨*element name*⟩ to be set to this template.

Example: \setbeamertemplate{bibliography item}[book] causes the bibliography items to become little book icons. This command causes a subsequent call of \usebeamertemplate{bibliography item} to insert the predefined code for inserting a book.

Some predefined template options take parameters themselves. In such a case, the parameters are given as ⟨*args*⟩.

Example: The ⟨*predefined option*⟩ grid for the template background takes an optional argument:

\setbeamertemplate{background}[grid][step=1cm]

In the example, the second argument in square brackets is the optional argument.

In the descriptions of elements, if there are possible ⟨*predefined option*⟩, the description shows how the ⟨*predefined option*⟩ can be used together with its arguments, but the \setbeamertemplate{xxxx} is omitted. Thus, the above example would be documented in the description of the background element like this:

- [grid] [⟨*step options*⟩] causes a light grid to be ...

\addtobeamertemplate{⟨*element name*⟩}{⟨*pre-text*⟩}{⟨*post-text*⟩}

This command adds the ⟨*pre-text*⟩ before the text that is currently installed as the template ⟨*element name*⟩ and the ⟨*post-text*⟩ after it. This allows you a limited form of modification of existing templates.

Example: The following commands have the same effect:

\setbeamertemplate{my template}{Hello world!}

\setbeamertemplate{my template}{world}
\addtobeamertemplate{my template}{Hello }{!}

If a new template is installed, any additions will be deleted. On the other hand, you can repeatedly use this command to add multiple things.

\defbeamertemplate<⟨*mode specification*⟩>*{⟨*element name*⟩}{⟨*predefined option*⟩}
[⟨*argument number*⟩] [⟨*default optional argument*⟩] {⟨*predefined text*⟩}
[action]{⟨*action command*⟩}

This command installs a *predefined option* for the template ⟨*element name*⟩. Once this command has been used, users can access the predefined template using the \setbeamertemplate command.

Example: \defbeamertemplate{itemize item}{double arrow}{$\Rightarrow$}

After the above command has been invoked, the following two commands will have the same effect:

\setbeamertemplate{itemize item}{$\Rightarrow$}
\setbeamertemplate{itemize item}[double arrow]

Sometimes, a predefined template needs to get an argument when it is installed. Suppose, for example, we want to define a predefined template that draws a square as the itemize item and we want to make this size of this square configurable. In this case, we can specify the ⟨*argument number*⟩ of the predefined option the same way one does for the \newcommand command:

\defbeamertemplate{itemize item}{square}[1]{\hrule width #1 height #1}

% The following have the same effect:
\setbeamertemplate{itemize item}[square]{3pt}
\setbeamertemplate{itemize item}{\hrule width 3pt height 3pt}

As for the \newcommand command, you can also specify a ⟨*default optional argument*⟩:

\defbeamertemplate{itemize item}{square}[1][1ex]{\hrule width #1 height #1}

% The following have the same effect:

```
\setbeamertemplate{itemize item}[square][3pt]
\setbeamertemplate{itemize item}{\hrule width 3pt height 3pt}

% So do the following:
\setbeamertemplate{itemize item}[square]
\setbeamertemplate{itemize item}{\hrule width 1ex height 1ex}
```

The starred version of the command installs the predefined template option, but then immediately calls \setbeamertemplate for this option. This is useful for the default templates. If there are any arguments necessary, these are set to \relax.

In certain cases, if a predefined template option is chosen, you do not only wish the template text to be installed, but certain extra "actions" must also be taken once. For example, a shading must be defined that should not be redefined every time the shading is used later on. To implement such "actions," you can use the optional argument ⟨action⟩ following the keyword [action]. Thus, after the normal use of the \defbeamertemplate you add the text [action] and then any commands that should be executed once when the ⟨predefined option⟩ is selected by the \setbeamertemplate command.

Example:

```
\defbeamertemplate{background canvas}{my shading}[2]
{
  \pgfuseshading{myshading}% simple enough
}
[action]
{
  \pgfdeclareverticalshading{myshading}{\the\paperwidth}
  {color(0cm)=(#1); color(\the\paperheight)=(#2)}
}
...

\setbeamertemplate{background canvas}{myshading}{red!10}{blue!10}
% Defines the shading myshading right here. Subsequent calls to
% \usebeamertemplate{background canvas} will yield
% ''\pgfuseshading{myshading}''.
```

ARTICLE Normally, this command has no effect in article mode. However, if a ⟨mode specification⟩ is given, this command is applied for the specified modes. Thus, this command behaves like the \\ command, which also gets the implicit mode specification <presentation> if no other specification is given.

Example: \defbeamertemplate{my template}{default}{something} has no effect in article mode.

Example: \defbeamertemplate<article>{my template}{default}{something} has no effect in presentation modes, but has an effect in article mode.

Example: \defbeamertemplate<all>{my template}{default}{something} applies to all modes.

It is often useful to have access to the same template option via different names. For this, you can use the following command to create aliases:

\defbeamertemplatealias{⟨element name⟩}{⟨new predefined option name⟩}{⟨existing predefined option name⟩}

Causes the two predefined options to have the same effect.

There is no inheritance relation among templates as there is for colors and fonts. This is due to the fact the templates for one element seldom make sense for another. However, sometimes certain elements "behave similarly" and one would like a \setbeamertemplate to apply to a whole set of templates via inheritance. For example, one might want that \setbeamertemplate{items}[circle] causes all items to use the circle option, though the effects for the itemize item as opposed to the itemize subsubitem as opposed to enumerate item must be slightly different.

The BEAMER-template mechanism implements a simple form of inheritance via *parent templates*. In element descriptions, parent templates are indicated via a check mark in parentheses.

171

`\defbeamertemplateparent{⟨parent template name⟩}[⟨predefined option name⟩]{⟨child template list⟩}` `[⟨argument number⟩][⟨default optional argument⟩]{⟨arguments for children⟩}`

The effect of this command is that whenever someone calls `\setbeamertemplate{⟨parent template name⟩}{⟨args⟩}`, the command `\setbeamertemplate{⟨child template name⟩}{⟨args⟩}` is called for each ⟨child template name⟩ in the ⟨child template list⟩.

The ⟨arguments for children⟩ come into play if the `\setbeamertemplate` command is called with a predefined option name (not necessarily the same as the ⟨predefined option name⟩, we'll come to that). If `\setbeamertemplate` is called with some predefined option name, the children are called with the ⟨arguments for children⟩ instead. Let's look at two examples:

Example: The following is the typical, simple usage:

```
\defbeamertemplateparent{itemize items}{itemize item,itemize subitem,itemize subsubitem}
{}

% The following command has the same effect as the three commands below:
\setbeamertemplate{itemize items}[circle]

\setbeamertemplate{itemite item}[circle] % actually, the ''empty'' argument is added
\setbeamertemplate{itemize subitem}[circle]
\setbeamertemplate{itemize subsubitem}[circle]
```

Example: In the following case, an argument is passed to the children:

```
\defbeamertemplateparent{sections/subsections in toc shaded}
{section in toc shaded,subsection in toc shaded}[1][20]
{[#1]}

% The following command has the same effect as the two commands below:
\setbeamertemplate{sections/subsections in toc shaded}[default][35]

\setbeamertemplate{section in toc shaded}[default][35]
\setbeamertemplate{subsection in toc shaded}[default][35]


% Again:
\setbeamertemplate{sections/subsections in toc shaded}[default]

\setbeamertemplate{section in toc shaded}[default][20]
\setbeamertemplate{subsection in toc shaded}[default][20]
```

In detail, the following happens: When `\setbeamertemplate` is encountered for a parent template, BEAMER first checks whether a predefined option follows. If not, a single argument is read and `\setbeamertemplate` is called for all children for this template. If there is a predefined template option set, BEAMER evaluates the ⟨argument for children⟩. It may contain parameters like #1 or #2. These parameters are filled with the arguments that follow the call of `\setbeamertemplate` for the parent template. The number of arguments must be the number given as ⟨argument number⟩. An optional argument can also be specified in the usual way. Once the ⟨arguments for the children⟩ have been computed, `\setbeamertemplate` is called for all children for the predefined template and with the computed arguments.

You may wonder what happens when certain predefined options take a certain number of arguments, but another predefined option takes a different number of arguments. In this case, the above-described mechanism cannot differentiate between the predefined options and it is unclear which or even how many arguments should be contained in ⟨arguments for children⟩. For this reason, you can give the optional argument ⟨predefined option name⟩ when calling `\defbeamertemplateparent`. If this optional argument is specified, the parenthood of the template applies only to this particular ⟨predefined option name⟩. Thus, if someone calls `\setbeamertemplate` for this ⟨predefined option name⟩, the given ⟨argument for children⟩ is used. For other predefined option names a possibly different definition is used. You can imaging that leaving out the optional ⟨*predefined option name*⟩ means "this ⟨*argument for children*⟩ applies to all predefined option names that have not been specially defined differently."

17 Colors

BEAMER's color management allows you to specify the color of every element (like, say, the color of the section entries in a table of contents or, say, the color of the subsection entries in a mini table of contents in a sidebar). While the system is quite powerful, it is not trivial to use. To simplify the usage of the color system, you should consider using a predefined color theme, which takes care of everything for you.

In the following, color themes are explained first. The rest of the section consists of explanations of how the color management works internally. You will need to read these sections only if you wish to write your own color themes; or if you are quite happy with the predefined themes but you absolutely insist that displayed mathematical text simply has to be typeset in a lovely pink.

17.1 Color Themes

In order to also show the effect of the different color themes on the sidebar, in the following examples the color themes are used together with the outer theme `sidebar`.

17.1.1 Default and Special-Purpose Color Themes

\usecolortheme{default}

Example:

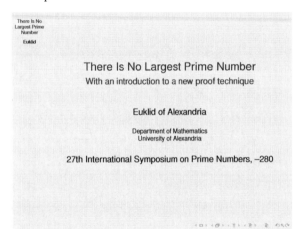 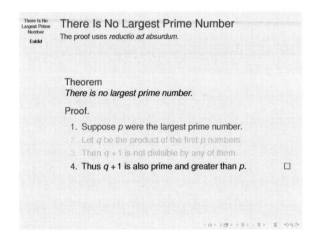

The `default` color theme is very sober. It installs little special colors and even less backgrounds. The default color theme sets up the default parent relations between the different BEAMER-colors.

The main colors set in the `default` color theme are the following:

- `normal text` is black on white.
- `alerted text` is red.
- `example text` is a dark green (green with 50% black).
- `structure` is set to a light version of MidnightBlue (more precisely, 20% red, 20% green, and 70% blue).

Use this theme for a no-nonsense presentation. Since this theme is loaded by default, you cannot "reload" it after having loaded another color theme.

\usecolortheme[⟨*options*⟩]{structure}

Example:

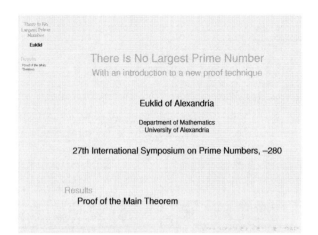 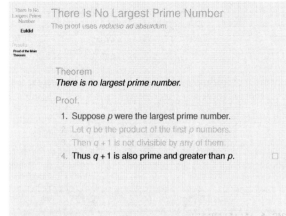

The example was created using \usecolortheme[named=SeaGreen]{structure}.

This theme offers a convenient way of changing the color used for structural elements. More precisely, it just changes the foreground of the BEAMER-color structure. You can also achieve this by directly invoking the function \setbeamercolor, but this color theme makes things a bit easier.

The theme offers several ⟨options⟩, which can be used to specify the color to be used for structural elements:

- rgb={⟨rgb tuple⟩} sets the structure foreground to the specified red-green-blue tuple. The numbers are given as decimals between 0 and 1. For example, rgb={0.5,0,0} yields a dark red.

- RGB={⟨rgb tuple⟩} does the same as rgb, except that the numbers range between 0 and 255. For example, RGB={128,0,0} yields a dark red.

- cmyk={⟨cmyk tuple⟩} sets the structure foreground to the specified cyan-magenta-yellow-black tuple. The numbers are given as decimals between 0 and 1. For example, cmyk={0,1,1,0.5} yields a dark red.

- cmy={⟨cmy tuple⟩} is similar to cmyk, except that the black component is not specified.

- hsb={⟨hsb tuple⟩} sets the structure foreground to the specified hue-saturation-brightness tuple. The numbers are given as decimals between 0 and 1. For example, hsb={0,1,.5} yields a dark red.

- named={⟨color name⟩} sets the structure foreground to a named color. This color must previously have been defined using the \DefineNamedColor command. Adding the class option xcolor=dvipsnames or xcolor=svgnames will install a long list of standard dvips or SVG color names (respectively). See the file dvipsnam.def for the list.

\usecolortheme{sidebartab}

Example:

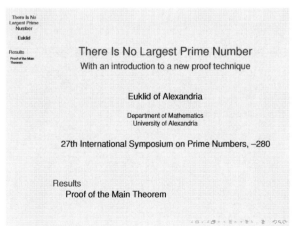 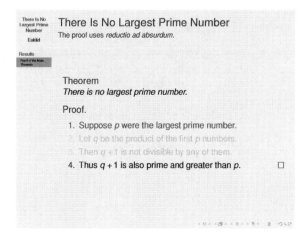

This theme changes the colors in a sidebar such that the current entry in a table of contents shown there gets highlighted by showing a different background behind it.

17.1.2 Complete Color Themes

A "complete" color theme is a color theme that completely specifies all colors for all parts of a frame. It installs specific colors and does not derive the colors from, say, the **structure** BEAMER-color. Complete color themes happen to have names of flying animals.

`\usecolortheme{albatross}`

Example:

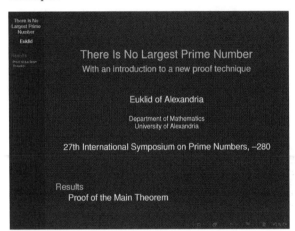 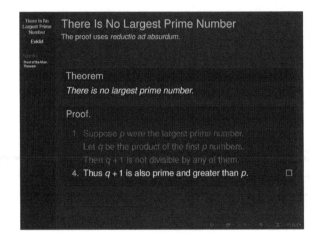

The color theme is a "dark" or "inverted" theme using yellow on blue as the main colors. The color theme also installs a slightly darker background color for blocks, which is necessary for presentation themes that use shadows, but which (in Till's opinion) is undesirable for all other presentation themes. By using the `lily` color theme together with this theme, the backgrounds for blocks can be removed.

When using a light-on-dark theme like this one, be aware that there are certain disadvantages:

- If the room in which the talk is given has been "darkened," using such a theme makes it more difficult for the audience to take or read notes.

- Since the room becomes darker, the pupil becomes larger, thus making it harder for the eye to focus. This *can* make text harder to read.

- Printing such slides is difficult at best.

On the other hand, a light-on-dark presentation often appears to be more "stylish" than a plain black-on-white one.

The following ⟨*options*⟩ may be given:

- `overlystylish` installs a background canvas that is, in Till's opinion, way too stylish. But then, it is not his intention to press his taste on other people. When using this option, it is probably a very good idea to also use the `lily` color theme.

Example: The `overlystylish` option together with the `lily` color theme:

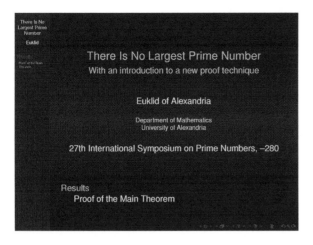 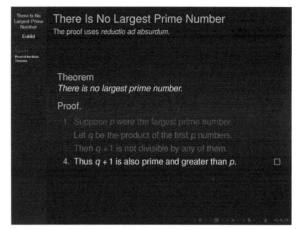

`\usecolortheme{beetle}`

Example:

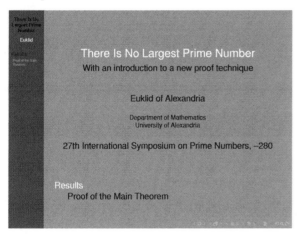 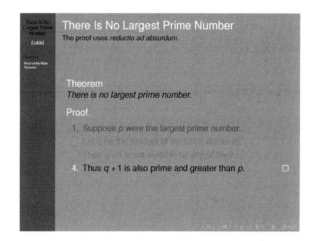

The main "theme behind this theme" is to use white and black text on gray background. The white text is used for special emphasis, the black text for normal text. The "outer stuff" like the headline and the footline use, however, a bluish color. To change this color, change the background of `palette primary`.

Great care must be taken with this theme since both the white/gray and the black/gray contrasts are much lower than with other themes. Make sure that the contrast is high enough for the actual presentation.

You can change the "grayish" background by changing the background of `normal text`.

`\usecolortheme{crane}`

Example:

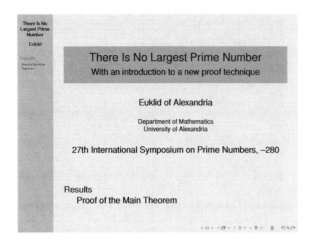 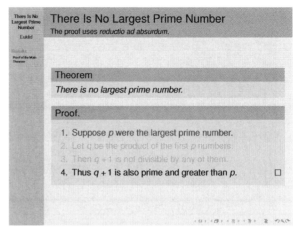

This theme uses the colors of Lufthansa, whose logo is a crane. It is *not* an official theme by that company, however.

\usecolortheme{dove}

Example:

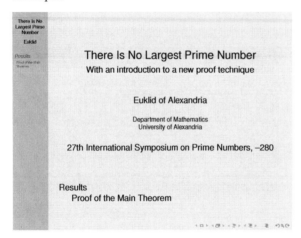 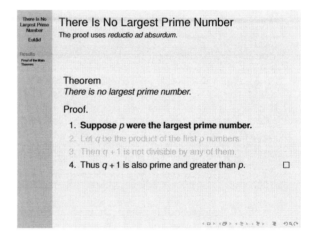

This theme is nearly a black and white theme and useful for creating presentations that are easy to print on a black-and-white printer. The theme uses grayscale in certain unavoidable cases, but never color. It also changes the font of alerted text to boldface.

When using this theme, you should consider using the class option gray, which ensures that all colors are converted to grayscale. Also consider using the structurebold font theme.

\usecolortheme{fly}

Example:

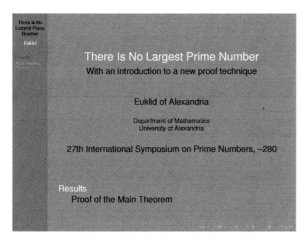 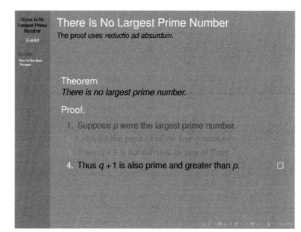

This theme is the "consequent" version of `beetle` and uses white/black/gray throughout. It does not go particularly well with themes that use shadows.

`\usecolortheme{`monarca`}`

Example:

beamerugcolorthememonarca1

beamerugcolorthememonarca2

The theme is based on the colors of the Monarch butterfly.

Theme author: Max Dohse.

`\usecolortheme{`seagull`}`

Example:

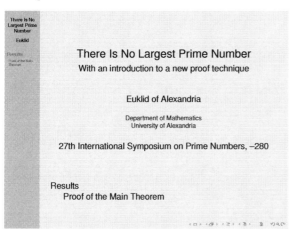 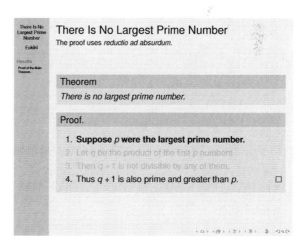

Like the `dove` color theme, this theme is useful for printing on a black-and-white printer. However, it uses different shades of gray extensively, which may or may not look good on a transparency.

`\usecolortheme{`wolverine`}`

Example:

179

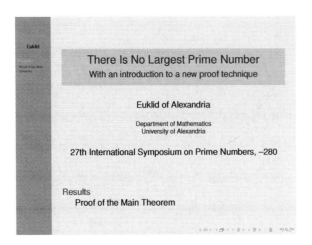 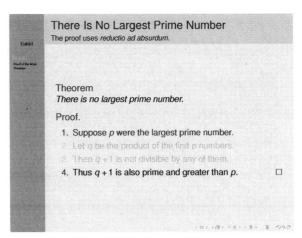

The theme is based on the colors of the University of Michigan's mascot, a wolverine.

Theme author: Madhusudan Singh.

\usecolortheme{beaver}

Example:

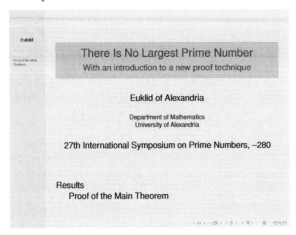 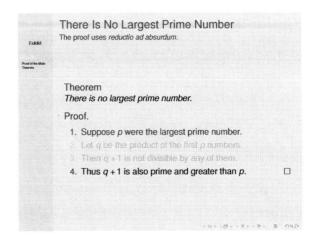

The theme is based on the colors of MIT's mascot, a beaver.

Theme author: Madhusudan Singh.

\usecolortheme{spruce}

Example:

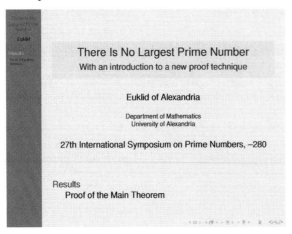 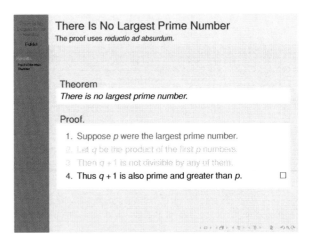

180

The theme is based on the colors of Michigan State University.

Theme author: Alan Munn.

17.1.3 Inner Color Themes

Inner color themes only specify the colors of elements used in inner themes. Most noticably, they specify the colors used for blocks. They can be used together with other (color) themes. If they are used to change the inner colors installed by a presentation theme or another color theme, they should obviously be specified *after* the other theme has been loaded. Inner color themes happen to have flower names.

`\usecolortheme{lily}`

Example:

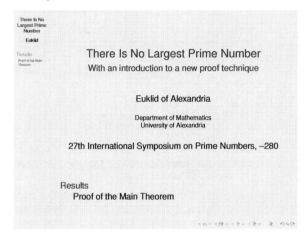 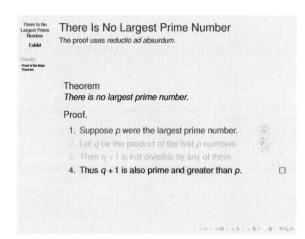

This theme is mainly used to *uninstall* any block colors setup by another theme, restoring the colors used in the `default` theme. In particular, using this theme will remove all background colors for blocks.

`\usecolortheme{orchid}`

Example:

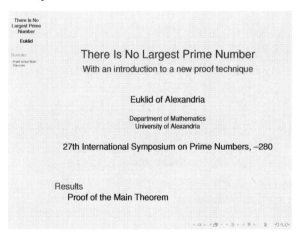 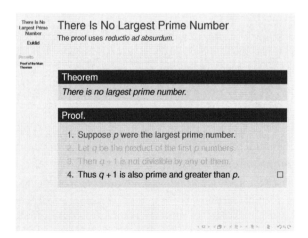

This theme installs white-on-dark block titles. The background of the title of a normal block is set to the foreground of the structure color, the foreground is set to white. The background of alerted blocks are set to red and of example blocks to green. The body of blocks get a nearly transparent background.

`\usecolortheme{rose}`

Example:

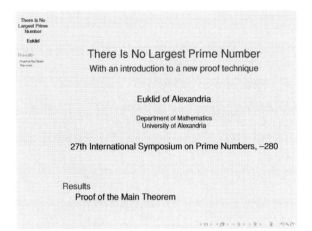
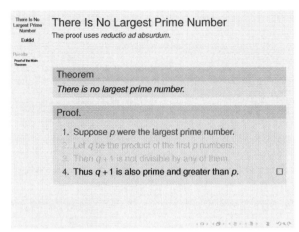

This theme installs nearly transparent backgrounds for both block titles and block bodies. This theme is much less "aggressive" than the orchid theme. The background colors are derived from the foreground of the structure BEAMER-color.

17.1.4 Outer Color Themes

An outer color theme changes the palette colors, on which the colors used in the headline, footline, and sidebar are based by default. Outer color themes normally do not change the color of inner elements, except possibly for titlelike. They happen to be sea-animal names.

\usecolortheme{whale}

Example:

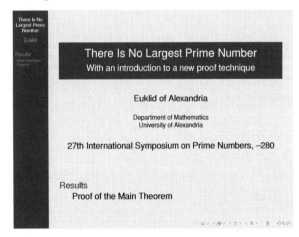
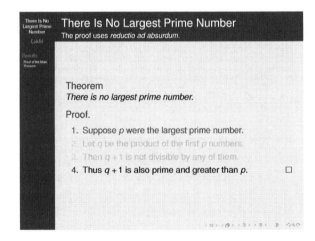

Installs a white-on-dark palette for the headline, footline, and sidebar. The backgrounds used there are set to shades between the structure BEAMER-color and black. The foreground is set to white.

While this color theme can appear to be aggressive, you should note that a dark bar at the border of a frame will have a somewhat different appearance during a presentation than it has on paper: During a presentation the projection on the wall is usually surrounded by blackness. Thus, a dark bar will not create a contrast as opposed to the way it does on paper. Indeed, using this theme will cause the main part of the frame to be more at the focus of attention.

The counterpart to the theme with respect to blocks is the orchid theme. However, pairing it with the rose color theme is also interesting.

\usecolortheme{seahorse}

Example:

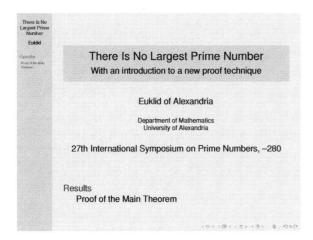 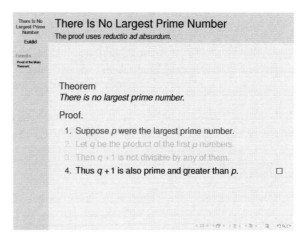

Installs a near-transparent backgrounds for the headline, footline, and sidebar. Using this theme will cause navigational elements to be much less "dominant" than when using the `whale` theme (see the discussion on contrast there, though).

It goes well with the `rose` or the `lily` color theme. Pairing it with the `orchid` overemphasizes blocks (in Till's opinion).

`\usecolortheme{dolphin}`

Example:

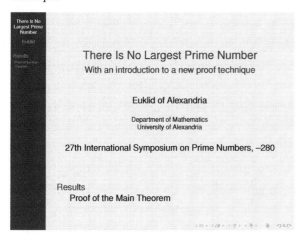 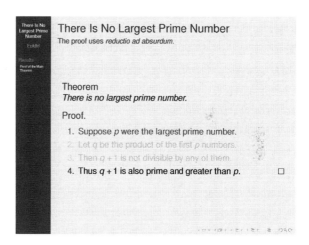

A color theme somewhere in the middle between the whale and the seahorse. It was graciously donated by Manuel Carro. Like the seahorse, it goes well with the `rose` and the `lily` color theme.

17.2 Changing the Colors Used for Different Elements of a Presentation

This section explains how BEAMER's color management works.

17.2.1 Overview of Beamer's Color Management

In BEAMER's philosophy, every element of a presentation can have a different color. Unfortunately, it turned out that simply assigning a single color to every element of a presentation is not such a good idea. First of all, we sometimes want colors of elements to change during a presentation, like the color of the item indicators when they become alerted or inside an example block. Second, some elements naturally have two colors, namely a foreground and a background, but not always. Third, sometimes elements somehow should not have any special color but should simply "run along" with the color of their surrounding. Finally, giving a special color to every element makes it very hard to globally change colors (like changing all the different kind-of-blue things into kind-of-red things) and it makes later extensions even harder.

For all these reasons, the color of an element in BEAMER is a structured object, which we call a BEAMER-*color*. Every BEAMER-color has two parts: a foreground and a background. Either of these may be "empty," which means that whatever foreground or background was active before should remain active when the color is used.

BEAMER-colors can *inherit* from other BEAMER-colors and the default themes make extensive use of this feature. For example, there is a BEAMER-color called `structure` and all sorts of elements inherit from this color. Thus, if someone changes `structure`, the color of all these elements automatically change accordingly. When a color inherits from another color, it can nevertheless still override only the foreground or the background.

It is also possible to "inherit" from another BEAMER-color in a more sophisticated way, which is more like *using* the other BEAMER-color in an indirect way. You can specify that, say, the background of the title should be a 90% of the background of normal text and 10% of the foreground of `structure`.

Inheritance and using of other BEAMER-colors is done dynamically. This means that if one of the parent BEAMER-colors changes during the presentation, the derived colors automatically also change.

The default color theme, which is always loaded, installs numerous BEAMER-colors and inheritance relations between them. These colors are explained throughout this guide. The color used for, say, frametitles is discussed in the section on frametitles, and so on.

17.2.2 Using Beamer's Colors

A BEAMER-color is not a normal color as defined by the `color` and `xcolor` packages and, accordingly, cannot be used directly as in commands like `\color` or `\colorlet`. Instead, in order to use a BEAMER-color, you should first call the command `\usebeamercolor`, which is explained below. This command will setup two (normal) colors called `fg` (for foreground) and `bg` (for, well, guess what). You can then say `\color{fg}` to install the foreground color and `\color{bg}` to install the background color. You can also use the colors `fg` and `bg` in any context in which you normally use a color like, say, `red`. If a BEAMER-color does not have a foreground or a background, the colors `fg` or `bg` (or both) remain unchanged.

Inside templates, this command will typically have already been called for you with the option `[fg]`.

`\usebeamercolor*[`⟨*fg or bg*⟩`]{`⟨*beamer-color name*⟩`}`

> This command (possibly) changes the two colors `fg` and `bg` to the foreground and background color of the ⟨*beamer-color name*⟩. If the BEAMER-color does not specify a foreground, `fg` is left unchanged; if does not specify a background, `bg` is left unchanged.
>
> You will often wish to directly use the color `fg` or `bg` after using this command. For this common situation, the optional argument ⟨*fg or bg*⟩ is useful, which may be either `fg` or `bg`. Giving this option will cause the foreground `fg` or the background `bg` to be immediately installed after they have been setup. Thus, the following command
>
> `\usebeamercolor[fg]{normal text}`
>
> is a shortcut for
>
> `\usebeamercolor{normal text}`
> `\color{fg}`
>
> If you use the starred version of this command, the BEAMER-color `normal text` is used before the command is invoked. This ensures that, barring evil trickery, the colors `fg` and `bg` will be setup independently of whatever colors happened to be in use when the command is invoked.
>
> This command has special side-effects. First, the (normal) color `parent.bg` is set to the value of `bg` prior to this call. Thus you can access the color that was in use prior to the call of this command via the color `parent.bg`.
>
> Second, the special color ⟨*beamer-color name*⟩`.fg` is *globally* set to the same value as `fg` and ⟨*beamer-color name*⟩`.bg` is globally set to the value of `bg`. This allows you to access the foreground or background of a certain ⟨*beamer-color name*⟩ after another BEAMER-color has been used. However, referring to these special global colors should be kept to the unavoidable minimum and should be done as locally as possible since a change of the BEAMER-color will not reflect in a change of the colors ⟨*beamer-color name*⟩`.fg` and ⟨*beamer-color name*⟩`.bg` until the next invocation of `\usebeamercolor`. Also, if the ⟨*beamer-color name*⟩

does not specify a foreground or a background color, then the values of the special colors are whatever happened to be the foreground or background at the time of the last invocation of \usebeamercolor.

So, try not to get into the habit of writing \color{structure.fg} all the time, at least not without a \usebeamercolor{structure} close by.

Example:

```
This text is {\usebeamercolor[fg]{alerted text} alerted}. The
following box uses the fore- and background of frametitles:
{
  \usebeamercolor[fg]{frametitle}
  \colorbox{bg}{Frame Title}
}
```

ARTICLE This command has no effect in `article` mode.

\ifbeamercolorempty[⟨*fg or bg*⟩]{⟨*beamer-color name*⟩}{⟨*if undefined*⟩}{⟨*if defined*⟩}

This command can be used to check whether the foreground or background of some ⟨*beamer-color name*⟩ is non-empty. If the foreground or background of ⟨*beamer-color name*⟩ is defined, ⟨*if defined*⟩ will be executed, otherwise the ⟨*if undefined*⟩ code.

Example:

```
\ifbeamercolorempty[bg]{frametitle}
{ % ''Transparent background''
  \usebeamercolor[fg]{frametitle}
  \insertframetitle
}
{ % Opaque background
  \usebeamercolor[fg]{frametitle}
  \colorbox{bg}{\insertframetitle}
}
```

17.2.3 Setting Beamer's Colors

To set or to change a BEAMER-color, you can use the command \setbeamercolor.

\setbeamercolor*{⟨*beamer-color name*⟩}{⟨*options*⟩}

Sets or changes a BEAMER-color. The ⟨*beamer-color name*⟩ should be a reasonably simple text (do not try too much trickery and avoid punctuation symbols), but it may contain spaces. Thus, `normal text` is a valid ⟨*beamer-color name*⟩ and so is `My Color Number 2`.

In the most simple case, you just specify a foreground by giving the `fg=` option and, possibly, also a background using the `bg=` option.

Example: \setbeamercolor{normal text}{fg=black,bg=mylightgrey}

Example: \setbeamercolor{alerted text}{fg=red!80!black}

The effect of this command is accumulative, thus the following two commands

```
\setbeamercolor{section in toc}{fg=blue}
\setbeamercolor{section in toc}{bg=white}
```

have the same effect as

```
\setbeamercolor{section in toc}{fg=blue,bg=white}
```

Naturally, a second call with the same kind of ⟨*option*⟩ set to a different value overrides a previous call.

The starred version first resets everything, thereby "switching off" the accumulative effect. Use this starred version to completely reset the definition of some BEAMER-color.

The following ⟨*options*⟩ may be given:

- fg=⟨*color*⟩ sets the foreground color of ⟨*beamer-color name*⟩ to the given (normal) ⟨*color*⟩. The ⟨*color*⟩ may also be a color expression like `red!50!black`, see the manual of the XCOLOR package. If ⟨*color*⟩ is empty, the ⟨*beamer-color name*⟩ "has no special foreground" and when the color is used, the foreground currently in force should not be changed.

  Specifying a foreground this way will override any inherited foreground color.

- bg=⟨*color*⟩ does the same as the `fg` option, but for the background.

- parent=⟨*parent beamer-color(s)*⟩ specifies that ⟨*beamer-color name*⟩ should inherit from the specified ⟨*parent beamer-color(s)*⟩. Any foreground and/or background color set by the parents will also be used when ⟨*beamer-color name*⟩ is used. If multiple parents specify a foreground, the last one "wins"; and likewise for the backgrounds.

  Example:

  ```
  \setbeamercolor{father}{fg=red}
  \setbeamercolor{mother}{bg=green}
  \setbeamercolor{child}{parent={father,mother}}
  \begin{beamercolorbox}{child}
    Terrible red on green text.
  \end{beamercolorbox}

  \setbeamercolor{father}{fg=blue}
  \begin{beamercolorbox}{child}
    Now terrible blue on green text, since parent was changed.
  \end{beamercolorbox}
  ```

  Note that a change of the foreground or background of a parent changes the corresponding foreground or background of the child (unless it is overruled).

  A BEAMER-color can not only have parents, but also grandparents and so on.

- use=⟨*another beamer-color*⟩ is used to make sure that another BEAMER-color is setup correctly before the foreground or background color specification are evaluated.

  Suppose you wish the foreground of items to be a mixture of 50% of the foreground of structural elements and 50% of the normal foreground color. You could try

  ```
  \setbeamercolor{item}{fg=structure.fg!50!normal text.fg}
  ```

  However, this will not necessarily give the desired result: If the BEAMER-color `structure` changes, the (normal) color `structure.fg` is not immediately updated. In order to ensure that the normal color `structure.fg` is correct, use the following:

  ```
  \setbeamercolor{item}{use={structure,normal text},fg=structure.fg!50!normal text.fg}
  ```

  This will guarantee that the colors `structure.fg` and `normal text.fg` are setup correctly when the foreground of `item` is computed.

  To show the difference, consider the following example:

  ```
  \setbeamercolor{grandfather}{fg=red}
  \setbeamercolor{grandmother}{bg=white}
  \setbeamercolor{father}{parent={grandfather,grandmother}}
  \setbeamercolor{mother}{fg=black}
  {
    \usebeamercolor{father}\usebeamercolor{mother}
    %% Defines father.fg and mother.fg globally
  }
  \setbeamercolor{my color A}{fg=father.fg!50!mother.fg}
  \setbeamercolor{my color B}{use={father,mother},fg=father.fg!50!mother.fg}

  {\usebeamercolor[fg]{my color A} dark red text}
  {\usebeamercolor[fg]{my color B} also dark red text}
  ```

```
\setbeamercolor{grandfather}{fg=green}

{\usebeamercolor[fg]{my color A} still dark red text}
{\usebeamercolor[fg]{my color B} now dark green text}
```

17.3   The Color of Mathematical Text

By default, mathematical text does not have any special color—it just inherits the "surrounding" color. Some people prefer mathematical text to have some special color. Though we do not recommend this (we believe mathematical text should *not* stand out amid the normal text), BEAMER makes it (reasonably) easy to change the color of mathematical text. Simply change the following colors:

Beamer-Color `math text`

> This color is the parent of `math text inlined` and `math text displayed`. It is empty by default. See those colors for details.

Beamer-Color `math text inlined`

> Color parents: `math text`

> If the foreground of this color is set, inlined mathematical text is typeset using this color. This is done via some `\everymath` hackery and may not work in all cases. If not, you'll have to try to find a way around the problem. The background is currently ignored.

Beamer-Color `math text displayed`

> Color parents: `math text`

> Like `math text inlined`, only for so-called "displayed" mathematical text. This is mathematical text between \[and \] or between $$ and $$ or inside environments like `equation` or `align`. The setup of this color is somewhat fragile, use at your own risk. The background is currently ignored.

Beamer-Color `normal text in math text`

> If the foreground of this color is set, normal text inside mathematical text (which is introduced using the `\text` command) will be typeset using this color. The background is currently ignored.

17.4   The Color Palettes

When one designs a color theme, one faces the following problem: Suppose we want the colors in the headline to gradually change from black to, say, blue. Whatever is at the very top of the headline should be black, what comes right below it should be dark blue, and at the bottom of the headline things should just be blue. Unfortunately, different outer themes will put different things at the top. One theme might put the author at the top, another theme might put the document title there. This makes it impossible to directly assign one of the three colors "black", "dark blue," and "blue" to the different elements that are typically rendered in the headline. No matter how we assign them, things will look wrong for certain outer themes.

To circumvent this problem, BEAMER uses a layer of *palette colors*. Color themes typically only change these palette colors. For example, a color theme might make the BEAMER-color `palette primary` blue, make `palette secondary` a dark blue, and make `palette tertiary` black. Outer themes can now setup things such that whatever they show at the top of the headline inherits from `palette primary`, what comes below inherits from `palette secondary`, and whatever is at the bottom inherits from `palette tertiary`. This way, color themes can change the way even complicated outer themes look and they can do so consistently.

Note that the user can still change the color of every element individually, simply by overriding the color(s) of the elements in the headline. In a sense, the palette colors are just a "suggestion" how things should be colored by an outer theme.

In detail, the following palette colors are used by outer themes.

Beamer-Color `palette primary`

Outer themes (should) base the color of navigational elements and, possibly, also of other elements, on the four palette colors. The "primary" palette should be used for the most important navigational elements, which are usually the ones that change most often and hence require the most attention by the audience. The "secondary" and "tertiary" are less important, the "quaternary" one is the least important.

By default, the palette colors do not have a background and the foreground ranges from `structure.fg` to `black`.

For the sidebar, there is an extra set of palette colors, see `palette sidebar primary`.

Beamer-Color `palette secondary`

See `palette primary`.

Beamer-Color `palette tertiary`

See `palette primary`.

Beamer-Color `palette quaternary`

See `palette primary`.

Beamer-Color `palette sidebar primary`

Similar to `palette primary`, only outer themes (should) base the colors of elements in the sidebar on the four sidebar palette colors.

Beamer-Color `palette sidebar secondary`

See `palette sidebar primary`.

Beamer-Color `palette sidebar tertiary`

See `palette sidebar primary`.

Beamer-Color `palette sidebar quaternary`

See `palette sidebar primary`.

17.5 Miscellaneous Colors

In this section some "basic" colors are listed that do not "belong" to any special commands.

Beamer-Color/-Font `normal text`

The color is used for normal text. At the beginning of the document the foreground color is installed as `\normalcolor`. The background of this color is used by the default background canvas for the background of the presentation, see Section 8.2.7. The background is also the default value of the normal color `bg`.

Since the color is the "root" of all other BEAMER-colors, both a foreground and a background must be installed. In particular, to get a transparent background canvas, make the background of the BEAMER-color `background canvas` empty, not the background of this color.

The BEAMER-font currently is not used. In particular, redefining this font will not have any effect. This is likely to change in the future.

Beamer-Color/-Font `example text`

The color/font is used when text is typeset inside an `example` block.

Beamer-Color/-Font `titlelike`

This color/font is a more specialized form of the `structure` color/font. It is the base for all elements that are "like titles." This includes the frame title and subtitle as well as the document title and subtitle.

Beamer-Color `separation line`

The foreground of this color is used for separating lines. If the foreground is empty, no separation line is drawn.

Beamer-Color `upper separation line head`

Color parents: `separation line`

Special case for the uppermost separation line in a headline.

Beamer-Color `middle separation line head`

Color parents: `separation line`

Special case for the middle separation line in a headline.

Beamer-Color `lower separation line head`

Color parents: `separation line`

Special case for the lower separation line in a headline.

Beamer-Color `upper separation line foot`

Color parents: `separation line`

Special case for the uppermost separation line in a footline.

Beamer-Color `middle separation line foot`

Color parents: `separation line`

Special case for the middle separation line in a footline.

Beamer-Color `lower separation line foot`

Color parents: `separation line`

Special case for the lower separation line in a footline.

17.6   Transparency Effects

By default, *covered* items are not shown during a presentation. Thus if you write `\uncover<2>{Text.}`, the text is not shown on any but the second slide. On the other slides, the text is not simply printed using the background color – it is not shown at all. This effect is most useful if your background does not have a uniform color.

Sometimes however, you might prefer that covered items are not completely covered. Rather, you would like them to be shown already in a very dim or shaded way. This allows your audience to get a feeling for what is yet to come, without getting distracted by it. Also, you might wish text that is covered "once more" still to be visible to some degree.

Ideally, there would be an option to make covered text "transparent." This would mean that when covered text is shown, it would instead be mixed with the background behind it. Unfortunately, `pgf` does not support real transparency yet. Instead, transparency is created by mixing the color of the object you want to show with the current background color (the color `bg`, which has hopefully been setup such that it is the average color of the background on which the object should be placed). To install this effect, you can use:

`\setbeamercovered{transparent}`

This command allows you to specify in a quite general way how a covered item should be rendered. You can even specify different ways of rendering the item depending on how long it will take before this item is shown or for how long it has already been covered once more. The transparency effect will automatically apply to all colors, *except* for the colors in images. For images there is a workaround, see the documentation of the PGF package.

`\setbeamercovered{⟨options⟩}`

This command offers several different options, the most important of which is `transparent`. All options are internally mapped to the two options `still covered` and `again covered`.

In detail, the following ⟨*options*⟩ may be given:

- `invisible` is the default and causes covered text to "completely disappear".

- `transparent`=⟨*opaqueness*⟩ causes covered text to be typset in a "transparent" way. By default, this means that 85% of the background color is mixed into all colors or that the ⟨*opaqueness*⟩ of the text is 15%. You can specify a different ⟨*percentage*⟩, where 0 means "totally transparent" and 100 means "totally opaque."

  Unfortunately, this value is kind of "specific" to every projector. What looks good on your screen need not look good during a presentation.

- `dynamic` Makes all covered text quite transparent, but in a dynamic way. The longer it will take till the text is uncovered, the stronger the transparency.

- `highly dynamic` Has the same effect as `dynamic`, but the effect is stronger.

- `still covered`=⟨*not yet list*⟩ specifies how to render covered items that have not yet been uncovered. The ⟨*not yet list*⟩ should be a list of `\opaqueness` commands, see the description of that command, below.

  Example:

  ```
  \setbeamercovered{%
    still covered={\opaqueness<1>{15}\opaqueness<2>{10}\opaqueness<3>{5}\opaqueness<4->{2}},
    again covered={\opaqueness<1->{15}}}
  ```

- `again covered`=⟨*once more list*⟩ specifies how to render covered items that have once more been covered, that is, that had been shown before but are now covered again.

`\opaqueness<⟨overlay specification⟩>{⟨percentage of opaqueness⟩}`

The ⟨*overlay specification*⟩ specifies on which slides covered text should have which ⟨*percentage of opaqueness*⟩. Unlike other overlay specifications, this ⟨*overlay specification*⟩ is a "relative" overlay specification. For example, the specification "3" here means "things that will be uncovered three slides ahead," respectively "things that have once more been covered for three slides." More precisely, if an item is uncovered for more than one slide and then covered once more, only the "first moment of uncovering" is used for the calculation of how long the item has been covered once more.

An opaqueness of 100 is fully opaque and 0 is fully transparent. Currently, since real transparency is not yet implemented, this command causes all colors to get a mixing of ⟨*percentage of opaqueness*⟩ of the current `bg`. At some future point this command might result in real transparency.

The alternate PGF extension used inside an opaque area is ⟨*percentage of opaqueness*⟩`opaque`. In case of nested calls, only the innermost opaqueness specification is used.

Example:

```
\setbeamercovered{still covered={\opaqueness<1->{15}},again covered={\opaqueness<1->{15}}}
\pgfdeclareimage{book}{book}
\pgfdeclareimage{book.!15opaque}{filenameforbooknearlytransparent}
```

Makes everything that is uncovered in two slides only 15 percent opaque.

18 Fonts

The first subsection introduces the predefined font themes that come with BEAMER and which make it easy to change the fonts used in a presentation. The next subsection describes further special commands for changing some basic attributes of the fonts used in a presentation. The last subsection explains how you can get a much more fine-grained control over the fonts used for every individual element of a presentation.

18.1 Font Themes

BEAMER comes with a set of font themes. When you use such a theme, certain fonts are changed as described below. You can use several font themes in concert. For historical reasons, you cannot change all aspects of the fonts used using font themes—in some cases special commands and options are needed, which are described in the next subsection.

The following font themes only change certain font attributes, they do not choose special font families (although that would also be possible and themes doing just that might be added in the future). Currently, to change the font family, you need to load special packages as explained in the next subsection.

`\usefonttheme{default}`

Example:

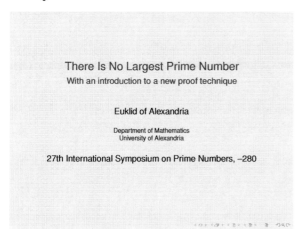 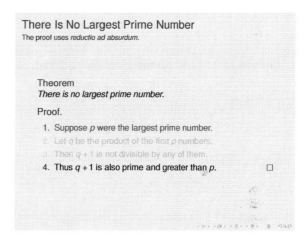

The default font theme installs a sans serif font for all text of the presentation. The default theme installs different font sizes for things like titles or head- and footlines, but does not use boldface or italics for "highlighting." To change some or all text to a serif font, use the `serif` theme.

Note: The command `\mathrm` will always produce upright (not slanted), serif text and the command `\mathsf` will always produce upright, sans-serif text. The command `\mathbf` will produce upright, boldface, sans-serif or serif text, depending on whether `mathsans` or `mathserif` is used.

To produce an upright, sans-serif or serif text, depending on whether `mathsans` or `mathserif` is used, you can use for instance the command `\operatorname` from the `amsmath` package. Using this command instead of `\mathrm` or `\mathsf` directly will automatically adjust upright mathematical text if you switch from sans-serif to serif or back.

`\usefonttheme{professionalfont}`

This font theme does not really change any fonts. Rather, it *suppresses* certain internal replacements performed by BEAMER. If you use "professional fonts" (fonts that you buy and that come with a complete set of every symbol in all modes), you do not want BEAMER to meddle with the fonts you use. BEAMER normally replaces certain character glyphs in mathematical text by more appropriate versions. For example, BEAMER will normally replace glyphs such that the italic characters from the main font are used for variables in mathematical text. If your professional font package takes care of this already, BEAMER's meddling should be switched off. Note that BEAMER's substitution is automatically turned off if one of the following packages is loaded: `arevmath`, `hvmath`, `kpfonts`, `lmodern`, `lucidabr`, `lucimatx`, `mathastext`, `mathpmnt`, `mathpple`, `mathtime`, `mtpro`, and `mtpro2`. If your favorite professional font package is not among these, use the `professionalfont` option (and write us an email, so that the package can be added).

\usefonttheme[⟨*options*⟩]{serif}

Example:

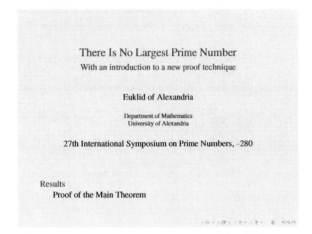 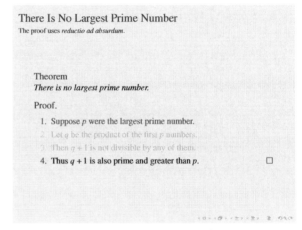

This theme causes all text to be typeset using the default serif font (except if you specify certain ⟨*options*⟩). You might wish to consult Section 5.6.2 on whether you should use serif fonts.

The following ⟨*options*⟩ may be given:

- `stillsansserifmath` causes mathematical text still to be typeset using sans serif. This option only makes sense if you also use the `stillsansseriftext` option since sans serif math inside serif text looks silly.

- `stillsansserifsmall` will cause "small" text to be still typeset using sans serif. This refers to the text in the headline, footline, and sidebars. Using this options is often advisable since small text is often easier to read in sans serif.

- `stillsansseriflarge` will cause "large" text like the presentation title or the frame title to be still typeset using sans serif. Sans serif titles with serif text are a popular combination in typography.

- `stillsansseriftext` will cause normal text (none of the above three) to be still typeset using sans serif. If you use this option, you should most likely also use the first two. However, by not using `stillsansseriflarge`, you get a serif (possibly italic) title over a sans serif text. This can be an interesting visual effect. Naturally, "interesting typographic effect" can mean "terrible typographic effect" if you choose the wrong fonts combinations or sizes. You'll need some typographic experience to judge this correctly. If in doubt, try asking someone who should know.

- `onlymath` is a short-cut for selecting all of the above options except for the first. Thus, using this option causes only mathematical text to by typeset using a serif font. Recall that, by default, mathematical formulas are also typeset using sans-serif letters. In most cases, this is visually the most pleasing and easily readable way of typesetting mathematical formulas if the surrounding text is typeset using sans serif. However, in mathematical texts the font used to render, say, a variable is sometimes used to differentiate between different meanings of this variable. In such case, it may be necessary to typeset mathematical text using serif letters. Also, if you have a lot of mathematical text, the audience may be quicker to "parse" it if it is typeset the way people usually read mathematical text: in a serif font.

\usefonttheme[⟨*options*⟩]{structurebold}

Example:

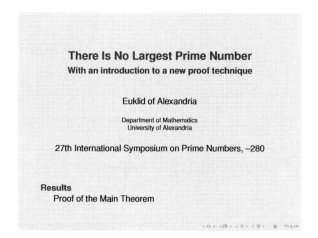
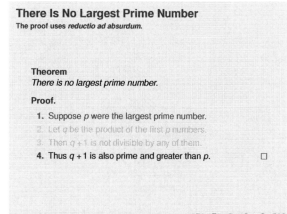

This font theme will cause titles and text in the headlines, footlines, and sidebars to be typeset in a bold font.

The following ⟨options⟩ may be given:

- `onlysmall` will cause only "small" text to be typeset in bold. More precisely, only the text in the headline, footline, and sidebars is changed to be typeset in bold. Large titles are not affected.

- `onlylarge` will cause only "large" text to be typeset in bold. These are the main title, frame titles, and section entries in the table of contents.

As pointed out in Section 5.6.1, you should use this theme (possibly with the `onlysmall` option) if your font is not scaled down properly or for light-on-dark text.

The normal themes do not install this theme by default, while the old compatibility themes do. Since you can reload the theme once it has been loaded, you cannot use this theme with the old compatibility themes to set also titles to a bold font.

\usefonttheme[⟨*options*⟩]{structureitalicserif}

Example:

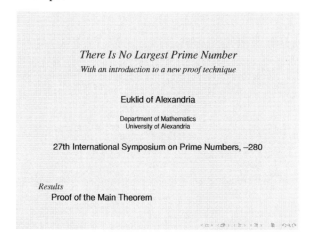
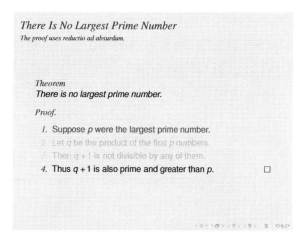

This theme is similarly as the `structurebold` font theme, but where `structurebold` makes text bold, this theme typesets it in italics and in the standard serif font. The same ⟨*options*⟩ as for the `structurebold` theme are supported. See Section 5.6.3 for the pros and cons of using italics.

\usefonttheme[⟨*options*⟩]{structuresmallcapsserif}

Example:

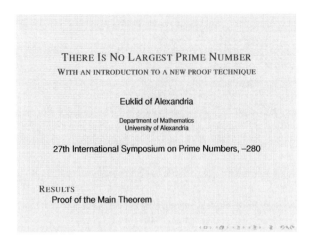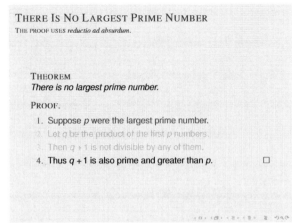

Again, this theme does exactly the same as the `structurebold` font theme, only this time text is set using small caps and a serif font. The same ⟨*options*⟩ as for the `structurebold` theme are supported. See Section 5.6.3 for the pros and cons of using small caps.

18.2 Font Changes Made Without Using Font Themes

While most font decisions can be made using font themes, for historical reasons some changes can only be made using class options or by loading special packages. These options are explained in the following. Possibly, these options will be replaced by themes in the future.

18.2.1 Choosing a Font Size for Normal Text

As pointed out in Section 5.6.1, measuring the default font size in points is not really a good idea for presentations. Nevertheless, BEAMER does just that, setting the default font size to 11pt as usual. This may seem ridiculously small, but the actual size of each frame size is by default just 128mm by 96mm and the viewer application enlarges the font. By specifying a default font size smaller than 11pt you can put more onto each slide, by specifying a larger font size you can fit on less.

To specify the font size, you can use the following class options:

`\documentclass[8pt]{beamer}`

This is way too small. Requires that the package `extsize` is installed.

`\documentclass[9pt]{beamer}`

This is also too small. Requires that the package `extsize` is installed.

`\documentclass[10pt]{beamer}`

If you really need to fit more onto each frame, use this option. Works without `extsize`.

`\documentclass[smaller]{beamer}`

Same as the 10pt option.

`\documentclass[11pt]{beamer}`

The default font size. You need not specify this option.

`\documentclass[12pt]{beamer}`

Makes all fonts a little bigger, which makes the text more readable. The downside is that less fits onto each frame.

`\documentclass[bigger]{beamer}`

Same as the 12pt option.

```
\documentclass[14pt]{beamer}
```
Makes all fonts somewhat bigger. Requires `extsize` to be installed.

```
\documentclass[17pt]{beamer}
```
This is about the default size of PowerPoint and OpenOffice.org Impress. Requires `extsize` to be installed.

```
\documentclass[20pt]{beamer}
```
This is really huge. Requires `extsize` to be installed.

18.2.2 Choosing a Font Family

By default, BEAMER uses the Computer Modern fonts. To change this, you can use one of the prepared packages of LaTeX's font mechanism. For example, to change to Times/Helvetica, simply add

```
\usepackage{mathptmx}
\usepackage{helvet}
```

in your preamble. Note that if you do not use the `serif` font theme, Helvetica (not Times) will be selected as the text font.

There may be many other fonts available on your installation. Typically, at least some of the following packages should be available: `arev`, `avant`, `bookman`, `chancery`, `charter`, `euler`, `helvet`, `lmodern`, `mathtime`, `mathptm`, `mathptmx`, `newcent`, `palatino`, `pifont`, `utopia`.

18.2.3 Choosing a Font Encodings

The same font can come in different encodings, which are (very roughly spoken) the ways the characters of a text are mapped to glyphs (the actual shape of a particular character in a particular font at a particular size). In TeX two encodings are often used with Latin characters: the T1 encoding and the OT1 encoding (old T1 encoding).

Conceptually, the newer T1 encoding is preferable over the old OT1 encoding. For example, hyphenation of words containing umlauts (like the famous German word Fräulein) will work only if you use the T1 encoding. Unfortunately, the EC fonts, that is, the T1-encoded Computer Modern fonts, are distributed on small installations just as MetaFont sources and only have bitmap renditions of each glyph. For this reason, using the T1-encoded EC fonts on such small installations will produce PDF files that render poorly.

TeX Live (cross-platform; replaced older `teTeX` for UNIX/Linux) and MiKTeX (for Windows platforms) can be installed with different levels of completeness. Concerning the Computer Modern fonts, the following packages can be installed: `cm-super` fonts, `lmodern` (Latin Modern) fonts, and `lgc` fonts, the latter containing the Latin, Greek, and Cyrillic alphabets. Concerning other fonts, the `txfonts` and `pxfonts` are two extended sets of the Times and the Palatino PostScript fonts, both packages containing extended sets of mathematical glyphs. Most other standard PostScript fonts are also available in T1 encoding.

Among the packages that make available the Computer Modern fonts in the T1 encoding, the package `lmodern` may be suggested. If you use `lmodern`, several extra fonts become available (like a sans-serif boldface math) and extra symbols (like proper guillemots).

To select the T1 encoding, use `\usepackage[T1]{fontenc}`. Thus, if you have the LM fonts installed, you could write

```
\usepackage[T1]{fontenc}
\usepackage{lmodern}
```

to get beautiful outline fonts and correct hyphenation. Note, however, that certain older versions of the LM bundle did not include correct glyphs for ligatures like "fi," which may cause trouble. Double check that all ligatures are displayed correctly and, if not, update your installation.

Everything mentioned above applies to `pdflatex` and `latex+dvips`. Unlike those engines, `xelatex` and `lualatex` support OpenType fonts, and that means that you can use system fonts in your documents relatively easy. Details will eventually be documented in this manual. For now, you can take a look at the documentation for the `fontspec` package which supports both engines. Also, note that when you use `lualatex` or `xelatex` with EU2 or EU1 encoding, respectively, by default you get OpenType Latin Modern fonts.

195

18.3 Changing the Fonts Used for Different Elements of a Presentation

This section explains how BEAMER's font management works.

18.3.1 Overview of Beamer's Font Management

BEAMER's font mechanism is somewhat similar to BEAMER's color mechanism, but not quite the same. As for colors, every BEAMER element, like the frame titles, the document title, the footnotes, and so on has a certain BEAMER-font. As for colors, on the one hand you can specify the font of each element individually; on the other hand fonts also use inheritance, thereby making it easy to globally change the fonts used for, say, "titlelike things" or for "itemizelike things."

While a BEAMER-color has a certain foreground and a certain background, either of which may be empty, a BEAMER-font has a size, a shape, a series, and a family, each of which may be empty. The inheritance relation among BEAMER-fonts is not necessarily the same as between BEAMER-colors, though we have tried to match them whenever possible.

Multiple inheritance plays a more important rule for fonts than it does for colors. A font might inherit the attributes of two different fonts. If one of them specifies that the font should be, say, boldface and the other specifies that the font should be, say, large, then the child font will be both large and bold.

As for fonts, the description of the font used for an element is given after the description of the element.

18.3.2 Using Beamer's Fonts

To use a BEAMER-font, you can use the command \usebeamerfont. Inside the templates for elements, this command will (typically) have already been called for you, so you will only seldomly have to use this command.

\usebeamerfont*{⟨beamer-font name⟩}

> This command changes the current font to the font specified by the ⟨beamer-font name⟩. The ⟨beamer-font name⟩ can be a not-too-fancyful text and may contain spaces. Typical examples are frametitle or section in toc or My Font 1. BEAMER-fonts can have (and should) have the same name as BEAMER-templates and BEAMER-colors.

> Example: \usebeamerfont{frametitle} In the unstarred version of this command, the font is changed according to the attributes specified in the ⟨beamer-font name⟩, but unspecified attributes remain unchanged. For example, if the font specifies that the font should be "bold," but specifies nothing else, and if the current font is large, then \usebeamerfont causes the current font to become large and bold.

> In the starred version of this command, the font is first reset before the font's attributes are applied. Thus, in the above example of a BEAMER-font having only the attribute "boldface" set, saying \usebeamerfont* will *always* cause the current font to become a normal-size, normal-shape, bold, default-family font.

18.3.3 Setting Beamer's Fonts

As for BEAMER-colors, there exists a central command for setting and changing BEAMER-fonts.

\setbeamerfont*{⟨beamer-font name⟩}{⟨attributes⟩}

> This command sets or resets certain attributes of the BEAMER-font ⟨beamer-font name⟩. In the unstarred version, this command just adds those attributes that have not been mentioned in a previous call and overwrites those that have been mentioned. Thus, the following two command blocks have the same effect:

> *Example:*
>
> ```
> \setbeamerfont{frametitle}{size=\large}
> \setbeamerfont{frametitle}{series=\bfseries}
> ```
>
> ```
> \setbeamerfont{frametitle}{size=\large,series=\bfseries}
> ```

> In the starred version, the font attributes are first completely reset, that is, set to be empty.

> The following ⟨attributes⟩ may be given:

- `size=⟨size command⟩` sets the size attribute of the BEAMER font. The ⟨size command⟩ should be a normal LaTeX-command used for setting the font size or it should be empty. Useful commands include `\tiny`, `\scriptsize`, `\footnotesize`, `\small`, `\normalsize`, `\large`, `\Large`, `\huge`, and `\Huge`. BEAMER also introduces the two font sizes `\Tiny` and `\TINY` for *really* small text. But you should know *exactly* what you are doing if you use them. You have been warned.

  Note that there is a difference between specifying an empty command and specifying `\normalsize`: Making the size attribute "empty" means that the font size should not be changed when this font is used, while specifying `\normalsize` means that the size should be set to the normal size whenever this font is used.

- `size*={⟨size in pt⟩}{⟨baselineskip⟩}` sets the size attribute of the font to the given ⟨size in pt⟩ and the baseline skip to the given value. Note that, depending on what kind of font you use, not all font sizes may be available. Also, certain font sizes are much less desirable than other ones; the standard commands take care of choosing appropriate sizes for you. Do not use this option unless you have a good reason. This command has the same effect as `size={\fontsize{⟨size in pt⟩}{⟨baselineskip⟩}}`.

- `shape=⟨shape command⟩` sets the shape attribute of the font. The command should be a command like `\itshape`, `\slshape`, `\scshape`, or `\upshape`.

- `shape*={⟨shape attribute abbreviation⟩}` sets the shape attribute of the font using the LaTeX's abbreviations for attributes. This command has the same effect as `shape={\fontshape{⟨shape attributes abbreviation⟩}}`.

- `series=⟨series command⟩` sets the "series" attribute of the font. The command should be a command like `\bfseries`.

- `series*={⟨series attribute abbreviation⟩}` has the same effect as `series={\fontseries{⟨series attributes abbreviation⟩}}`.

- `family=⟨family command⟩` sets the font family attribute. The command should be a LaTeX-font command like `\rmfamily` or `\sffamily`.

- `family*={⟨family name⟩}` sets the font family attribute to the given ⟨family name⟩. The command has the same effect as `family={\fontfamily{⟨family name⟩}}`. The ⟨family name⟩ is, normally, a somewhat cryptic abbreviation of a font family name that installed somewhere on the system. For example, the ⟨family name⟩ for Times happens to be `ptm`. No one can remember these names, so it's perfectly normal if you have to look them up laboriously.

- `parent={⟨parent list⟩}` specifies a list of parent fonts. When the BEAMER-font is used, the parents are used first. Thus, any font attributes set by one of the parents is inherited by the BEAMER-font, except if this attribute is overwritten by the font.

Example:
```
\setbeamerfont{parent A}{size=\large}
\setbeamerfont{parent B}{series=\bfseries}
\setbeamerfont{child}{parent={parent A, parent B},size=\small}

\normalfont
This text is in a normal font.
\usebeamerfont{parent A}
This text is large.
\usebeamerfont{parent B}
This text is large and bold.
\usebeamerfont{parent B}
This text is still large and bold.
\usebeamerfont*{parent B}
This text is only bold, but not large.
\usebeamerfont{child}
This text is small and bold.
```

Part IV
Creating Supporting Material

The objective of the BEAMER class is to simplify the creation of presentations using a projector. However, a presentation rarely exists in isolation. Material that accompanies a presentation includes:

- Presentations should normally be accompanied by *handouts*, written text that the audience can read during and/or after your presentation is given.

- You might wish to create notes for yourself that, ideally, are shown to you on your computer screen while the audience sees the presentation.

- You might wish to create a printout of your talk, either for yourself or for checking for errors.

- You might wish to create a transparencies version of your talk as a fall-back.

This part dicusses how BEAMER helps you with the creation of the above.

19   Adding Notes for Yourself

A *note* is text that is intended as a reminder to yourself of what you should say or should keep in mind when presenting a slide. Notes are usually printed out on paper, but with two-screen support they can also be shown on your laptop screen while the main presentation is shown on the projector.

19.1   Specifying Note Contents

To add a note to a slide or a frame, use the \note command. This command can be used both inside and outside frames, but it has quite different behaviors then: Inside frames, \note commands accumulate and append a single note page after the current slide; outside frames each \note directly inserts a single note page with the given parameter as contents. Using the \note command inside frames is usually preferably over using them outside, since only commands issued inside frames profit from the class option onlyslideswithnotes, see below.

Inside a frame, the effect of \note⟨*text*⟩ is the following: When you use it somewhere inside the frame on a specific slide, a note page is created after the slide, containing the ⟨*text*⟩. Since you can add an overlay specification to the \note command, you can specify after which slide the note should be shown. If you use multiple \note commands on one slide, they "accumulate" and are all shown on the same note.

To make the accumulation of notes more convenient, you can use the \note command with the option [item]. The notes added with this option are accumulated in an enumerate list that follows any text inserted using \note.

The following example will produce one note page that follows the second slide and has two entries.

```
\begin{frame}
  \begin{itemize}
  \item<1-> Eggs
  \item<2-> Plants
    \note[item]<2>{Tell joke about plants.}
    \note[item]<2>{Make it short.}
  \item<3-> Animals
  \end{itemize}
\end{frame}
```

Outside frames, the command \note creates a single note page. It is "independent" of any usage of the \note commands inside the previous frame. If you say \note inside a frame and \note right after it, *two* note pages are created.

In the following, the syntax and effects of the \note command *inside* frames are described:

\note<⟨*overlay specification*⟩>[⟨*options*⟩]{⟨*note text*⟩}

> Effects *inside* frames:
>
> This command appends the ⟨*note text*⟩ to the note that follows the current slide. Multiple uses of this command on a slide accumulate. If you do not specify an ⟨*overlay specification*⟩, the note will be added to *all* slides of the current frame. This is often not what you want, so adding a specification like <1> is usually a good idea.
>
> The following ⟨*options*⟩ may be given:
>
> - item causes the note to be put as an item in a list that is shown at the end of the note page.
>
> *Example:* \note<2>{Do not talk longer than 2 minutes about this.}

ARTICLE Notes are ignored in article mode.

Next, the syntax and effects of the \note command *outside* frames are described:

\note[⟨*options*⟩]{⟨*note text*⟩}

> Outside frames, this command creates a note page. This command is *not* affected by the option notes=onlyframeswithnotes, see below.
>
> The following ⟨*options*⟩ may be given:

- `itemize` will enclose the whole note page in an `itemize` environment. This is just a convenience.

- `enumerate` will enclose the whole note page in an `enumerate` environment.

Example:
```
\frame{some text}
\note{Talk no more than 1 minute.}

\note[enumerate]
{
\item Stress this first.
\item Then this.
}
```
ARTICLE Notes are ignored in `article` mode.

The following element dictates how the note pages are rendered:

Beamer-Template/-Color/-Font `note page`

This template is used to typeset a note page. The template should contain a mentioning of the insert `\insertnote`, which will contain the note text. To squeeze more onto note pages you might consider changing the size of the BEAMER-font `note page` to something small. The default is `\small`.

The following template options are predefined:

- [`default`] The default template shows the last slide in the upper right corner and some "hints" that should help you match a note page to the slide that is currently shown.

- [`compress`] The option produces an output that is similar to the default, only more fits onto each note page at the price of legibility.

- [`plain`] Just inserts the note text, no fancy hints.

The following two inserts are useful for note pages:

- `\insertnote` Inserts the text of the current note into the template.

- `\insertslideintonotes{⟨magnification⟩}` Inserts a "mini picture" of the last slide into the current note. The slide will be scaled by the given magnification.

  Example: `\insertslideintonotes{0.25}`
  This will give a mini slide whose width and height are one fourth of the usual size.

19.2 Specifying Contents for Multiple Notes

Sometimes you wish some text to be shown on every note or at least on every note in a long series of notes. To achieve this effect, you can use the following two commands:

`\AtBeginNote{⟨text⟩}`

The ⟨text⟩ will be inserted at the beginning of every note in the scope of the command. To stop the effect, either use `\AtBeginNote{}` or enclose the area in a TeX group.

It is advisable to add a `\par` command or an empty line at the end of the ⟨text⟩ since otherwise any note text will directly follow the ⟨text⟩ without a line break.

Example:
```
\section{My Section}

\AtBeginNote{Finish this section by 14:35.\par}
\begin{frame}
  ...
  \note{some note}
```

```
\end{frame}
\begin{frame}
  ...
  \note{some other note}
\end{frame}
\AtBeginNote{}
```

`\AtEndNote{⟨text⟩}`

This command behaves the same way as `\AtBeginNote`, except that the text is inserted at the end (bottom). You may wish to add a `\par` at the beginning of ⟨text⟩.

19.3 Specifying Which Notes and Frames Are Shown

Since you normally do not wish the notes to be part of your presentation, you must explicitly say so in the preamble if notes should be included in your presentation. You can use the following BEAMER options for this:

`\setbeameroption{hide notes}`

Notes are not shown. This is the default in a presentation.

`\setbeameroption{show notes}`

Include notes in the output file. Normal slides are also included and the note pages are interleaved with them.

`\setbeameroption{show notes on second screen=⟨location⟩}`

When this option is given, a two screen version of your talk is created, see Section 22 for further details. The second screen, which is displayed on the right by default, shows your notes. By specifying a different ⟨location⟩, you can also place the second screen on the left, bottom, or top.

Example:

```
\documentclass{beamer}
\usepackage{pgfpages}
\setbeameroption{show notes on second screen}
\begin{document}
\begin{frame}
  A frame.
  \note{This is shown on the right.}
\end{frame}
\end{document}
```

In detail, the following happens: The presentation is typeset normally and shown on the main screen or, to be precise, on `pgfpages`'s logical page number zero. The second screen (logical screen number one) is initialized to be empty.

Whenever a note page is to be typeset, either because a frame contained `\note` commands or because the frame was followed by a `\note` command, the note page is normally typeset. Then the note page is put on the second screen. Then the whole page is shipped out. (The exact details are bit more complex, but that is what happens, basically.)

An important effect of this behavior is that a note page *following* a frame is shown next to this frame. Normally, this is exactly what you want and expect. However, if there are multiple note pages for a single slide only the last one is shown, currently. This may change in the future, so do not rely on this effect.

Example:

```
\begin{frame}
  First frame.
\end{frame}
\note{This note is not shown at all (currently).}
\note{This note is shown together with the first frame.}
```

```
\begin{frame}
  Second frame.
  \note{This note is shown together with the second frame.}
\end{frame}

\begin{frame}
  No note text is shown for this frame.
\end{frame}
```

If you really need multiple note pages for a single slide, you will have to use something more complicated like this:

```
\begin{frame}<1-3>
  First frame.
  \note<1>{First page of notes for this frame.}
  \note<2>{Second page of notes for this frame.}
  \note<3>{Third page of notes for this frame.}
\end{frame}
```

\setbeameroption{show only notes}

Include only the notes in the output file and suppresses all frames. This options is useful for printing them. If you specify this command, the .aux and .toc files are *not* updated. So, if you add a section and reTeX your presentation, this will not be reflected in the navigation bars (which you do not see anyway since only notes are output).

20 Creating Transparencies

The main aim of the BEAMER class is to create presentations for projectors (sometimes called beamers, hence the name). However, it is often useful to print transparencies as backup, in case the hardware fails. A transparencies version of a talk often has less slides than the main version, since it takes more time to switch slides, but it may have more slides than the handout version. For example, while in a handout an animation might be condensed to a single slide, you might wish to print several slides for the transparency version.

In order to create a transparencies version, specify the class option `trans`. If you do not specify anything else, this will cause all overlay specifications to be suppressed. For most cases this will create exactly the desired result.

`\documentclass[trans]{beamer}`

   Create a version that uses the `trans` overlay specifications.

In some cases, you may want a more complex behavior. For example, if you use many `\only` commands to draw an animation. In this case, suppressing all overlay specifications is not such a good idea, since this will cause all steps of the animation to be shown at the same time. In some cases this is not desirable. Also, it might be desirable to suppress some `\alert` commands that apply only to specific slides in the handout.

For a fine-grained control of what is shown on a handout, you can use *mode specifications*. They specify which slides of a frame should be shown for a special version, for example for the handout version. As explained in Section 9.2, a mode specification is written alongside the normal overlay specification inside the pointed brackets. It is separated from the normal specification by a vertical bar and a space. Here is an example:

`\only<1-3,5-9| trans:2-3,5>{Text}`

This specification says: "Normally (in `beamer` mode), insert the text on slides 1–3 and 5–9. For the transparencies version, insert the text only on slides 2, 3, and 5." If no special mode specification is given for `trans` mode, the default is "always." This causes the desirable effect that if you do not specify anything, the overlay specification is effectively suppressed for the handout.

An especially useful specification is the following:

`\only<3| trans:0>{Not shown on transparencies.}`

Since there is no zeroth slide, the text is not shown. Likewise, `\alert<3| trans:0>{Text}` will not alert the text on a transparency.

You can also use a mode specification for the overlay specification of the `{frame}` environment as in the following example.

```
\begin{frame}<1-| trans:0>
  Text...
\end{frame}
```

This causes the frame to be suppressed in the transparencies version. Also, you can restrict the presentation such that only specific slides of the frame are shown on the handout:

```
\begin{frame}<1-| trans:4-5>
  Text...
\end{frame}
```

It is also possible to give only an alternate overlay specification. For example, `\alert<trans:0>{...}` causes the text to be always highlighted during the presentation, but never on the transparencies version. Likewise, `\frame<trans:0>{...}` causes the frame to be suppressed for the handout.

Finally, note that it is possible to give more than one alternate overlay specification and in any order. For example, the following specification states that the text should be inserted on the first three slides in the presentation, in the first two slides of the transparency version, and not at all in the handout.

`\only<trans:1-2| 1-3| handout:0>{Text}`

If you wish to give the same specification in all versions, you can do so by specifying `all:` as the version. For example,

`\frame<all:1-2>{blah...}`

ensures that the frame has two slides in all versions.

21 Creating Handouts and Lecture Notes

During a presentation it is very much desirable that the audience has a *handout* or even *lecture notes* available to it. A handout allows everyone in the audience to individually go back to things he or she has not understood.

Always provide handouts *as early as possible*, preferably weeks before the talk. Do *not* retain the handout till the end of the talk.

The BEAMER package offers two different ways of creating special versions of your talk; they are discussed in the following. The first, easy, way is to create a handout version by adding the handout option, which will cause the document to be typeset in handout mode. It will "look like" a presentation, but it can be printed more easily (the overlays are "flattened"). The second, more complicated and more powerful way is to create an independent "article" version of your presentation. This version coexists in your main file.

21.1 Creating Handouts Using the Handout Mode

The easiest way of creating a handout for your audience (though not the most desirable one) is to use the handout option. This option works exactly like the trans option.

`\documentclass[handout]{beamer}`

Create a version that uses the handout overlay specifications.

You might wish to choose a different color and/or presentation theme for the handout.

When printing a handout created this way, you will typically wish to print at least two and possibly four slides on each page. The easiest way of doing so is presumably to use pgfpages as follows:

```
\usepackage{pgfpages}
\pgfpagesuselayout{2 on 1}[a4paper,border shrink=5mm]
```

Instead of 2 on 1 you can use 4 on 1 (but then you have to add landscape to the list of options) and you can use, say, letterpaper instead of a4paper.

21.2 Creating Handouts Using the Article Mode

In the following, the "article version" of your presentation refers to a normal TeX text typeset using, for example, the document class article or perhaps llncs or a similar document class. This version of the presentation will typically follow different typesetting rules and may even have a different structure. Nevertheless, you may wish to have this version coexist with your presentation in one file and you may wish to share some part of it (like a figure or a formula) with your presentation.

In general, the article version of a talk is better suited as a handout than a handout created using the simple handout mode since it is more economic and can include more in-depth information.

21.2.1 Starting the Article Mode

The article mode of a presentation is created by specifying article or book or some other class as the document class instead of beamer and by then loading the package beamerarticle.

The package beamerarticle defines virtually all of BEAMER's commands in a way that is sensible for the article mode. Also, overlay specifications can be given to commands like \textbf or \item once beamerarticle has been loaded. Note that, except for \item, these overlay specifications also work: by writing \section<presentation>{Name} you will suppress this section command in the article version. For the exact effects overlay specifications have in article mode, please see the descriptions of the commands to which you wish to apply them.

`\usepackage[`⟨*options*⟩`]{beamerarticle}`

Makes most BEAMER commands available for another document class.

The following ⟨*options*⟩ may be given:

- `activeospeccharacters` will leave the character code of the pointed brackets as specified by other packages. Normally, BEAMER will turn off the special behavior of the two characters < and >. Using this option, you can reinstall the original behavior at the price of possible problems when using overlay specifications in the `article` mode.

- `noamssymb` will suppress the automatic loading of the `amssymb` package. Normally, BEAMER will load this package since many themes use AMS symbols. This option allows you to opt-out from this behavior in article mode, thus preventing clashes with some classes and font packages that conflict with `amssymb`. Note that, if you use this option, you will have to care for yourself that `amssymb` or an alternative package is loaded if you use respective symbols.

- `noamsthm` will suppress the loading of the `amsthm` package. No theorems will be defined.

- `notheorems` will suppress the definition of standard environments like `theorem`, but `amsthm` is still loaded and the `\newtheorem` command still makes the defined environments overlay-specification-aware. Using this option allows you to define the standard environments in whatever way you like while retaining the power of the extensions to `amsthm`.

- `envcountsect` causes theorem, definitions and the like to be numbered with each section. Thus instead of Theorem 1 you get Theorem 1.1. We recommend using this option.

- `noxcolor` will suppress the loading of the `xcolor` package. No colors will be defined.

Example:

```
\documentclass{article}
\usepackage{beamerarticle}
\begin{document}
\begin{frame}
  \frametitle{A frame title}
  \begin{itemize}
\item<1-> You can use overlay specifications.
\item<2-> This is useful.
  \end{itemize}
\end{frame}
\end{document}
```

There is one remaining problem: While the `article` version can easily TeX the whole file, even in the presence of commands like `\frame<2>`, we do not want the special article text to be inserted into our original BEAMER presentation. That means, we would like all text *between* frames to be suppressed. More precisely, we want all text except for commands like `\section` and so on to be suppressed. This behavior can be enforced by specifying the option `ignorenonframetext` in the presentation version. The option will insert a `\mode*` at the beginning of your presentation.

The following example shows a simple usage of the `article` mode:

```
\documentclass[a4paper]{article}
\usepackage{beamerarticle}
%\documentclass[ignorenonframetext,red]{beamer}

\mode<article>{\usepackage{fullpage}}
\mode<presentation>{\usetheme{Berlin}}

% everyone:
\usepackage[english]{babel}
\usepackage{pgf}

\pgfdeclareimage[height=1cm]{myimage}{filename}

\begin{document}

\section{Introduction}
```

```
This is the introduction text. This text is not shown in the
presentation, but will be part of the article.

\begin{frame}
  \begin{figure}
    % In the article, this is a floating figure,
    % In the presentation, this figure is shown in the first frame
    \pgfuseimage{myimage}
  \end{figure}
\end{frame}

This text is once more not shown in the presentation.

\section{Main Part}

While this text is not shown in the presentation, the section command
also applies to the presentation.

We can add a subsection that is only part of the article like this:

\subsection<article>{Article-Only Section}

With some more text.

\begin{frame}
  This text is part both of the article and of the presentation.
  \begin{itemize}
\item This stuff is also shown in both version.
\item This too.
  \only<article>{\item This particular item is only part
      of the article version.}
\item<presentation:only@0> This text is also only part of the article.
  \end{itemize}
\end{frame}
\end{document}
```

There is one command whose behavior is a bit special in `article` mode: The line break command \\. Inside frames, this command has no effect in `article` mode, except if an overlay specification is present. Then it has the normal effect dictated by the specification. The reason for this behavior is that you will typically inserts lots of \\ commands in a presentation in order to get control over all line breaks. These line breaks are mostly superfluous in `article` mode. If you really want a line break to apply in all versions, say \\<all>. Note that the command \\ is often redefined by certain environments, so it may not always be overlay-specification-aware. In such a case you have to write something like \only<presentation>{\\}.

21.2.2 Workflow

The following workflow steps are optional, but they can simplify the creation of the article version.

- In the main file `main.tex`, delete the first line, which sets the document class.

- Create a file named, say, `main.beamer.tex` with the following content:

  ```
  \documentclass[ignorenonframetext]{beamer}
  \input{main.tex}
  ```

- Create an extra file named, say, `main.article.tex` with the following content:

```
\documentclass{article}
\usepackage{beamerarticle}
\setjobnamebeamerversion{main.beamer}
\input{main.tex}
```

- You can now run `pdflatex` or `latex` on the two files `main.beamer.tex` and `main.article.tex`.

The command `\setjobnamebeamerversion` tells the article version where to find the presentation version. This is necessary if you wish to include slides from the presentation version in an article as figures.

`\setjobnamebeamerversion{⟨filename without extension⟩}`

  Tells the BEAMER class where to find the presentation version of the current file.

21.2.3 Including Slides from the Presentation Version in the Article Version

If you use the package `beamerarticle`, the `\frame` command becomes available in `article` mode. By adjusting the frame template, you can "mimic" the appearance of frames typeset by BEAMER in your articles. However, sometimes you may wish to insert "the real thing" into the `article` version, that is, a precise "screenshot" of a slide from the presentation. The commands introduced in the following help you do exactly this.

In order to include a slide from your presentation in your article version, you must do two things: First, you must place a normal LATEX label on the slide using the `\label` command. Since this command is overlay-specification-aware, you can also select specific slides of a frame. Also, by adding the option `label=⟨name⟩` to a frame, a label ⟨name⟩<⟨slide number⟩> is automatically added to each slide of the frame.

Once you have labeled a slide, you can use the following command in your article version to insert the slide into it:

`\includeslide[⟨options⟩]{⟨label name⟩}`

  This command calls `\pgfimage` with the given ⟨options⟩ for the file specified by

    `\setjobnamebeamerversion⟨filename⟩`

Furthermore, the option `page=⟨page of label name⟩` is passed to `\pgfimage`, where the ⟨page of label name⟩ is read internally from the file ⟨filename⟩`.snm`.

Example:
```
\article
  \begin{figure}
    \begin{center}
      \includeslide[height=5cm]{slide1}
    \end{center}
    \caption{The first slide (height 5cm). Note the partly covered second item.}
  \end{figure}
  \begin{figure}
    \begin{center}
      \includeslide{slide2}
    \end{center}
    \caption{The second slide (original size). Now the second item is also shown.}
  \end{figure}
```

The exact effect of passing the option `page=⟨page of label name⟩` to the command `\pgfimage` is explained in the documentation of `pgf`. In essence, the following happens:

- For old versions of `pdflatex` and for any version of `latex` together with `dvips`, the `pgf` package will look for a file named

    ⟨filename⟩`.page`⟨page of label name⟩`.`⟨extension⟩

207

For each page of your .pdf or .ps file that is to be included in this way, you must create such a file by hand. For example, if the PostScript file of your presentation version is named `main.beamer.ps` and you wish to include the slides with page numbers 2 and 3, you must create (single page) files `main.beamer.page2.ps` and `main.beamer.page3.ps` "by hand" (or using some script). If these files cannot be found, `pgf` will complain.

- For new versions of `pdflatex`, `pdflatex` also looks for the files according to the above naming scheme. However, if it fails to find them (because you have not produced them), it uses a special mechanism to directly extract the desired page from the presentation file `main.beamer.pdf`.

21.3 Details on Modes

This subsection describes how modes work exactly and how you can use the `\mode` command to control what part of your text belongs to which mode.

When BEAMER typesets your text, it is always in one of the following five modes:

- `beamer` is the default mode.

- `second` is the mode used when a slide for an optional second screen is being typeset.

- `handout` is the mode for creating handouts.

- `trans` is the mode for creating transparencies.

- `article` is the mode when control has been transferred to another class, like `article.cls`. Note that the mode is also `article` if control is transferred to, say, `book.cls`.

In addition to these modes, BEAMER recognizes the following names for modes sets:

- `all` refers to all modes.

- `presentation` refers to the first four modes, that is, to all modes except for the `article` mode.

Depending on the current mode, you may wish to have certain text inserted only in that mode. For example, you might wish a certain frame or a certain table to be left out of your article version. In some situations, you can use the `\only` command for this purpose. However, the command `\mode`, which is described in the following, is much more powerful than `\only`.

The command actually comes in three "flavors," which only slightly differ in syntax. The first, and simplest, is the version that takes one argument. It behaves essentially the same way as `\only`.

`\mode<`⟨*mode specification*⟩`>{`⟨*text*⟩`}`

Causes the ⟨*text*⟩ to be inserted only for the specified modes. Recall that a ⟨*mode specification*⟩ is just an overlay specification in which no slides are mentioned.

The ⟨*text*⟩ should not do anything fancy that involves mode switches or including other files. In particular, you should not put an `\include` command inside ⟨*text*⟩. Use the argument-free form below, instead.

Example:

`\mode<article>{Extra detail mentioned only in the article version.}`

```
\mode
<beamer| trans>
{\frame{\tableofcontents[currentsection]}}
```

The second flavor of the `\mode` command takes no argument. "No argument" means that it is not followed by an opening brace, but any other symbol.

\mode<_⟨mode specification⟩_**>**

In the specified mode, this command actually has no effect. The interesting part is the effect in the non-specified modes: In these modes, the command causes TeX to enter a kind of "gobbling" state. It will now ignore all following lines until the next line that has a sole occurrence of one of the following commands: \mode, \mode*, \begin{document}, \end{document}. Even a comment on this line will make TeX skip it. Note that the line with the special commands that make TeX stop gobbling may not directly follow the line where the gobbling is started. Rather, there must either be one non-empty line before the special command or at least two empty lines.

When TeX encounters a single \mode command, it will execute this command. If the command is \mode command of the first flavor, TeX will resume its "gobbling" state after having inserted (or not inserted) the argument of the \mode command. If the \mode command is of the second flavor, it takes over.

Using this second flavor of \mode is less convenient than the first, but there are different reasons why you might need to use it:

- The line-wise gobbling is much faster than the gobble of the third flavor, explained below.
- The first flavor reads its argument completely. This means, it cannot contain any verbatim text that contains unbalanced braces.
- The first flavor cannot cope with arguments that contain \include.
- If the text mainly belongs to one mode with only small amounts of text from another mode inserted, this second flavor is nice to use.

Note: When searching line-wise for a \mode command to shake it out of its gobbling state, TeX will not recognize a \mode command if a mode specification follows on the same line. Thus, such a specification must be given on the next line.

Note: When a TeX file ends, TeX must not be in the gobbling state. Switch this state off using \mode on one line and <all> on the next.

Example:

```
\mode<article>

This text is typeset only in |article| mode.
\verb!verbatim text is ok {!

\mode
<presentation>
{ % this text is inserted only in presentation mode
\frame{\tableofcontents[currentsection]}}

Here we are back to article mode stuff. This text
is not inserted in presentation mode

\mode
<presentation>

This text is only inserted in presentation mode.
```

The last flavor of the mode command behaves quite differently.

\mode*

The effect of this mode is to ignore all text outside frames in the **presentation** modes. In **article** mode it has no effect.

This mode should only be entered outside of frames. Once entered, if the current mode is a **presentation** mode, TeX will enter a gobbling state similar to the gobbling state of the second "flavor" of the \mode command. The difference is that the text is now read token-wise, not line-wise. The text is gobbled token by token until one of the following tokens is found: \mode, \frame, \againframe, \part, \section, \subsection, \appendix, \note, \begin{frame}, and \end{document} (the last two are not really tokens, but they are recognized anyway).

Once one of these commands is encountered, the gobbling stops and the command is executed. However, all of these commands restore the mode that was in effect when they started. Thus, once the command is finished, TEX returns to its gobbling.

Normally, \mode* is exactly what you want TEX to do outside of frames: ignore everything except for the above-mentioned commands outside frames in presentation mode. However, there are cases in which you have to use the second flavor of the \mode command instead: If you have verbatim text that contains one of the commands, if you have very long text outside frames, or if you wish some text outside a frame (like a definition) to be executed also in presentation mode.

The class option ignorenonframetext will switch on \mode* at the beginning of the document.

Example:
```
\begin{document}
\mode*

This text is not shown in the presentation.

\begin{frame}
  This text is shown both in article and presentation mode.
\end{frame}

this text is not shown in the presentation again.

\section{This command also has effect in presentation mode}

Back to article stuff again.

\frame<presentation>
{ this frame is shown only in the presentation. }
\end{document}
```

Example: The following example shows how you can include other files in a main file. The contents of a main.tex:

```
\documentclass[ignorenonframetext]{beamer}
\begin{document}
This is star mode stuff.

Let's include files:
\mode<all>
\include{a}
\include{b}
\mode*

Back to star mode
\end{document}
```

And a.tex (and likewise b.tex):

```
\mode*
\section{First section}
Extra text in article version.
\begin{frame}
  Some text.
\end{frame}
\mode<all>
```

22   Taking Advantage of Multiple Screens

This section describes options provided by BEAMER for taking advantage of computers that have more than one video output and can display different outputs on them. For such systems, one video output can be attached to a projector and the main presentation is shown there. The second video output is attached to a small extra monitor (or is just shown on the display of the computer) and shows, for example, special notes for you. Alternatively, the two outputs might be attached to two different projectors. One can then show the main presentation on the first projection and, say, the table of contents on the second. Or the second projection might show a version translated into a different language. Or the seoncd projection might always show the "previous" slide. Or . . . —we are sure you can think of further useful things.

The basic idea behind BEAMER's support of two video outputs is the following: Using special options you can ask BEAMER to create a PDF-file in which the "pages" are unusually wide or high. By default, their height will still be 128mm, but their width will be 192mm (twice the usual default 96mm). These "superwide" pages will show the slides of the main presentation on the left and auxilliary material on the right (this can be switched using appropriate options, though hyperlinks will only work if the presentation is on the left and the second screen on the right).

For the presentation you attach two screens to the system. The windowing system believes that the screen is twice as wide as it actually is. Everything the windowing system puts on the left half of this big virtual screen is redirected to the first video output, everything on the right half is redirected to the second video output.

When the presentation program displays the specially prepared superwide BEAMER-presentation, exactly the left half of the screen will be filled with the main presentation, the right part is filled with the auxilliary material—voilà. Not all presentation programs support this special feature. For example, the Acrobat Reader 6.0.2 will only use one screen in fullscreen mode on MacOS X. On the other hand, a program named PDF Presenter supports showing dual-screen presentations. Generally, you will have to find out for yourself whether your display program and system support showing superwide presentations stretching over two screens.

BEAMER uses the package `pgfpages` to typeset two-screen presentations. Because of this, your first step when creating a two-screen presentation is to include this package:

```
\documentclass{beamer}
\usepackage{pgfpages}
```

The next step is to choose an appropriate option for showing something special on the second screen. These options are discussed in the following sections.

One of the things these options do is to setup a certain `pgfpages`-layout that is appropriate for two-screen presentations. However, you can still change the `pgfpages`-layout arbitrarily, afterwards. For example, you might wish to enlarge the virtual pages. For details, see the documentation of `pgfpages`.

22.1   Showing Notes on the Second Screen

The first way to use a second screen is to show the presentation on the main screen and to show your notes on the second screen. The option `show notes on second screen` can be used for this. It is described on page 201.

22.2   Showing Second Mode Material on the Second Screen

The second way to use the second screen is to show "a different vesion" of the presentation on the second screen. This different version might be a translation or it might just always be the current table of contents.

To specify what is shown on the second screen, you can use a special BEAMER-mode called `second`. This mode behaves similar to modes like `handout` or `beamer`, but its effect depends on the exact options used:

`\setbeameroption{second mode text on second screen=`⟨*location*⟩`}`

> This option causes the second screen to show the second mode material. The ⟨*location*⟩ of the second screen can be `left`, `right`, `bottom`, or `top`.

> In detail, the following happens: When a new frame needs to be typeset, BEAMER checks whether the special option `typeset second` is given. If not, the frame is typeset normally and the slides are put on the main

presentation screen (more precisely, on the logical `pgfpages`-page number zero). The second screen (logical page number one) shows whatever it showed before the frame was typeset.

If the special frame option `typeset second` is given, after each slide of the frame the frame contents is typeset once more, but this time for the mode `second`. This results in another slide, which is put on the second screen (on logical page number one). Then the whole page is shipped out.

The `second` mode behaves more like the `beamer` mode than other modes: Any overlay specification for `beamer` will also apply to `second` mode, unless an explicit `second` mode specification is also given. In particular, `\only<1-2>{Text}` will be shown on slides 1 and 2 in `second` mode, but only on the first slide in `handout` mode or `trans` mode.

Example:

```
\documentclass{beamer}
\usepackage{pgfpages}
\setbeameroption{second mode text on second screen}
\begin{document}
\begin{frame}[typeset second]
  This text is shown on the left and on the right.
  \only<second>{This text is only shown on the right.}
  \only<second:0>{This text is only shown on the left.}
\end{frame}
\begin{frame}
  This text is shown on the left. The right shows the same as for the
  previous frame.
\end{frame}
\begin{frame}[typeset second]
  \alt<second>{The \string\alt command is useful for second
    mode. Let's show the table of contents, here: \tableofcontents}
  {Here comes some normal text for the first slide.}
\end{frame}
\end{document}
```

Example: The following example shows how translations can be added in a comfortable way.

```
\documentclass{beamer}
\usepackage{pgfpages}
\setbeameroption{second mode text on second screen}
\DeclareRobustCommand\translation[1]{\mytranslation#1\relax}
\long\def\mytranslation#1|#2\relax{\alt<second>{#2}{#1}}
\title{\translation{Preparing Presentations|Vortr\"age vorbereiten}}
\author{Till Tantau}
\begin{document}
\begin{frame}[typeset second]
  \titlepage
\end{frame}
\begin{frame}[typeset second]
  \frametitle{\translation{This is the frame title.|Dies ist der Titel des Rahmens.}}
  \begin{itemize}
  \item<1-> \translation{First|Erstens}.
  \item<2-> \translation{Second|Zweitens}.
  \item<3-> \translation{Third|Drittens}.
  \end{itemize}
  \translation{Do not use line-by-line uncovering.|Man sollte Text nicht
  Zeile f\"ur Zeile aufdecken.}
\end{frame}
\end{document}
```

In the last of the above example, it is a bit bothersome that the option `typeset second` has to be added to each frame. The following option globally sets this option:

`\setbeameroption{always typeset second mode=`*⟨true or false⟩*`}`

> When this option is set to true, every following frame will have the option `typeset second` set to true.

22.3 Showing the Previous Slide on the Second Screen

`\setbeameroption{previous slide on second screen=`*⟨location⟩*`}`

> This option causes the second screen to show the previous slide that was typeset, unless this is overruled by a frame with the [`typeset second`] option set. The idea is that if you have two projectors you can always present "the last two" slides simultaneously and talk about them.
>
> Using this option will switch off the updating of external files like the table of contents.

Part V
Howtos

This part contains explanations-of-how-to-do-things (commonly known as *howtos*). These explanations are not really part of the "BEAMER core." Rather, they explain how to use BEAMER to achieve a certain effect or how get something special done.

The first howto is about tricky uncovering situations.

The second howto explains how you can import (parts or) presentations created using some other LATEX-presentation class, like PROSPER.

The third and final howto talks about TRANSLATOR, a package BEAMER uses for translating simple strings.

23 How To Uncover Things Piecewise

23.1 Uncovering an Enumeration Piecewise

A common usage of overlays is to show a list of points in an enumeration in a piecewise fashion. The easiest and most flexible way to do this is the following:

```
\begin{itemize}
\item<1-> First point.
\item<2-> Second point.
\item<3-> Third point.
\end{itemize}
```

The advantage of this approach is that you retain total control over the order in which items are shown. By changing, for example, the last specification to <2->, you can have the last two points uncovered at the same time.

A disadvantage of the approach is that you will have to renumber everything if you add a new item. This is usually not such a big problem, but it can be a nuisance.

To automatize the uncovering, you can use the following code:

```
\begin{itemize}[<+->]
\item First point.
\item Second point.
\item Third point.
\end{itemize}
```

The effect of the [<+->] is to install a *default overlay specification*, see the definition of itemize for details.

Now, suppose you wish the second and third point to be shown at the same time. You could achieve this by adding the specification <2-> to either the second or third \item command. However, then you still have to do some renumbering if you add a new item at the beginning. A better approach is to temporarily use a different overlay specification and the dot-notation:

```
\begin{itemize}[<+->]
\item First point.
\item[<.->] Second point.
\item Third point.
\end{itemize}
```

You might wish to build your own macros based on these ideas (like an itemstep environment or a \itemlikeprevious command).

23.2 Highlighting the Current Item in an Enumeration

If you uncover an enumeration piecewise, it is sometimes a good idea to highlight the last uncovered point to draw the audience's attention to it. This is best achieved as follows:

```
\begin{itemize}
\item<1-| alert@1> First point.
\item<2-| alert@2> Second point.
\item<3-| alert@3> Third point.
\end{itemize}
```

or

```
\begin{itemize}[<+-| alert@+>]
\item First point.
\item Second point.
\item Third point.
\end{itemize}
```

Note that this will draw the little item symbol also in red.

23.3 Changing Symbol Before an Enumeration

When uncovering a list of tasks or problems, you may desire that the symbol in front of the last uncovered symbol is, say, a ballot X, while for the previous items it is a check mark (you'll find these characters in some Dingbats fonts).

The best way to achieve this is to implement a new action environment. If this action is activated, it temporarily changes the item symbol template to the other symbol:

```
\newenvironment{ballotenv}
{\only{%
  \setbeamertemplate{itemize item}{code for showing a ballot}%
  \setbeamertemplate{itemize subitem}{code for showing a smaller ballot}%
  \setbeamertemplate{itemize subsubitem}{code for showing a smaller ballot}}}
{}

\setbeamertemplate{itemize item}{code for showing a check mark}
\setbeamertemplate{itemize subitem}{code for showing a smaller check mark}
\setbeamertemplate{itemize subsubitem}{code for showing a smaller check mark}
```

The effect of the code is to install a check mark as the default template. If the action `ballot` is now requested for some item, this template will temporarily be replaced by the ballot templates.

Note that the `ballotenv` is invoked with the overlay specification given for the action directly following it. This causes the `\only` to be invoked exactly for the specified overlays.

Here are example usages:

```
\begin{itemize}
\item<1-| ballot@1> First point.
\item<2-| ballot@2> Second point.
\item<3-| ballot@3> Third point.
\end{itemize}
```

and

```
\begin{itemize}[<+-| ballot@+>]
\item First point.
\item Second point.
\item Third point.
\end{itemize}
```

In the following example, more and more items become "checked" from slide to slide:

```
\begin{itemize}[<ballot@+-| visible@1-,+(1)>]
\item First point.
\item Second point.
\item Third point.
\end{itemize}
```

The important point is `ballot@+`. The funny `visible@1-,+(1)` has the following effect: Although it has no effect with respect to what is shown (after all, it applies to all slides), it ensures that in the enumeration the slide number 4 is mentioned. Thus there will also be a slide in which all three points are checked.

23.4 Uncovering Tagged Formulas Piecewise

Suppose you have a three-line formula as the following:

```
\begin{align}
  A &= B \\
    &= C \\
    &= D
\end{align}
```

Uncovering this formula line-by-line is a little tricky. A first idea is to use the \pause or \onslide commands. Unfortunately, these do not work since align internally reprocesses its input several times, which messes up the delicate internals of the commands. The next idea is the following, which works a little better:

```
\begin{align}
  A &= B \\
    \uncover<2->{&= C \\}
    \uncover<3->{&= D}
\end{align}
```

Unfortunately, this does not work in the presence of tags (so it works for the align* environment). What happens is that the tag of the last line is shown on all slides. The problem here is that the tag is created when \\ is encountered or when \end{align} is encountered. In the last line these are already "behind" the \uncover.

To solve this problem, you can add an empty line without a tag and then insert a negative vertical skip to undo the last line:

```
\begin{align}
  A &= B \\
    \uncover<2->{&= C \\}
    \uncover<3->{&= D \\}
    \notag
  \end{align}
\vskip-1.5em
```

23.5 Uncovering a Table Rowwise

When you wish to uncover a table line-by-line, you will run into all sorts of problems if there are vertical and horizontal lines in the table. The reason is that the first vertical line at the left end is drawn before the line is even read (and thus, in particular, before any \onslide command can be read). However, placing a \pause or \uncover at the end of the line before is also not helpful since it will then suppress the horizontal line below the last uncovered line.

A possible way to solve this problem is not to use either horizontal or vertical lines. Instead, coloring the lines using the colortbl package is a good alternative to structure the table. Here is an optically pleasing example, where the table is uncovered line-wise:

```
\rowcolors[]{1}{blue!20}{blue!10}
\begin{tabular}{l!{\vrule}cccc}
  Class & A & B & C & D \\\hline
  X     & 1 & 2 & 3 & 4 \pause\\
  Y     & 3 & 4 & 5 & 6 \pause\\
  Z     & 5 & 6 & 7 & 8
\end{tabular}
```

By using \onslide instead of \pause, you can get more fine-grained control over which line is shown on which slide.

23.6 Uncovering a Table Columnwise

The same problems as for uncovering a table linewise arise for uncovering it columnwise.

Once more, using the colortbl package offers a solution. In the following example, the tabular header is used to insert \onslide commands, one for each column, that cover the entries in the column from a certain slide on. At the end of the last column, the \onslide without a specification ensures that the first column on the next row is once more shown normally.

Inserting a horizontal line is tricky since it will protrude over the full width of the table also in the covered version. The best idea is just not to use horizontal bars.

```
\rowcolors[]{1}{blue!20}{blue!10}
\begin{tabular}{l!{\vrule}c<{\onslide<2->}c<{\onslide<3->}c<{\onslide<4->}c<{\onslide}c}
  Class & A & B & C & D \\
```

```
  X      & 1 & 2 & 3 & 4 \\
  Y      & 3 & 4 & 5 & 6 \\
  Z      & 5 & 6 & 7 & 8
\end{tabular}
```

24 How To Import Presentations Based on Other Packages and Classes

The BEAMER class comes with a number of emulation layers for classes or packages that do not support BEAMER directly. For example, the package `beamerseminar` maps some (not all) commands of the SEMINAR class to appropriate BEAMER commands. This way, individual slides or whole sets of slides that have been prepared for a presentation using SEMINAR can be used inside BEAMER, provided they are reasonably simple.

None of the emulation layers is a perfect substitute for the original (emulations seldom are) and it is not intended that they ever will be. If you want/need/prefer the features of another class, use that class for preparing your presentations. The intention of these layers is just to help speed up creating BEAMER presentations that use parts of old presentations. You can simply copy these parts in verbatim, without having to worry about the subtle differences in syntax.

A useful effect of using an emulation layer is that you get access to all the features of BEAMER while using the syntax of another class. For example, you can use the `article` mode to create a nice article version of a PROSPER talk.

24.1 Prosper, HA-Prosper and Powerdot

The package `beamerprosper` maps the commands of the PROSPER package, developed by Frédéric Goualard, to BEAMER commands. Also, some commands of the HA-PROSPER and POWERDOT packages, developed by Hendri Adriaens, are mapped to BEAMER commands. *These mappings cannot perfectly emulate all of Prosper!* Rather, these mappings are intended as an aid when porting parts of presentations created using PROSPER to BEAMER. *No styles are implemented that mimick Prosper styles.* Rather, the normal BEAMER themes must be used (although, one could implement BEAMER themes that mimicks existing PROSPER styles; we have not done that and do not intend to).

The workflow for creating a BEAMER presentation that uses PROSPER code is the following:

1. Use the document class `beamer`, not `prosper`. Most options passed to `prosper` do not apply to `beamer` and should be omitted.

2. Add a `\usepackage{beamerprosper}` to start the emulation.

3. If you add slides relying on HA-PROSPER, you may wish to add the option `framesassubsections` to `beamerprosper`, though we do not recommend it (use the normal `\subsection` command instead; it gives you more fine-grained control).

4. If you also copy the title commands, it may be necessary to adjust the content of commands like `\title` or `\author`. Note that in PROSPER the `\email` command is given outside the `\author` command, whereas in BEAMER and also in HA-PROSPER it is given inside.

5. When copying slides containing the command `\includegraphics`, you will almost surely have to adjust its usage. If you use pdfLATEX to typeset the presentation, than you cannot include PostScript files. You should convert them to `.pdf` or to `.png` and adjust any usage of `\includegraphics` accordingly.

6. When starting to change things, you can use all of BEAMER's commands and even mix them with PROSPER commands.

An example can be found in the file `beamerexample-prosper.tex`.

There are, unfortunately, quite a few places where you may run into problems:

- In BEAMER, the command `\PDForPS` will do exactly what the name suggests: insert the first argument when run by `pdflatex`, insert the second argument when run by `latex`. However, in PROSPER, the code inserted for the PDF case is actually PostScript code, which is only later converted to PDF by some external program. You will need to adjust this PostScript code such that it works with `pdflatex` (which is not always possible).

- If you used fine-grained spacing commands, like adding a little horizontal skip here and a big negative vertical skip there, the typesetting of the text may be poor. It may be a good idea to just remove these spacing commands.

- If you use `pstricks` commands, you will either have to stick to using `latex` and `dvips` or will have to work around them using, for example, `pgf`. Porting lots of `pstricks` code is bound to be difficult, if you wish to switch over to `pdflatex`, so be warned. You can read more about that in Section 13 that talks about graphics.

- If the file cannot be compiled because some PROSPER command is not implemented, you will have to delete this command and try to mimick its behavior using some BEAMER command.

`\usepackage{beamerprosper}`

Include this package in a `beamer` presentation to get access to PROSPER commands. Use `beamer` as the document class, not `prosper`. Most of the options passed to the class `prosper` make no sense in `beamer`, so just delete them.

This package takes the following options:

- `framesassubsections` causes each frame to create its own subsection with the frame title as subsection name. This behavior mimicks HA-PROSPER's behavior. In a long talk this will create way too many subsections.

ARTICLE   The `framesassubsections` option has no effect in `article` mode.

Example:

```
\documentclass[notes]{beamer}

\usepackage[framesassubsections]{beamerprosper}

\title{A Beamer Presentation Using (HA-)Prosper Commands}
\subtitle{Subtitles Are Also Supported}
\author{Till Tantau}
\institution{The Institution is Mapped To Institute}

\begin{document}

\maketitle

\tsectionandpart{Introduction}

\overlays{2}{
\begin{slide}{About this file}
  \begin{itemstep}
  \item
    This is a beamer presentation.
  \item
    You can use the prosper and the HA-prosper syntax.
  \item
    This is done by mapping prosper and HA-prosper commands to beamer
    commands.
  \item
    The emulation is by no means perfect.
  \end{itemstep}
\end{slide}
}

\section{Second Section}
\subsection{A subsection}
```

```
\begin{frame}
  \frametitle{A frame created using the \texttt{frame} environment.}

  \begin{itemize}[<+->]
  \item You can still use the original beamer syntax.
  \item The emulation is intended only to make recycling slides
    easier, not to install a whole new syntax for beamer.
  \end{itemize}
\end{frame}

\begin{notes}{Notes for these slides}
My notes for these slides.
\end{notes}
\end{document}
```

You can run, for example, pdfLaTeX on the file to get a BEAMER presentation with overlays. Adding the `notes` option will also show the notes. Certain commands, like `\LeftFoot`, are ignored. You can change the theme using the usual commands. You can also use all normal BEAMER commands and concepts, like overlay-specifications, in the file. You can also create an `article` version by using the class `article` and including the package `beamerarticle`.

In the following, the effects of PROSPER commands in BEAMER are listed.

`\email{⟨text⟩}`

Simply typesets its argument in typewriter text. Should hence be given *inside* the `\author` command.

`\institution{⟨text⟩}`

This command is mapped to BEAMER's `\institute` command if given *outside* the `\author` command, otherwise it typesets its argument in a smaller font.

`\Logo(⟨x⟩,⟨y⟩){⟨logo text⟩}`

This is mapped to `\logo{⟨logo text⟩}`. The coordinates are ignored.

`\begin{slide}[⟨options⟩]{⟨frame title⟩}`
  `⟨environment contents⟩`
`\end{slide}`

Inserts a frame with the `fragile=singleslide` option set. The ⟨frame title⟩ will be enclosed in a `\frametitle` command.

The following ⟨options⟩ may be given:

- `trans=⟨prosper transition⟩` installs the specified ⟨prosper transition⟩ as the transition effect when showing the slide.
- ⟨prosper transition⟩ has the same effect as `trans=⟨prosper transition⟩`.
- `toc=⟨entry⟩` overrides the subsection table of contents entry created by this slide by ⟨entry⟩. Note that a subsection entry is created for a slide only if the `framesassubsections` options is specified.
- `template=⟨text⟩` is ignored.

Example: The following two texts have the same effect:

```
\begin{slide}[trans=Glitter,toc=short]{A Title}
  Hi!
\end{slide}
```

and

```
\subsection{short} % omitted, if framesassubsections is not specified
\begin{frame}[fragile=singleslide]
  \transglitter
```

```
  \frametitle{A Title}
    Hi!
\end{frame}
```

`\overlays{`⟨*number*⟩`}{`⟨*slide environment*⟩`}`

This will put the ⟨*slide environment*⟩ into a frame that does not have the `fragile` option and which can hence contain overlayed text. The ⟨*number*⟩ is ignored since the number of necessary overlays is computed automatically by BEAMER.

Example: The following code fragments have the same effect:

```
\overlays{2}{
\begin{slide}{A Title}
  \begin{itemstep}
  \item Hi!
  \item Ho!
  \end{itemstep}
\end{slide}}
```

and

```
\subsection{A Title} % omitted, if framesassubsections is not specified
\begin{frame}
  \frametitle{A Title}
  \begin{itemstep}
  \item Hi!
  \item Ho!
  \end{itemstep}
\end{frame}
```

`\fromSlide{`⟨*slide number*⟩`}{`⟨*text*⟩`}`

This is mapped to `\uncover<`⟨*slide number*⟩`->{`⟨*text*⟩`}`.

`\fromSlide*{`⟨*slide number*⟩`}{`⟨*text*⟩`}`

This is mapped to `\only<`⟨*slide number*⟩`->{`⟨*text*⟩`}`.

`\onlySlide{`⟨*slide number*⟩`}{`⟨*text*⟩`}`

This is mapped to `\uncover<`⟨*slide number*⟩`>{`⟨*text*⟩`}`.

`\onlySlide*{`⟨*slide number*⟩`}{`⟨*text*⟩`}`

This is mapped to `\only<`⟨*slide number*⟩`>{`⟨*text*⟩`}`.

`\untilSlide{`⟨*slide number*⟩`}{`⟨*text*⟩`}`

This is mapped to `\uncover<-`⟨*slide number*⟩`>{`⟨*text*⟩`}`.

`\untilSlide*{`⟨*slide number*⟩`}{`⟨*text*⟩`}`

This is mapped to `\only<-`⟨*slide number*⟩`>{`⟨*text*⟩`}`.

`\FromSlide{`⟨*slide number*⟩`}`

This is mapped to `\onslide<`⟨*slide number*⟩`->`.

`\OnlySlide{`⟨*slide number*⟩`}`

This is mapped to `\onslide<`⟨*slide number*⟩`>`.

`\UntilSlide{`⟨*slide number*⟩`}`

This is mapped to `\onslide<-`⟨*slide number*⟩`>`.

`\slideCaption{⟨text⟩}`

> This is mapped to `\date{⟨text⟩}`.

`\fontTitle{⟨text⟩}`

> Simply inserts ⟨text⟩.

`\fontText{⟨text⟩}`

> Simply inserts ⟨text⟩.

`\PDFtransition{⟨prosper transition⟩}`

> Maps the ⟨prosper transition⟩ to an appropriate `\transxxxx` command.

`\begin{Itemize}`
`⟨environment contents⟩`
`\end{Itemize}`

> This is mapped to `itemize`.

`\begin{itemstep}`
`⟨environment contents⟩`
`\end{itemstep}`

> This is mapped to `itemize` with the option `[<+->]`.

`\begin{enumstep}`
`⟨environment contents⟩`
`\end{enumstep}`

> This is mapped to `enumerate` with the option `[<+->]`.

`\hiddenitem`

> This is mapped to `\addtocounter{beamerpauses}{1}`.

`\prosperpart[⟨options⟩]{⟨text⟩}`

> This command has the same effect as PROSPER's `\part` command. BEAMER's normal `\part` command retains its normal semantics. Thus, you might wish to replace all occurrences of `\part` by `\prosperpart`.

`\tsection*{⟨section name⟩}`

> Creates a section named ⟨section name⟩. The star, if present, is ignored.

`\tsectionandpart*{⟨part text⟩}`

> Mapped to a `\section` command followed by a `\prosperpart` command.

ARTICLE In `article` mode, no part page is added.

`\dualslide[⟨x⟩][⟨y⟩][⟨z⟩]{⟨options⟩}{⟨left column⟩}{⟨right column⟩}`

> This command is mapped to a `columns` environment. The ⟨left column⟩ text is shown in the left column, the ⟨right column⟩ text is shown in the right column. The options ⟨x⟩, ⟨y⟩, and ⟨z⟩ are ignored. Also, all ⟨options⟩ are ignored, except for `lcolwidth=` and `rcolwidth=`. These set the width of the left or right column, respectively.

`\PDForPS{⟨PostScript text⟩}{⟨PDF text⟩}`

> Inserts either the ⟨PostScript text⟩ or the ⟨PDF text⟩, depending on whether `latex` or `pdflatex` is used. When porting, the ⟨PDF text⟩ will most likely be *incorrect*, since in PROSPER the ⟨PDF text⟩ is actually PostScript text that is later transformed to PDF by some external program.
>
> If the ⟨PDF text⟩ contains an `\includegraphics` command (which is its usual use), you should change the name of the graphic file that is included to a name ending `.pdf`, `.png`, or `.jpg`. Typically, you will have to convert your graphic to this format.

`\onlyInPDF`⟨*PDF text*⟩

The ⟨*PDF text*⟩ is only included if `pdflatex` is used. The same as for the command `\PDForPS` applies here.

`\onlyInPS`⟨*PS text*⟩

The ⟨*PS text*⟩ is only included if `latex` is used.

`\begin{notes}{`⟨*title*⟩`}`
  ⟨*environment contents*⟩
`\end{notes}`

Mapped to `\note{\textbf{`⟨*title*⟩`}`⟨*environment contents*⟩`}` (more or less).

The following commands are parsed by BEAMER, but have no effect:

- `\myitem`,
- `\FontTitle`,
- `\FontText`,
- `\ColorFoot`,
- `\DefaultTransition`,
- `\NoFrenchBabelItemize`,
- `\TitleSlideNav`,
- `\NormalSlideNav`,
- `\HAPsetup`,
- `\LeftFoot`, and
- `\RightFoot`.

24.2 Seminar

The package `beamerseminar` maps a subset of the commands of the SEMINAR package to BEAMER. As for PROSPER, the emulation cannot be perfect. For example, no portrait slides are supported, no automatic page breaking, the framing of slides is not emulated. Unfortunately, for all frames (`slide` environments) that contain overlays, you have to put the environment into a `frame` environment "by hand" and must remove all occurrences of `\newslide` inside the environment by closing the slide and opening a new one (and then putting these into `frame` environments).

The workflow for the migration is the following:

1. Use the document class `beamer`, not `seminar`. Most options passed to `seminar` do not apply to `beamer` and should be omitted.

2. If you copy parts of a presentation that is mixed with normal text, add the `ignorenonframetext` option and place *every* `slide` environment inside a `frame` since BEAMER will not recognize the `\begin{slide}` as the beginning of a frame.

3. Add a `\usepackage{beamerseminar}` to start the emulation. Add the option `accumulated` if you wish to create a presentation to be held with a video projector.

4. Possibly add commands to install themes and templates.

5. There should not be commands in the preamble having to do with page and slide styles. They do not apply to `beamer`.

6. If a `\newslide` command is used in a `slide` (or similarly `slide*`) environment that contains an overlay, you must replace it by a closing `\end{slide}` and an opening `\begin{slide}`.

7. Next, for each `slide` or `slide*` environment that contains an overlay, you must place a `frame` environment around it. You can remove the `slide` environment (and hence effectively replace it by `frame`), unless you use the `accumulated` option.

8. If you use `\section` or `\subsection` commands inside slides, you will have to move them *outside* the frames. It may then be necessary to add a `\frametitle` command to the slide.

9. If you use pdfLATEX to typeset the presentation, you cannot include PostScript files. You should convert them to `.pdf` or to `.png` and adjust any usage of `\includegraphics` accordingly.

10. When starting to change things, you can use all of BEAMER's commands and even mix them with SEMINAR commands.

An example can be found in the file `beamerexample-seminar.tex`.
There are, unfortunately, numerous places where you may run into problems:

- The whole `note` management of `seminar` is so different from `beamer`'s, that you will have to edit notes "by hand." In particular, commands like `\ifslidesonly` and `\ifslide` may not do exactly what you expect.

- If you use `pstricks` commands, you will either have to stick to using `latex` and `dvips` or will have to work around them using, for example, `pgf`. Porting lots of `pstricks` code is bound to be difficult, if you wish to switch over to `pdflatex`, so be warned.

- If the file cannot be compiled because some SEMINAR command is not implemented, you will have to delete this command and try to mimick its behavior using some BEAMER command.

`\usepackage{beamerseminar}`

Include this package in a `beamer` presentation to get access to SEMINAR commands. Use `beamer` as the document class, not `seminar`. Most of the options passed to the class `seminar` make no sense in `beamer`, so just delete them.

This package takes the following options:

- `accumulated` causes overlays to be accumulated. The original behavior of the SEMINAR package is that in each overlay only the really "new" part of the overlay is shown. This makes sense, if you really print out the overlays on transparencies and then really stack overlays on top of each other. For a presentation with a video projector, you rather want to present an "accumulated" version of the overlays. This is what this option does: When the new material of the i-th overlay is shown, the material of all previous overlays is also shown.

Example: The following example is an extract of `beamerexample-seminar.tex`:

```
\documentclass[ignorenonframetext]{beamer}
\usepackage[accumulated]{beamerseminar}
\usepackage{beamerthemeclassic}

\title{A beamer presentation using seminar commands}
\author{Till Tantau}

\let\heading=\frametitle

\begin{document}

\begin{frame}
  \maketitle
\end{frame}

This is some text outside any frame. It will only be shown in the
article version.

\begin{frame}
  \begin{slide}
    \heading{This is a frame title.}
```

```
      \begin{enumerate}
        {\overlay1
        \item Overlays are a little tricky in seminar.
          {\overlay2
          \item But it is possible to use them in beamer.
          }
        }
      \end{enumerate}
    \end{slide}
  \end{frame}
\end{document}
```

You can use all normal BEAMER commands and concepts, like overlay-specifications, in the file. You can also create an `article` version by using the class `article` and including the package `beamerarticle`.

In the following, the effects of SEMINAR commands in BEAMER are listed.

\overlay{⟨*number*⟩}

Shows the material till the end of the current TeX group only on overlay numbered ⟨*number*⟩ + 1 or, if the `accumulated` option is given, from that overlay on. Usages of this command may be nested (as in SEMINAR). If an \overlay command is given inside another, it temporarily "overrules" the outer one as demonstrated in the following example, where it is assumed that the `accumulated` option is given.

Example:

```
\begin{frame}
  \begin{slide}
    This is shown from the first slide on.
    {\overlay{2}
      This is shown from the third slide on.
      {\overlay{1}
        This is shown from the second slide on.
      }
      This is shown once more from the third slide on.
    }
  \end{slide}
\end{frame}
```

\begin{slide}*
  ⟨*environment contents*⟩
\end{slide}

Mainly installs an \overlay{0} around the ⟨*environment contents*⟩. If the `accumulated` option is given, this has no effect, but otherwise it will cause the main text of the slide to be shown *only* on the first slide. This is useful if you really wish to physically place slides on top of each other.

The starred version does the same as the nonstarred one.

If this command is not issued inside a \frame, it sets up a frame with the `fragile=singleframe` option set. Thus, this frame will contain only a single slide.

Example:

```
\begin{slide}
  Some text.
\end{slide}

\frame{
\begin{slide}
  Some text. And an {\overlay{1} overlay}.
\end{slide}
}
```

\red

> Mapped to \color{red}.

\blue

> Mapped to \color{blue}.

\green

> Mapped to \color{green}.

\ifslide

> True in the presentation modes, false in the article mode.

\ifslidesonly

> Same as \ifslide.

\ifarticle

> False in the presentation modes, true in the article mode.

\ifportrait

> Always false.

The following commands are parsed by BEAMER, but have no effect:

- \ptsize.

24.3   FoilTEX

The package beamerfoils maps a subset of the commands of the FOILS package to BEAMER. Since this package defines only few non-standard TEX commands and since BEAMER implements all the standard commands, the emulation layer is pretty simple.

A copyright notice: The FoilTEX package has a restricted license. For this reason, no example from the FOILS package is included in the BEAMER class. The emulation itself does not use the code of the FOILS package (rather, it just maps FOILS commands to BEAMER commands). For this reason, our understanding is that the *emulation* offered by the BEAMER class is "free" and legally so. IBM has a copyright on the FOILS class, not on the effect the commands of this class have. (At least, that's our understanding of things.)

The workflow for the migration is the following:

1. Use the document class beamer, not foils.

2. Add a \usepackage{beamerfoils} to start the emulation.

3. Possibly add commands to install themes and templates.

4. If the command \foilhead is used inside a \frame command or frame environment, it behaves like \frametitle. If it used outside a frame, it will start a new frame (with the allowframebreaks option, thus no overlays are allowed). This frame will persist till the next occurrence of \foilhead or of the new command \endfoil. Note that a \frame command will *not* end a frame started using \foilhead.

5. If you rely on automatic frame creation based on \foilhead, you will need to insert an \endfoil before the end of the document to end the last frame.

6. If you use pdfLATEX to typeset the presentation, than you cannot include PostScript files. You should convert them to .pdf or to .png and adjust any usage of \includegraphics accordingly.

7. Sizes of objects are different in BEAMER, since the scaling is done by the viewer, not by the class. Thus a framebox of size 6 inches will be way too big in a BEAMER presentation. You will have to manually adjust explicit dimension occurring in a foilTEX presentation.

`\usepackage{`beamerfoils`}`

Include this package in a beamer presentation to get access to FOILS commands. Use beamer as the document class, not foils.

Example: In the following example, frames are automatically created. The `\endfoil` at the end is needed to close the last frame.

```
\documentclass{beamer}
\usepackage{beamerfoils}

\begin{document}

\maketitle

\foilhead{First Frame}

This is on the first frame.
\pagebreak
This is on the second frame, which is a continuation of the first.

\foilhead{Third Frame}

This is on the third frame.

\endfoil
\end{document}
```

Example: In this example, frames are manually inserted. No `\endfoil` is needed.

```
\documentclass{beamer}
\usepackage{beamerfoils}

\begin{document}

\frame{\maketitle}

\frame{
\foilhead{First Frame}
This is on the first frame.
}

\frame{
\foilhead{Second Frame}
This is on the second frame.
}
\end{document}
```

In the following, the effects of FOILS commands in BEAMER are listed.

`\MyLogo{`⟨*logo text*⟩`}`

This is mapped to `\logo`, though the logo is internally stored, such that it can be switched on and off using `\LogoOn` and `\LogoOff`.

`\LogoOn`

Makes the logo visible.

`\LogoOff`

Makes the logo invisible.

`\foilhead[`⟨*dimension*⟩`]{`⟨*frame title*⟩`}`

> If used inside a `\frame` command or `frame` environment, this is mapped to `\frametitle{`⟨*frame title*⟩`}`. If used outside any frames, a new frame is started with the option `allowframebreaks`. If a frame was previously started using this command, it will be closed before the next frame is started. The ⟨*dimension*⟩ is ignored.

`\rotatefoilhead[`⟨*dimension*⟩`]{`⟨*frame title*⟩`}`

> This command has exactly the same effect as `\foilhead`.

`\endfoil`

> This is a command that is *not* available in FOILS. In BEAMER, it can be used to end a frame that has automatically been opened using `\foildhead`. This command must be given before the end of the document if the last frame was opened using `\foildhead`.

`\begin{boldequation}*`
⟨*environment contents*⟩
`\end{boldequation}`

> This is mapped to the `equation` or the `equation*` environment, with `\boldmath` switched on.

`\FoilTeX`

> Typesets the foilTeX name as in the FOILS package.

`\bm{`⟨*text*⟩`}`

> Implemented as in the FOILS package.

`\bmstyle{`⟨*text*⟩`}{`⟨*more text*⟩`}`

> Implemented as in the FOILS package.

The following additional theorem-like environments are predefined:

- `Theorem*`,
- `Lemma*`,
- `Corollary*`,
- `Proposition*`, and
- `Definition*`.

For example, the first is defined using `\newtheorem*{Theorem*}{Theorem}`.

The following commands are parsed by BEAMER, but have no effect:

- `\leftheader`,
- `\rightheader`,
- `\leftfooter`,
- `\rightfooter`,
- `\Restriction`, and
- `\marginpar`.

24.4 TEXPower

The package `beamertexpower` maps a subset of the commands of the TEXPOWER package, due to Stephan Lehmke, to BEAMER. This subset is currently rather small, so a lot of adaptions may be necessary. Note that TEXPOWER is not a full class by itself, but a package that needs another class, like `seminar` or `prosper` to do the actual typesetting. It may thus be necessary to additionally load an emulation layer for these also. Indeed, it *might* be possible to directly use TEXPOWER inside BEAMER, but we have not tried that. Perhaps this will be possible in the future.

Currently, the package `beamertexpower` mostly just maps the `\stepwise` and related commands to appropriate BEAMER commands. The `\pause` command need not be mapped since it is directly implemented by BEAMER anyway.

The workflow for the migration is the following:

1. Replace the document class by `beamer`. If the document class is `seminar` or `prosper`, you can use the above emulation layers, that is, you can include the files `beamerseminar` or `beamerprosper` to emulate the class.

   All notes on what to do for the emulation of SEMINAR or PROSPER also apply here.

2. Additionally, add `\usepackage{beamertexpower}` to start the emulation.

`\usepackage{beamertexpower}`

Include this package in a `beamer` presentation to get access to the TEXPOWER commands having to do with the `\stepwise` command.

A note on the `\pause` command: Both BEAMER and TEXPOWER implement this command and they have the same semantics; so there is no need to map this command to anything different in `beamertexpower`. However, a difference is that `\pause` can be used almost anywhere in BEAMER, whereas it may only be used in non-nested situations in TEXPOWER. Since BEAMER is only more flexible than TEXPOWER here, this will not cause problems when porting.

In the following, the effect of TEXPOWER commands in BEAMER are listed.

`\stepwise{⟨text⟩}`

As in TEXPOWER, this initiates text in which commands like `\step` or `\switch` may be given. Text contained in a `\step` command will be enclosed in an `\only` command with the overlay specification `<+(1)->`. This means that the text of the first `\step` is inserted from the second slide onward, the text of the second `\step` is inserted from the third slide onward, and so on.

`\parstepwise{⟨text⟩}`

Same as `\stepwise`, only `\uncover` is used instead of `\only` when mapping the `\step` command.

`\liststepwise{⟨text⟩}`

Same as `\stepwise`, only an invisible horizontal line is inserted before the ⟨text⟩. This is presumably useful for solving some problems related to vertical spacing in TEXPOWER.

`\step{⟨text⟩}`

This is either mapped to `\only<+(1)->⟨text⟩` or to `\uncover<+(1)->⟨text⟩`, depending on whether this command is used inside a `\stepwise` environment or inside a `\parstepwise` environment.

`\steponce{⟨text⟩}`

This is either mapped to `\only<+(1)>⟨text⟩` or to `\uncover<+(1)>⟨text⟩`, depending on whether this command is used inside a `\stepwise` environment or inside a `\parstepwise` environment.

`\switch{⟨alternate text⟩}{⟨text⟩}`

This is mapped to `\alt<+(1)->{⟨text⟩}{⟨alternate text⟩}`. Note that the arguments are swapped.

\bstep{⟨*text*⟩}

> This is always mapped to \uncover<+(1)->⟨*text*⟩.

\dstep

> This just advances the counter beamerpauses by one. It has no other effect.

\vstep

> Same as \dstep.

\restep{⟨*text*⟩}

> Same as \step, but the ⟨*text*⟩ is shown on the same slide as the previous \step command. This is implemented by first decreasing the counter beamerpauses by one before calling \step.

\reswitch{⟨*alternate text*⟩}⟨*text*⟩

> Like \restep, only for the \switch command.

\rebstep⟨*text*⟩

> Like \restep, only for the \bstep command.

\redstep

> This command has no effect.

\revstep

> This command has no effect.

\boxedsteps

> Temporarily (for the current TeX group) changes the effect of \step to issue an \uncover, even if used inside a \stepwise environment.

\nonboxedsteps

> Temporarily (for the current TeX group) changes the effect of \step to issue an \only, even if used inside a \parstepwise environment.

\code{⟨*text*⟩}

> Typesets the argument using a boldface typewriter font.

\codeswitch

> Switches to a boldface typewriter font.

25 Translating Strings

25.1 Introduction

25.1.1 Overview of the Package

The TRANSLATOR package is a LaTeX package that provides a flexible mechanism for translating individual words into different languages. For example, it can be used to translate a word like "figure" into, say, the German word "Abbildung". Such a translation mechanism is useful when the author of some package would like to localize the package such that texts are correctly translated into the language preferred by the user. The TRANSLATOR package is *not* intended to be used to automatically translate more than a few words.

You may wonder whether the TRANSLATOR package is really necessary since there is the (very nice) babel package available for LaTeX. This package already provides translations for words like "figure". Unfortunately, the architecture of the babel package was designed in such a way that there is no way of adding translations of new words to the (very short) list of translations directly built into babel.

The TRANSLATOR package was specifically designed to allow an easy extension of the vocabulary. It is both possible to add new words that should be translated and translations of these words.

The TRANSLATOR package can be used together with babel. In this case, babel is used for language-specific things like special quotation marks and input shortcuts, while TRANSLATOR is used for the translation of words.

25.1.2 How to Read This Section

This section explains the commands of the TRANSLATOR package and its usage. The "public" commands and environments provided by the `translator` package are described throughout the text. In each such description, the described command, environment or option is printed in red. Text shown in green is optional and can be left out.

In the following documentation, the installation is explained first, followed by an overview of the basic concepts used. Then, we explain the usage of the package.

25.1.3 Contributing

Since this package is about internationalization, it needs input from people who can contribute translations to their native tongue.

In order to submit dictionaries, please do the following:

1. Read this manual and make sure you understand the basic concepts.

2. Find out whether the translations should be part of the TRANSLATOR package or part of another package. In general, submit translations and new keys to the TRANSLATOR project only if they are of public interest.

   For example, translations for keys like `figure` should be send to the TRANSLATOR project. Translations for keys that are part of a special package should be send to the author of the package.

3. If you are sure that the translations should go to the TRANSLATOR package, create a dictionary of the correct name (see this documentation once more).

4. Finally, submit the dictionary using the correct forum on the development site.

25.1.4 Installation

This package is distributed with BEAMER. Typically, if you have BEAMER installed, the package will already be installed on your system. If not, look in Section 2 for instructions on how to install BEAMER.

25.2 Basic Concepts

25.2.1 Keys

The main purpose of the TRANSLATOR package is to provide translations for *keys*. Typically, a key is an English word like `Figure` and the German translation for this key is "Abbildung".

For a concept like "figures" a single key typically is not enough:

1. It is sometimes necessary to translate a group of words like "Table of figures" as a whole. While these are three words in English, the German translation in just a single word: "Abbildungsverzeichnis".

2. Uppercase and lowercase letters may cause problems. Suppose we provide a translation for the key `Figure`. Then what happens when we want to use this word in normal text, spelled with a lowercase first letter? We could use TEX's functions to turn the translation into lowercase, but that would be wrong with the German translation "Abbildung", which is always spelled with a capital letter.

3. Plurals may also cause problems. If we know the translation for "Figure", that does not mean that we know the translation for "Figures" (which is "Abbildungen" in German).

Because of these problems, there are many keys for the single concept of "figures": `Figure`, `figure`, `Figures`, and `figures`. The first key is used for translations of "figure" when used in a headline in singular. The last key is used for translations of "figure" when used in normal text in plural.

A key may contain spaces, so `Table of figures` is a permissible key.

Keys are normally English texts whose English translation is the same as the key, but this need not be the case. Theoretically, a key could be anything. However, since the key is used as a last fallback when no translation whatsoever is available, a key should be readable by itself.

25.2.2 Language Names

The TRANSLATOR package uses names for languages that are different from the names used by other packages like babel. The reason for this is that the names used by babel are a bit of a mess, so Till decided to clean things up for the TRANSLATOR package. However, mappings from babel names to TRANSLATOR names are provided.

The names used by the TRANSLATOR package are the English names commonly used for these languages. Thus, the name for the English language is `English`, the name for German is `German`.

Variants of a language get their own name: The British version of English is called `BritishEnglish`, the US-version is called `AmericanEnglish`.

For German there is the special problem of pre-1998 as opposed to the current (not yet fixed) spelling. The language `German` reflects the current official spelling, but `German1997` refers to the spelling used in 1997.

25.2.3 Language Paths

When you request a translation for a key, the TRANSLATOR package will try to provide the translation for the current *language*. Examples of languages are German or English.

When the TRANSLATOR looks up the translation for the given key in the current language, it may fail to find a translation. In this case, the TRANSLATOR will try a fallback strategy: It keeps track of a *language path* and successively tries to find translations for each language on this path.

Language paths are not only useful for fallbacks. They are also used for situations where a language is a variant of another language. For example, when the TRANSLATOR looks for the translation for a key in Austrian, the language path starts with Austrian, followed by German. Then, a dictionary for Austrian only needs to provide translations for those keys where Austrian differs from German.

25.2.4 Dictionaries

The translations of keys are typically provided by *dictionaries*. A dictionary contains the translations of a specific set of keys into a specific language. For example, a dictionary might contain the translations of the names of months into the language German. Another dictionary might contain the translations of the numbers into French.

25.3 Usage

25.3.1 Basic Usage

Here is a typical example of how to use the package:

```
\documentclass[german]{article}

\usepackage{babel}
\usepackage{some-package-that-uses-translator}

\begin{document}
...
\end{document}
```

As can be seen, things really happen behind the scenes, so, typically, you do not really need to do anything. It is the job of other package to load the TRANSLATOR package, to load the dictionaries and to request translations of keys.

25.3.2 Providing Translations

There are several commands to tell the TRANSLATOR package what the translation of a given key is. As said before, as a normal author you typically need not provide such translations explicitly, they are loaded automatically. However, there are two situations in which you need to provide translations:

1. You do not like the existing translation and you would like to provide a new one.

2. You are writing a dictionary.

You provide a translation using one of the following commands:

\newtranslation[⟨*options*⟩]{⟨*key*⟩}{⟨*translation*⟩}

This command defines the translation of ⟨*key*⟩ to be ⟨*translation*⟩ in the language specified by the ⟨*options*⟩.

You can only use this command if the translation is really "new" in the sense that no translation for the keys has yet been given for the language. If there is already a translation, an error message will be printed.

The following ⟨*options*⟩ may be given:

- [to]=⟨*language*⟩ This options tells the TRANSLATOR, that the translation ⟨*translation*⟩ of ⟨*keys*⟩ applies to the language ⟨*language*⟩.

  Inside a dictionary file (see Section 25.3.3), this option is set automatically to the language of the dictionary.

Example: \newtranslation[to=German]{figure}{Abbildung}

Example: \newtranslation[to=German]{Figures}{Abbildungen}

\renewtranslation[⟨*options*⟩]{⟨*key*⟩}{⟨*translation*⟩}

This command works like \newtranslation, only it will redefine an existing translation.

\providetranslation[⟨*options*⟩]{⟨*key*⟩}{⟨*translation*⟩}

This command works like \newtranslation, but no error message will be printed if the translation already exists. It this case, the existing translation is not changed.

This command should be used by dictionary authors since their translations should not overrule any translations given by document authors or other dictionary authors.

\deftranslation[⟨*options*⟩]{⟨*key*⟩}{⟨*translation*⟩}

This command defines the translation "no matter what". An existing translation will be overwritten.

This command should typically used by document authors to install their preferred translations.

Example: \deftranslation[to=German]{figure}{Figur}

Here is an example where a translation is provided by a document author:

```
\documentclass[ngerman]{article}

\usepackage{babel}
\usepackage{some-package-that-uses-translator}

\deftranslation[to=German]{Sketch of proof}{Beweisskizze}

\begin{document}
  ...
\end{document}
```

25.3.3 Creating and Using Dictionaries

Two kind of people will create *dictionaries*: First, package authors will create dictionaries containing translations for the (new) keys used in the package. Second, document authors can create their own private dictionaries that overrule settings from other dictionaries or that provide missing translations.

There is not only one dictionary per language. Rather, many different dictionaries may be used by TRANSLATOR when it tries to find a translation. This makes it easy to add new translations: Instead of having to change TRANSLATOR's main dictionaries (which involves, among other things, the release of a new version of the `translator` package), package authors can just add a new dictionary containing just the keys needed for the package.

Dictionaries are named according to the following rule: The name of the dictionary must start with its *kind*. The kind tells TRANSLATOR which kind of keys the dictionary contains. For example, the dictionaries of the kind `translator-months-dictionary` contain keys like `January` (note that this is a key, not a translation). Following the kind, the name of a dictionary must have a dash. Then comes the language for which the dictionary file provides translations. Finally, the file name must end with `.dict`.

To continue the example of the month dictionary, for the German language the dictionary is called

```
translator-months-dictionary-German.dict
```

Its contents is the following:

```
\ProvidesDictionary{translator-months-dictionary}{German}

\providetranslation{January}{Januar}
\providetranslation{February}{Februar}
\providetranslation{March}{M\"arz}
\providetranslation{April}{April}
\providetranslation{May}{Mai}
\providetranslation{June}{Juni}
\providetranslation{July}{Juli}
\providetranslation{August}{August}
\providetranslation{September}{September}
\providetranslation{October}{Oktober}
\providetranslation{November}{November}
\providetranslation{December}{Dezember}
```

Note that the `\providetranslation` command does not need the option `[to=German]`. Inside a dictionary file TRANSLATOR will always set the default translation language to the language provided by the dictionary. However, you can still specify the language, if you prefer.

The `\ProvidesDictionary` command currently only prints a message in the log-files.

`\ProvidesDictionary{⟨kind⟩}{⟨language⟩}[⟨version⟩]`

> This command currently only prints a message in the log-files. The format is the same as for LaTeX's `\ProvidesPackage` command.

Dictionaries are stored in a decentralized manner: A special dictionary for a package will typically be stored somewhere in the vicinity of the package. For this reasons, TRANSLATOR needs to be told which *kinds* of dictionaries should be loaded and which *languages* should be used. This is accomplished using the following two commands:

\usedictionary{⟨*kind*⟩}

> This command tells the `translator` package, that at the beginning of the document it should load all dictionaries of kind ⟨*kind*⟩ for the languages used in the document. Note that the dictionaries are not loaded immediately, but only at the beginning of the document.
>
> If no dictionary of the given *kind* exists for one of the language, nothing bad happens.
>
> Invocations of this command accumulate, that is, you can call it multiple times for different dictionaries.

\uselanguage{⟨*list of languages*⟩}

> This command tells the `translator` package that it should load the dictionaries for all languages in the ⟨*list of languages*⟩. The dictionaries are loaded at the beginning of the document.

Here is an example of how all of this works: Suppose you wish to create a new package for drawing, say, chess boards. Let us call this package `chess`. In the file `chess.sty` we could now write the following:

```
// This is chess.sty

\RequirePackage{translator}
\usedictionary{chess}

...

\newcommand\MoveKnight[2]{%
  ...
  \translate{knight}
  ...
}
```

Now we create dictionaries like the following:

```
// This is chess-German.dict
\ProvidesDictionary{chess}{German}

\providetranslation{chess}{Schach}
\providetranslation{knight}{Springer}
\providetranslation{bishop}{L\"aufer}
...
```

and

```
// This is chess-English.dict
\ProvidesDictionary{chess}{English}

\providetranslation{chess}{chass}
\providetranslation{knight}{knight}
\providetranslation{bishop}{bishop}
...
```

Here are a few things to note:

- The package `chess.sty` does not use the command \uselanguage. After all, the package does not know (or care) about the language used in the final document. It only needs to tell the TRANSLATOR package that it will use the dictionary `chess`.

- You may wonder why we need an English dictionary. After all, the keys themselves are the ultimate fallbacks if no other translation is available. The answer to this question is that, first of all, English should be treated like any other language. Second, there are some situations in which there is a "better" English translation than the key itself. An example is explained next.

- The keys we chose may not be optimal. What happens, if some other package, perhaps on medieval architecture, also needs translations of knights and bishops. However, in this different context, the translations of knight and bishop are totally different, namely `Ritter` and `Bischof`.

  Thus, it might be a good idea to add something to the key to make it clear that the "chess bishop" is meant:

```
// This is chess-German.dict
\providetranslation{knight (chess)}{Springer}
\providetranslation{bishop (chess)}{L\"aufer}


// This is chess-English.dict
\providetranslation{knight (chess)}{knight}
\providetranslation{bishop (chess)}{bishop}
```

25.3.4 Creating a User Dictionary

There are two ways of creating a personal set of translations. First, you can simply add commands like

```
\deftranslation[to=German]{figure}{Figur}
```

to your personal macro files.

Second, you can create a personal dictionary file as follows: In your document you say

```
\documentclass[ngerman]{article}

\usepackage{translator}
\usedictionary{my-personal-dictionary}
```

and then you create the following file somewhere where TeX can find it:

```
// This is file my-personal-dictionary-German.dict
\ProvidesDictionary{my-personal-dictionary}{German}

\deftranslation{figure}{Figur}
```

25.3.5 Translating Keys

Once the dictionaries and languages have been setup, you can translate keys using the following commands:

`\translate[⟨options⟩]{⟨key⟩}`

This command will insert the translation of the ⟨key⟩ at the current position into the text. The command is robust.

The translation process of ⟨key⟩ works as follows: TRANSLATOR iterates over all languages on the current *language path* (see Section 25.3.6). For each language on the path, TRANSLATOR checks whether a translation is available for the ⟨key⟩. For the first language for which this is the case, the translation is used. If there is no translation available for any language on the path, the ⟨key⟩ itself is used as the translation.

Example: `\caption{\translate{Figure}~2.}`

The following options may be given:

- [to]=⟨language⟩ This option overrules the language path setting and installs ⟨language⟩ as the target language(s) for which TRANSLATOR tries to find a translation.

`\translatelet[⟨options⟩]{⟨macro⟩}{⟨key⟩}`

> This command works like the `\translate` command, only it will not insert the translation into the text, but will set the macro ⟨macro⟩ to the translation found by the `\translate` command.
>
> *Example:* `\translatelet\localfigure{figure}`

25.3.6 Language Path and Language Substitution

`\languagepath{⟨language path⟩}`

> This command sets the language path that is searched when TRANSLATOR looks for a key.
>
> The default value of the language path is `\languagename,English`. The `\languagename` is the standard TeX macro that expands to the current language. Typically, this is exactly what you want and there is no real need to change this default language path.

There is a problem with the names used in the macro `\languagename`. These names, like ngerman, are not the ones used by TRANSLATOR and we somehow have to tell the TRANSLATOR about aliases for cryptic language names like ngerman. This is done using the following command:

`\languagealias{⟨name⟩}{⟨language list⟩}`

> This command tells the TRANSLATOR that the language ⟨name⟩ should be replaced by the language in the ⟨language list⟩.
>
> *Example:* `\languagealias{ngerman}{German}`
>
> *Example:* `\languagealias{german}{German1997,German}`

For the languages used by the babel package, the aliases are automatically setup, so you typically do not need to call either `\languagepath` or `\languagealias`.

25.3.7 Package Loading Process

The TRANSLATOR package is loaded "in stages":

1. First, some package or the document author requests the TRANSLATOR package is loaded.

2. The TRANSLATOR package allows options like ngerman to be given. These options cause the necessary aliases and the correct TRANSLATOR languages to be requested.

3. During the preamble, packages and the document author request creating dictionary kinds and certain languages to be used. There requests are protocoled.

4. At the beginning of the document (`\begin{document}`) the requested dictionary-language-pairs are loaded.

The first thing that needs to be done is to load the package. Typically, this is done automatically by some other package, but you may wish to include it directly:

`\usepackage{translator}`

> When you load the package, you can specify (multiple) babel languages as ⟨options⟩. The effect of giving such an option is the following: It causes the TRANSLATOR package to call `\uselanguage` for the appropriate translation of the babel language names to TRANSLATOR's language names. It also causes `\languagealias` to be called for the languages.

Index

This index only contains automatically generated entries, sorry. A good index should also contain carefully selected keywords.

51218080R00139

Made in the USA
Middletown, DE
01 July 2019